Drunk-ish

Also by Stefanie Wilder-Taylor

Sippy Cups Are Not for Chardonnay

Naptime Is the New Happy Hour

It's Not Me, It's You

I'm Kind of a Big Deal

Gummi Bears Should Not Be Organic

Drunk-ish

A Memoir of Loving and
Leaving Alcohol

Stefanie Wilder-Taylor

G

GALLERY BOOKS

New York   London   Toronto   Sydney   New Delhi

G

Gallery Books
An Imprint of Simon & Schuster, Inc.
1230 Avenue of the Americas
New York, NY 10020

First Gallery Books hardcover edition January 2024

GALLERY BOOKS and colophon are registered trademarks of Simon & Schuster, Inc.

Simon & Schuster: Celebrating 100 Years of Publishing in 2024

For information about special discounts for bulk purchases, please contact Simon & Schuster Special Sales at 1-866-506-1949 or business@simonandschuster.com.

The Simon & Schuster Speakers Bureau can bring authors to your live event. For more information or to book an event, contact the Simon & Schuster Speakers Bureau at 1-866-248-3049 or visit our website at www.simonspeakers.com.

Interior design by Kathryn A. Kenney-Peterson

Manufactured in the United States of America

10 9 8 7 6 5 4 3 2 1

Library of Congress Cataloging-in-Publication Data
Names: Wilder-Taylor, Stefanie, author.
Title: Drunk-ish : loving and leaving alcohol / Stefanie Wilder-Taylor.
Description: New York : Gallery Books, 2024. |
Identifiers: LCCN 2023031362 (print) | LCCN 2023031363 (ebook) | ISBN 9781668019412 (hardcover) | ISBN 9781668019436 (ebook)
Subjects: LCSH: Alcoholism—Prevention. | Substance abuse—Prevention. | Dependency (Psychology) | Wilder-Taylor, Stefanie.
Classification: LCC HV5035 .W365 2024 (print) | LCC HV5035 (ebook) | DDC 362.292—dc23/eng/20230929
LC record available at https://lccn.loc.gov/2023031362
LC ebook record available at https://lccn.loc.gov/2023031363

ISBN 978-1-6680-1941-2
ISBN 978-1-6680-1943-6 (ebook)

For Elby, Sadie, and Xander:
You are the how and the why of it.

CONTENTS

1. Motherhood: The Beginning of the End (Before Conception, After Delivery)   1

2. Is This an Intervention?   21

3. Sugar, We're Goin' Down   27

4. I Remember My First Beer   43

5. I Drink Because I'm a Comic   59

6. Let's Play Twenty Questions   71

7. DUI (Dating Under the Influence)   83

8. Do I Have to Quit or Can I Just Cut Down?   99

9. How I Almost Became a Lifetime Movie   111

10. Asking for Help   123

11. The "A" Word   133

12. What's God Got to Do with It?   143

13. A Year of Firsts   151

14. Where Everybody Knows Your (First) Name   165

15. Not Without My Xanax   173

16. Sober Wife, Happy Life?   189

17. The Moms on the Other Side of the Fence   203

18. Outed   213

19. Whac-A-Mole   229

20. Tools of the Trade   239

21. Sorry About Your Bachelorette Party   251

Epilogue: In the End, There Is Gratitude   265

Acknowledgments   269

Drunk-ish

1. Motherhood: The Beginning of the End

2004 B.C. (Before Conception)

My first thought when the plus sign appeared on the EPT was *Oh shit!* You would have thought I was a fifteen-year-old sophomore in high school looking down the barrel at teen mom life and not a thirty-six-going-on-thirty-seven-year-old adult woman. Truthfully, I was a massive mix of emotions: giddy, happy, terrified, and secretly relieved. Although we'd never 100 percent committed to trying to have a baby, and were just going to "see if it happened naturally" by pulling the goalie, I was worried it might take a Herculean effort to get pregnant at my "advanced maternal age." I didn't know if I'd be up for fertility drugs, specialty doctors, and everything the process might entail, so, yeah, I was relieved but a little shocked that it happened so fast.

A big part of my reluctance to go all in on trying to conceive was that I never quite felt like a grown-up myself. I'd been in the habit of drinking most nights in the one-bedroom Santa Monica apartment I shared with my then boyfriend, very recently turned husband, Jon. We lived like twenty-somethings even though we were both in our late thirties, drinking cabernet and eating takeout at eleven p.m. in front of *The Sopranos* or *The Daily Show*. It wasn't unusual for us to run out of wine and go grab another bottle from the grocery store whose parking lot was conveniently connected to our back alley. We stayed up every night until one or two a.m., yet somehow we could easily wake up for our TV jobs the next morning if we drank enough coffee.

On weekends we went to parties or out to dinner with our friends who also had no kids. My husband was usually the designated driver because even when I offered to stay sober, despite my best intentions, I'd be luggage by the end of the night.

I did worry about my drinking sometimes. I got brutal hangovers that didn't seem quite normal. I often blacked out and couldn't remember anything that happened the night before. In high school I got into two car accidents where I'd been drinking, although I never got in trouble, and it's quite possible I hadn't even been drunk! In my estimation, I hadn't suffered any real consequences of my drinking besides occasionally embarrassing myself. One night I got so drunk that when we got home I fell asleep mid–blow job. Jon made a joke the next day that I'd taken a "cock nap." I was mortified but had to admit it was sort of funny.

Luckily, Santa Monica is densely populated with restaurants and bars we could easily reach on foot, as long as I didn't wear heels. Our favorite dive bar, Chez Jay, was the place my husband first said, "I love you," and where we often ended the night with a final beer or three. We saw movies, we went to concerts, and we ate at Noah's Bagels for breakfast every weekend. We could walk to our favorite sushi restaurant, where we would start out with a large house sake and a large Sapporo. We began a tradition where we would always pour each other's sake into our little glazed cups because it shows honor and reverence to the other person and also, it's fun. If one of us forgot, the other would just wait, cup empty, until the other one noticed. Then we'd have at least three more rounds, mostly instigated by me. "Let's go for one more large sake!" I'd say, already fairly drunk, and Jon would oblige. One time we got drunk enough to try blowfish, a Japanese delicacy they call fugu, which is poisonous, and can kill you if it's not prepared properly. We fed each other the mildly flavored fish on its little bed of sweet rice and then stared each other down while we waited to see if we'd live or die. Life was good.

I wasn't sure if I wanted kids, but because I was edging into my mid-thirties, I felt obligated to give it major consideration. It seemed like the next logical step in life, and although Jon would have been fine waiting another ten years, I knew I didn't have that kind of leeway. I knew for sure I wanted to get married. I'd pushed for it for years, bringing it up constantly. Jon was very slow moving and methodical when it came to making decisions, which only sped me up. Marriage was the real goal: A proposal would mean I was chosen, wanted. But most importantly and selfishly, I'd feel secure—a feeling I'd wanted since childhood. I'd know someone loved me most of all. I knew I loved Jon—he was a great guy, easygoing and funny and the smartest person I'd ever met—but it was also easy to love him because I wasn't 100 percent convinced he loved me quite as much as I loved him. I had this nagging feeling that Jon would definitely survive if I broke up with him, and that made me want to punch him, but also made the relationship less threatening. His security and self-sufficiency made him desirable, even at my own expense.

Babies, on the other hand, are needy. In my estimation, you have to be pretty selfless to be a parent. I didn't always view myself as a natural nurturer—I wasn't the friend who thought to set up the meal train when your life went sideways; I was the "someone who's better at this stuff will set it up and then they'll let me know how to help" friend. But I grew up being told I was selfish and self-centered, so I couldn't be sure if that was actually who I was or if that was just how I believed I was. Maybe I could step up?

Once I was engaged, the question of whether I should try for a baby loomed even larger: Now that I was thirty-six, my eggs were almost eligible for an AARP card and I needed to decide on a plan of action. I brought it up with my therapist, Linda, during a session. She sat in her comfy chair and I sat across from her on a love seat adorned with two cross-stitched decorative pillows, one of which said "Hope," and the other "Healing." I picked up the Healing pillow and clutched it on my lap.

"How do I know if I'm ready to have a baby? I mean, I'm just not sure. Maybe something's wrong with me. I feel like I should want it more." I trusted Linda, which was unusual for me because I have a bad history with therapists. The way some women always end up dating douchebags, I always end up with bad therapists. One tried to set me up with a married doctor at the hospital where she worked, one canceled a session because she got a potato chip in her eye yet still billed me, and one yelled at me because I wasn't getting in touch with my anger. But Linda was different. She was kind and empathetic but also no-nonsense when necessary. She once shocked me by referring to my biological father as a motherfucker because she knew swearing was my love language.

She had short, no-fuss gray hair but counterbalanced it with expansive multicolored maxi skirts. The resulting look was "theater major who went back to school to learn to treat PTSD." The only thing that set my teeth on edge was that there was a framed poster on the wall of her waiting room listing the twelve steps of Alcoholics Anonymous. The rest of the space was calming, with neutral-colored walls, a painting of a windswept sand dune, and a few hanging philodendrons—but that poster was like a tiny bloodstain on an otherwise pristine white sheet. I often felt as if the poster was taunting me, daring me to look at my drinking, but I had no intention of doing that; I had bigger fish to fry.

I looked at Linda, ready for her trademark therapeutic advice.

"When it comes to having a baby, most people don't decide, they just do it," was all she had for me. "You'll be okay either way, eventually."

Two months later I was married, newly pregnant, and moving to the suburbs.

I had worried that it would be difficult to abandon our lifestyle at the drop of a hat. In particular, I worried about quitting drinking while I was pregnant—*not because I had a problem*, but because it was such a big part of my life. These days the common wisdom is that no amount of alcohol is safe during pregnancy—at least according to some little-known authorities like, oh, the CDC and the American College of Obstetrics. But at that time, people were a little looser, and my OB said I could have one or two drinks a week, which was good news to me. And for anyone who's scandalized by that, let's keep in mind that it wasn't until 1981 that women were advised drinking while pregnant might not be a great idea. And only thirty or forty years before that, Winston ran ads telling women to smoke cigarettes because it would keep their babies slim and make for an easier delivery. I imagine a happy obstetrician in the hospital, ciggy dangling from their mouth, letting out a victorious "Yes!" as they catch a tiny baby that just slid out of its mother's birth canal with barely a push because she smoked two packs a day.

Ironically, the first nine weeks of pregnancy felt exactly like an extended hangover minus the alcohol, and I felt too sick to want to drink anyway. I couldn't do much more than lie on the couch, getting up every so often to dry-heave or eat a Saltine. But once I no longer felt incapacitated by nausea 24/7, the sun rose high into the sky and my anxiety faded out as if someone had hit the dimmer switch. The slight edge of irritability that I'd always figured was just part of my DNA was suddenly gone. No drinking? No problem! I didn't know why I'd ever felt like drinking every weeknight was something I needed to do.

And I didn't feel deprived! After all, I could still have two drinks a week! I found that I was terrific at self-control. Of course I got a little obsessed with those two drinks and plotted when I would have them: both on a Friday night? Spread evenly throughout the week? Maybe one on a Tuesday and one on a Saturday? I had nervous thoughts like, *What if I blow my alcohol wad on Monday and lock myself out of a single glass of wine for the upcoming weekend?* But I never went above those two glasses. I was a moderation rock star! I didn't think too far into the future about the actual "having a baby" part. It still felt so far away . . .

2004 A.D. (After Delivery)

When I got home from the hospital, I realized the elevated hormone levels that buoyed me through pregnancy had made an Irish exit, slipping out with my placenta. The baby swung in like a seven-pound-two-ounce wrecking ball, leveling any semblance of the life I'd built for myself.

Sleep deprivation hit me hard. My daughter was up all night and slept all day, like she lived in some Vegas casino. I'd barely slept in the hospital, and now I wasn't sleeping at home either, because the baby wouldn't so much as catnap unless she was in our bed. I'd had no idea how much I took sleep for granted until it was no longer an option.

Breastfeeding was incredibly difficult due to a breast-reduction surgery twenty years prior. At the time I had given zero fucks that detaching my nipples and then sewing them back on could negatively affect my ability to breastfeed—I just didn't want to look like Dolly Parton. But now that I was stuck with malfunctioning boobs unable to produce more than a NyQuil cup's worth of milk, I felt like a failure.

I *wanted* parenting to be good. I loved this tiny creature and felt a primal need to protect her, but my experience was clouded by crushing anxiety. Was she hungry? Tired? Cold? Hot? Bored? Scared? Sad? Was I holding her correctly? Feeding her correctly? Burping her correctly? If I had any maternal instinct, it was hidden behind a veil of fear. I started buying up books on Amazon: *Healthy Sleep Habits, Happy Child; The Happiest Baby on the Block; What to Expect the First Year*. I know what you're thinking: Why didn't I get those books *before* I had a baby? Because I didn't have a baby then! I was pregnant! I bought pregnancy books. Duh.

My husband took the first couple of weeks off of his sixty-hour-a-week job after the baby came home, and he really tried to help. One evening he sent me to bed and slept on the couch all night with our daughter on his chest. It was the best six hours of my life up to that point. Once I was fully formula feeding, he also took on many of the late-night feedings, fueling himself on coffee and Rockstar energy drinks. But as much as he pitched in, it didn't stop my anxiety, which was getting worse. During those sleepless nights, I worried it might never get better. What if I'd made a monumental mistake that I couldn't take back? And then I'd feel guilty for even having that awful thought. Would I be forced to pretend I was happy and fine with my choices for the foreseeable future?

Very quickly Jon's time off timed out and he was able to escape watching me cry and complain. He went back to his TV production office, and he often didn't get home until after nine p.m. or nine thirty, sometimes even ten. Although he complained about the long hours and *said* he wanted to get home earlier, I found that hard to believe. I imagined long languorous lunches, an endless supply of Starbucks lattes at his disposal, frequent chats with his fun coworkers—probably cute female coworkers who weren't sporting cellulite on their arms from recently giving birth. When he walked in the door exhausted from helping with the late-night feedings and then working a twelve-hour day, I didn't feel bad for him, I felt jealous and slightly resentful.

One thing I found to take the edge off was a glass of wine. It was something to look forward to, something for me—a treat to celebrate white-knuckling it through another day of infant care. And since I was no longer pregnant, I could drink again. It was a beautiful reunion. Wine was like an ex-boyfriend I'd been on break from when I was pregnant, and now that we were back together I couldn't understand how I'd lived without him. I'd always liked wine but now I *really liked* wine. It was reliable, accessible, and socially acceptable.

One glass definitely helped but I found that two or even three worked better. When I would ask Jon to stop by the store on his way home from work every night to grab a bottle, it raised no alarm bells—it's not as if I was checking if he could score a gram of coke! It was normal! All of us moms were doing it! Well almost.

The first time I realized not every mom drank like me, I was having lunch at a Mexican restaurant near my house, with my new mom friend, Lara, and our six-month-old babies. Lara and I had met at a Mommy & Me class held at a temple in my neighborhood. I wasn't religious so much as desperate to make some friends with babies. I liked Lara. We had bonded over our mutual irritation at having to sing *all* the verses of "Wheels on the Bus." We agreed everything after *the wipers on the bus go swish swish swish* was excessive—by the time you get to *the babies on the bus go wah wah wah* it's just diminishing returns. She was someone I felt I could hang with; she seemed like she got me, like we had an understanding, which was that even though we'd just had babies, we wanted to still be ourselves. It was a relief to have connected with someone, because I was definitely struggling.

As soon as we were seated at our patio table with our babies situated in two high chairs, Lara pulled out a disposable *Sesame Street* place mat, laid it on her daughter's high chair tray, then broke out hand sanitizer for both us and the babies. "Here, put out your hand," she said. This was pre-Covid, so it felt a little extra. She squirted gel into all of our hands and then sat back, satisfied. This poor woman clearly dealt with her own brand of anxiety. But I knew what would help.

"Let's get a margarita," I said, like it was a done deal, like of course we're getting a margarita because we're out of the house, in a

Mexican restaurant, and already with our babies, momming. Plus, what else did we have to do? It wasn't like either of us had pressing plans. Where were we going besides home to do more of the same?

A frozen margarita sounded so damn good I could taste it already, the icy sweet, tart flavor with just the perfect kick to let me know there was a good amount of alcohol and I'd soon feel the familiar softening, the quiet confidence that would set in, whispering to me in a soft margarita voice, "You got this, mama. See, it's not all so hard. There are moments of bliss like this. You're doing great! Your baby is in a possibly clean diaper happily eating shredded cheese. There's nothing to worry about! Motherhood is not so bad right?" But Lara interrupted my drink's soothing monologue. "Oh no. Not for me. I'm such a lightweight since the baby. I wouldn't be able to drive home."

What the fuck? What was wrong with her? Was she on antibiotics?

"Not even just one?"

"I *really* can't. Even a half a drink would make me feel drunk these days. But you go ahead."

Go ahead? I wasn't going to *just go ahead.* Drink alone? That seemed really lushy. I tried to hide that it mattered so much. Inwardly I cursed the fact that I have one of those faces where you can always read my expression. It had always been a problem with teachers and bosses, and at poker games. The last thing I wanted to seem was desperate for a drink—because I definitely wasn't. I'd just thought it would be *fun* to let loose a little. I wanted to feel like a grown woman out for lunch with a girlfriend and not a Mom with a capital "M" who had spent the better part of an hour packing a diaper bag with a fucking duck on it, premixing bottles, preemptively changing a diaper, applying Orajel, making sure I had my Hyland's teething tablets, which I compulsively fed my baby like she was a teenage boy popping

Tic Tacs on a first date. This was all so much harder and way more responsibility than I'd thought it would be, and sitting at that table with the stupid *Sesame Street* place mats, seeing orange cheese strewn all over the floor despite the fact we'd been seated less than ten minutes felt downright depressing.

Fuck it. I deserved it. I ordered the drink and I drank it alone.

I found being a stay-at-home mom incredibly isolating. I'd worked since I was sixteen and had gotten my first job at Burger King. Over the next twenty years I waited tables, sold office supplies over the phone, clerked at a life insurance company, did stand-up comedy while waiting tables some more, drove a limo, and eventually found my place working in television. I felt the most like myself when I was at work. It gave me identity, a sense of community, and *a lot* of snacks.

I'd always imagined myself squeezing out the kid and being back at work after six weeks, but even though Jon was progressive in every other way, he thought that someone should be home with the baby at least for the first year. That person was going to have to be me, since Jon had an ongoing job and I was working on a pilot that would be over before my due date.

It had made sense in the abstract while I was still pregnant, and I'd agreed it was probably for the best. It wasn't as if I relished the idea of leaving a six-week-old with a stranger. I imagined coming home from a day at work and finding the babysitter breastfeeding my baby à la Rebecca De Mornay in *The Hand That Rocks the Cradle*. But now that it was reality, I felt like staying home was a mistake. I wasn't about this life! I needed community, I needed purpose, I needed a break from the monotony. But the problem was since I didn't technically have a job I'd have to try to get one, and any TV jobs I put myself out for would entail a ten-to-twelve-hour day, possibly more if there were a commute. Plus, in my experience, TV jobs were no place for new moms.

At that time in the culture, moms in a writers' room were more rare than natural boobs. I remember working on *Family Feud* and my coworkers making fun of a new mom who had worked there for a brief time. Apparently most of her submissions were things like, "Name a gift you would bring to a baby shower," or, "Name a reason an infant might be crying." At the time, I laughed along with the guys: New moms are ridiculous! One-track minds! Of course, now I think that woman was a genius. I mean, who's watching *Family Feud*? Moms!

One night, when the baby was only a few months old, feeling desperate for connection to other moms, starved for a creative outlet and brave from two or three glasses of chardonnay, I started a blog on a whim. I called it *Baby on Bored*. I used it to get my edgy yet comedic thoughts on parenting out of my head and into the world. Luckily it struck a chord with other moms: other new moms who were also a few glasses in, sitting in front of their computers reading blogs and trying to figure out just what the fuck had happened to their lives. These other moms and I would read each other's posts and leave comments, and slowly we formed a little community. I could share things on my blog I didn't feel comfortable saying to people in real life.

My blog led to a book deal, and a year or so later I published *Sippy Cups Are Not for Chardonnay*. The book did pretty well, and after numerous appearances on the *Today* show, I was known for being ruthlessly honest about everything from breastfeeding to not falling in love with my baby at first sight, and I was also known for talking about drinking *a lot*. But when I was writing the book, even though I was relieved to have a little gig, I had no idea if anything would come of it, plus it wasn't a lot of money and I wasn't in an office with coworkers, so I still felt disconnected. I made it my business to find some like-minded friends.

I met Susan at My Gym, one of the few organized activities I did with my daughter. I just wasn't one of those go-getter moms who went from toddler tap dance to swim lessons to T-ball; I was more like browse the Dollar Tree, hit the park for an hour, and call it a full day. Susan was cool. She had a son about the same age as my toddler daughter and her husband was a lawyer who worked an insane amount of hours like mine, so she was alone most of the day and into the evening and therefore pretty bored like me. I'd invite myself over a few afternoons a week and make myself at home on a swivel stool at her kitchen counter. We'd boil the kids some pasta, serve it up to them with butter and shaky cheese along with a juice box, and crack open a bottle of chardonnay for ourselves. I was so grateful for the company and somewhere to go.

Lara and I still hung out, but she was way more of a plan maker, wanting to book activities a week in advance, and I was more of a plan canceler who liked to decide if I felt like doing something at the last minute. Susan was as laid-back as I was high-strung and, although she didn't seem to need wine the way I did, she didn't call attention to it either. Since she lived less than a mile from my house, it never seemed risky to have a drink. Sometimes I would have two and need to wait to drive my daughter home because I felt buzzed.

Sometimes I drove home anyway.

Having a glass of wine at Susan's made me feel more relaxed, more patient; it made things seem almost fun, and I thought it gave me the ability to be more in the moment, less focused on my worry that this might be how I would feel for the rest of my life. What was I supposed to do, not drink? That seemed an unreasonable expectation of myself. After all, I was providing my daughter with an enriching afternoon. Sometimes we'd fill an inflatable baby pool, slather our kids with broad-spectrum SPF 50 sunscreen, and let them splash and play for hours while standing over them watching them like hawks. Didn't we deserve a little fun as well?

The thing was that having wine in the late afternoon was nice but I also needed wine to get through the evening. So I would get home from Susan's, do bath time, read *The Very Hungry Caterpillar*, and wait for Jon to get home from work so I could open a new bottle with him, as if this was the first of the evening. "Hi, honey. Let me open some wine!" Of course, since many nights Jon didn't come home from work until nine or ten o'clock, I had to open a bottle of wine before that if I wanted to float through the late afternoon straight to everyone's bedtime. I hated the feeling of my buzz wearing off. But, for me, staying buzzed without getting sloppy was a tough balancing act. Knowing when I've had enough was never my strong suit.

The Halloween just before my daughter turned two, Susan, who was a regular at craft stores and chichi baby shops, brought over a little puffy bumblebee costume—the kind perfect for photo ops—so we could go trick-or-treating together. It was going to be me; Jon; Susan; her husband, Billy; and Susan's mom. Since we were entertaining, I decided festive Halloween cocktails were in order. On the Internet I found a recipe for something called a Tootsie Roll using Kahlúa and orange juice—Halloween colors! It sounded good. Unfortunately, the other folks in our trick-or-treating troupe thought the combination sounded disgusting and stuck to a beer or water, which really seemed lame, but whatever, more for me.

I scooped some ice from the freezer tray and poured myself a big glass of Kahlúa, adding a splash of OJ. Damn, it really tasted just like a Tootsie Roll! I'd discovered a new drink! Maybe I'd put together some kind of holiday drink recipe coffee-table book! These people were really missing out. By the time we hit the streets I was feeling amazing. Afterward, I saw the pictures of us walking down the side-walk, my little girl and Susan's little dude, their plastic orange pump-kin buckets in hand to collect their candy earnings, but I couldn't remember any of it—well, not more than a few flashes. I remembered bonding with Susan's mom, who was only about ten years older than me, actually slightly closer in age to me than Susan. But the next day I was told exactly how much we'd bonded. In my drunken state, I'd made her my bestie, monopolizing her attention, exchanging stories and contact info, claiming that we were "definitely going to stay in touch."

Even though no one else seemed too bothered by my behavior, I was mortified. Not only had I embarrassed myself once again, I'd missed Halloween. I'd missed the experience with my baby, missed seeing her walking up to the neighbors' front doors, missed hearing them say, "Are you a little bee? How cute!" I'd been there, I'd walked her up to those front doors, I'd held her little hand, but I'd robbed myself of the experience. Those memories would forever be missing.

Through my hangover I lashed out at myself. *What's wrong with me? Is this the kind of mother I want to be?* I decided to quit drinking. Completely. I was done. This was the wake-up call I needed. And I did stop. I even went to a few recovery meetings, but I quickly de-cided I had overshot the mark. My issue wasn't so bad that it required a *program*: books and meetings and discussing my issues with other people. It was all too much. No, I could do this on my own.

Six weeks later, still alcohol-free, I found out I was pregnant with twins.

The ultrasound tech was all smiles. "Two babies!" But it didn't seem like good news to me. Jon had been on board to try for another baby, but I had vacillated between feeling overwhelmed with just the one and occasionally feeling perhaps I could handle one more, so during one "fuck it, let's go" moment, we'd tried. But twins felt like suddenly being signed up for a marathon when I'd just wrapped my head around jogging. Two new babies meant we'd need to either move or add space to our house, which we couldn't afford. Twins meant twice the diapers, twice the stress, and half the sleep of one baby. Although I had been put on Zoloft for postpartum anxiety, it had shot through the roof.

Jon, on the other hand, was decidedly more chill about it. He'd been enjoying being a dad. He read bedtime stories, carried our baby in a backpack until she was heavy enough to threaten spine damage, and was always up for a trip to Disneyland. You know, dad shit. He looked at having twins as something that would be difficult for the first few years but pay off in the long run when we're old. Maybe I was shortsighted (although I prefer to think of it as realistic), but I wasn't at all sure I'd survive those "first few years" and I was resentful that Jon wasn't as worried.

Two days after the startling news, I felt like I was going crazy. An insane amount of hormones were flooding my system, the bad hormones; the ones that left me paranoid and anxious, wanting to crawl out of my skin. I needed something to counter that lethal cocktail of estrogen and progesterone that was killing my optimism. I decided I needed one drink.

I took stock of the dusty bottles of booze in our liquor cabinet. I didn't even like the taste of Grand Marnier, but it was the lesser evil among the jugs of hard liquor left in the house, which included extra-dry vermouth, triple sec, and cooking sherry. What kind of sad alcoholic drinks cooking sherry? So I grabbed a glass of OJ, added in a healthy shot of Grand Marnier, slugged it down, and waited to feel like having twins could be a workable situation. But nothing happened. All I felt was guilty. I was more determined not to drink at all.

Luckily, like with my previous pregnancy, the good hormones kicked in and made it easy to be sober. The pregnancy went smoothly until my twentieth week, when I was alerted that one of the twins was quite a bit smaller than the other. I was told to lie on one side to increase blood flow to the smaller twin for three to four hours a day. I tried my best but I also had a two-year-old, a book deadline, and construction going on in order to make our house accommodate more kids. I had frequent visits with a doctor who specialized in high-risk pregnancies and was finally put on hospital bed rest at thirty weeks so that my little twin's blood flow could be monitored 24/7.

Hanging out in the high-risk ward of the hospital wasn't half bad. I was still under the hormonal delusion that my little twin could pop out full sized, surprising us all, if I just ate enough hospital pudding. But three weeks later I delivered prematurely at thirty-three weeks. The bigger baby was a monstrous four pounds but the little one was only two pounds, the size of a men's loafer. Both twins were promptly placed in the neonatal intensive care unit.

The next month was a blur of stressful daily NICU visits with the babies while our older daughter attended preschool a few days a week. Once my C-section was healed enough that I could drive myself back and forth to the hospital, Jon returned to work, hoping to save his time off for when the babies came home. I made many of those visits alone, pushing past the heavy double NICU doors, scrubbing my hands in the hospital sink until they were raw and irritated, and taking turns holding my bigger baby and staring at my tinier girl in her Isolette. I still hadn't had a drop of alcohol.

After two weeks, the bigger twin came home, and after a month, the smaller twin was sent home to us at only three pounds, having not yet perfected her suck/swallow technique, which, as it would turn out, is a fairly important life skill.

Once both babies were home and the sleep deprivation was kicking my ass, it suddenly occurred to me that, besides that *teeny tiny* Grand Marnier slip-up, I hadn't had any alcohol in almost nine months. It meant that I didn't really have an alcohol problem! If I were an alcoholic, there was no way I could have gone that long without drinking and not missed it at all. This was a huge relief, because I now had newborn preemie twins and a three-year-old; if there was ever a time I needed to drink, it was right now.

Although breastfeeding hadn't worked out with my older daughter and wasn't working for my twins, I invested in a hospital-grade pump in an attempt to eke out even an ounce of breast milk. I'd have done anything to help them grow.

The first thing I drank once I started again was beer, because I read that dark beer stimulates the hormone prolactin, which can increase your milk supply. This was probably bullshit, but at the time, it seemed like as good an excuse as any. You'll be shocked to find out beer didn't turn me into a miracle milk machine, but even if it had, my little twin wasn't eating.

By the time she was four months old she only weighed eight pounds, as much as a normal newborn. Feeding her was a struggle, and doctors couldn't figure out why. It was around this time we realized she had other challenges as well and we were assigned a number of therapists to intervene: an occupational therapist, physical therapist, a child development specialist, and a nutritionist. Meanwhile, I didn't even have a hairstylist. Besides all that was going on with her, my book was due and I had two other kids. Yeah, I had a lot on my plate. Thank God I wasn't an alcoholic!

2. Is This an Intervention?

I didn't see it coming. My sister-in-law, Racquel, along with my brother, Michael, had been coming over a few times a week to help me with my colicky infant twins while Jon was at work. I had a nanny during the day because I was on a book deadline, but she had a hard out at five p.m., which coincidentally marked the beginning of the witching hour, somehow signaling to my twins that it was time to start crying nonstop for approximately three hours. The witching hour also signaled to my brain that it was time to break open the pinot grigio.

Racquel and Michael lived about three minutes away from me, and once they both got home from work they'd come by and take turns holding red-faced, shrieking infants. When I tell you these babies were inconsolable, I'm not exaggerating. If you've never had a colicky baby, I would describe it like that scene in *Ozark* where Jason Bateman takes over as leader of the Mexican cartel and tortures a guy by throwing him in a cell and blasting earsplitting death metal music through speakers until he finally makes a false confession just to make it stop—except you can't make it stop. By the time Racquel and Mike would get to my house at about six thirty p.m., I was waist-deep in white wine and had at least a half a Xanny on board. I was in survival mode.

On one particular visit, Racquel asked if she could talk to me for a minute, *alone*. We left my brother in the living room to attend to both crying babies and walked into the kitchen together to talk about what I assumed would be a new Weight Watchers muffin recipe or the latest episode of *The Bachelor*, and that's when it happened:

"Hey, so I've been worried about you, babe. Obviously you have a lot on your plate right now and I'm sure you're insanely stressed, but I've been noticing that you seem to be drinking a lot every night and it's concerning."

Whoa. I didn't even know what to say or how to respond. I replayed what she'd just said in my mind: *Drinking every night? She was worried about me?* I had infant twins and a toddler. I wasn't sleeping. I was worried about me too. She didn't even have kids. What the fuck did she know? She was in "trying to get pregnant" mode, so her vision of having a baby was of the "idealistic photo that comes with the frame" variety. When she did get pregnant, I knew she'd be one of those people who sends out mass emails telling everyone in her contacts that BabyCenter.com said her fetus is the size of a sweet potato now. She'd definitely decorate her nursery with a theme like Under the Sea or Outer Space. She'd probably do a professional pregnancy photo shoot where she'd wear maternity clothes from A Pea in the Pod and take shot after shot of her looking down at her belly while touching it tenderly, imagining being mom of the fucking year. That's the type of person she was: put-together, accessorized, living a picture-perfect life in a house that was always clean. She knew what fucking wainscoting was.

She had no idea what actual life with kids was like or how I was *hanging on by a thread*. I had postpartum depression and premature babies with *goddamned fucking colic*. Did she not have ears? Could she not hear them screaming bloody murder? She got to go home after helping me. I *was* home. Was it that hard to understand how much I needed something, *anything* to take the edge off? No, she didn't know how I felt. She *couldn't* know how I felt.

She'd never been someone who drank. She was one of those people who talked a good game and *claimed* to love going out with the girls and guzzling an exotic flavored martini; she spoke of times she'd overindulged, but I'd never seen her drunk, and anytime I offered her a glass of sparkling Contadino pinot grigio, my latest obsession, she always said, "No thanks," like it was weird to offer company a glass of wine at three in the afternoon.

But, at the same time, I knew it couldn't have been easy for her to confront me, so she must've been truly worried about me. She wasn't a shitty sister-in-law; we were actually very close. She was my family and she loved me and did want what was best for me, so I knew her intentions weren't bad and that this must've taken a lot of guts, especially not knowing how I was going to react.

If we're keeping it real, this wasn't my first intervention rodeo. When my older daughter was still a baby, before I had twins, two of my friends, Karina and Chloe, invited me over to Karina's condo to have girl talk and supposedly allow me a baby-free hour. But before I could even get into gossiping about all the sex I wasn't having, Karina jumped into her real reason for the invite: "You've seemed out of it lately," she began. I just sat there on the sofa, sipping my tap water, stunned, while she accused me of taking too much Xanax. "I can tell when you've taken it, because you seem pilled out." Now, this was incredibly galling, since Karina was the one who turned me onto benzos in the first place. She'd taken them for years in small amounts in the past. When I'd dealt with bouts of anxiety, she'd offer me a .25-milligram Klonopin, which, truthfully, barely touched my anxiety and only got me thinking how much better a whole-ass milligram would feel. But at that time, I'd had no doctor or diagnosable issues to warrant my getting my own prescription, so I'd had to settle for bumming one off her once in a while.

But now, having been officially diagnosed with postpartum anxiety, I'd been taking Xanax *as needed*, sometimes more, sometimes less. Point being, I hadn't been *abusing* them! But if I thought about it, this accusation tracked: Karina was newly sober and thought she needed to save everyone else. You know those extremists? The friends who join a new religion or try intermittent fasting or discover transcendental meditation and suddenly *it's the only answer and you must do it immediately because it will change your life*? Yeah, that was Karina. She'd found sobriety and now she was basically in a cult and was actively recruiting new members. No thanks.

I'd known Karina since I was in my mid-twenties. We had become close friends, the kind of friends who hung out several nights a week and supported each other through breakups, career upsets, and the time she had a manic episode and became a totally different person for a few months before getting put on medication. But now she was sitting there judging my life and I was pissed. "I'm fine. Please don't worry about me. Worry about your own life." My voice oozed with irritation, but Karina wasn't going to drop it. "I really think you have a problem and I'm going to say something to Jon." Now she was crossing the line! I wasn't going to sit there and listen to that nonsense. Everything was under control. What was she even talking about? You'd think I was leaving my baby in the car while I went barhopping, or that I was losing teeth due to a meth addiction. This wasn't fucking *Trainspotting*!

"You have no clue what you're even talking about! You know

nothing about my life or what I'm doing." I was on my feet, ready to leave, but Chloe came over and grabbed my hand.

"Hey, hey, sit back down. It's fine. We were just worried and wanted to talk to you, but only because we care. Let's just take this down a notch and hang out." To my credit, I did calm down, and I promised to think about what they'd said. And about a year after that I quit drinking and taking Xanax for about six weeks, proving I was fine. Then I'd gotten knocked up with twins, and now here I was, in my kitchen, getting "the talk" once again.

I saw myself from above, listening and nodding and trying to hear my sister-in-law out, while inside my body, everything was churning and hot. This was embarrassing. Who else thought this? Was Racquel leaving my house after helping me with my babies and driving home with my brother talking about my drinking? I imagined their conversations. "Did you notice how out of it your sister was tonight?" Racquel would say. My brother would probably agree but be too scared to say anything to me. He *should* be too scared to say anything! Many years before, when he was still in high school, I'd found his high school yearbook, which was chock-full of references to his drinking, and I'd found out he'd been keeping liquor bottles in his closet, so I had to have a talk with *him*—I'd even had to get my mother involved, although she refused to acknowledge there could be a problem. But the point was, he'd gone through some times when he drank waaay too much, so who the hell did he think he was, judging *me*? I loved my brother. He was my foundation, one of the few people I trusted implicitly! But even though he wasn't the one who said something to me, I doubted he stood up for me either.

One thing was for sure: I'd have to watch the way I drank around her. In fact, even though I needed the support desperately because my husband was back at work sixty hours a week, leaving me alone with the twin terrors, I probably wouldn't be inviting her over to help me anymore, not if she was going to be keeping tabs on me, noticing every time I went in the kitchen and opened the refrigerator, probably thinking I was sneaking a sip of wine. I wouldn't be able to just enjoy an adult beverage like a fucking normal person with her around.

Despite feeling like a cornered rat, I told myself not to panic and get ahead of myself. She was worried. I didn't want to discount that. Maybe she had reason to be concerned. I did have two little babies and a toddler and I cared for them more than anything. I felt so protective over them, like a mama bear. I would never want to hurt them.

And right then and there, I had a moment of clarity. It was the Xanax. That was the problem. I was taking my Xanax as directed, but when you combine that with the couple glasses of wine I had at night, it was probably making me seem out of it, like she said. Okay. That made sense. This was a good thing. I was actually really happy she'd brought it to my attention. And I had to pat myself on the back for being so willing to take in what she was saying without getting defensive. I would need to take a harder look at my combining Xanax with wine, but the good news was I wasn't an alcoholic—definitely not. Nothing really had to change. Phew.

3. Sugar, We're Goin' Down

Sugar was my very first full-on addiction. It can't get you arrested the way booze, crack, heroin, or opiates can, but it has led to some risky behavior on my part. When I was four years old I stole some Halloween candy from our kitchen pantry. Halloween was only a few days away but I couldn't wait. I knew my mother had hidden the bag of assorted Hershey bars high up out of my reach because I wasn't supposed to have them—they were meant for trick-or-treaters—but I'd seen her do it and now it was all I thought about. All day long, the bag called to me from its top shelf, until I finally had to take action.

I summited our pantry's white-painted wooden shelves like a seasoned climber scaling Mount Whitney—securing my foot on the first level, where the boxes of healthy cereal were kept, then grabbing on to the next shelf, which held the dry rice, uncooked beans, pasta, and cans of Yuban coffee. Next I managed to boost myself up to the canned goods: tuna, Campbell's chicken noodle soup and, even better, chicken and dumplings. I bypassed the baking-goods shelf, since I'd once been traumatized after sneaking a bite of bitter unsweetened chocolate. Higher still I climbed, to the cookies. Normally the box of Fig Newtons would have been the goal, but today I needed to reach the peak. With one foot on the Newton's shelf, I reached high up over my head and at last secured the bag of chocolate.

I was terrified of getting in trouble, but I figured if I could have just one—one little mini Hershey bar—I'd be able to get it off my mind and survive until Halloween. So I made a *very small* hole in the plastic with my tiny four-year-old baby teeth, carefully slid one bite-sized candy bar out, unwrapped it with one hand, and ate it right there, while still holding on to the top shelf with my other hand. And then I ate another one, because who are we kidding, one wasn't going to do it. Then I ate ten more because, hell, I was already up there, wasn't I?

Once I climbed down, I was immediately seized with regret. I didn't feel better after eating all that chocolate; I felt worse. Now that I was no longer obsessing on getting my fix, I was petrified of getting found out. I worried about it constantly until the afternoon of Halloween, when I watched my mom stand on a stepstool and get the candy down in order to put it in a bowl for the neighborhood kids. She knew immediately what I'd done and she was furious. "Goddamn it, Stefanie! How could you do that? You knew that candy was not for you! You're so selfish!" My face reddened and I started to cry. I was so ashamed but I couldn't explain it to her; she wouldn't understand that I just couldn't help myself. My need for relief was stronger than my fear of consequences.

Even at four years old I knew I loved candy more than other people did, even other kids. Sure I realized every kid loves candy, but for me it was on a whole other level. I *had* to have candy. I thought about candy, dreamed about candy and how it made me feel. Candy calmed my soul, and even as a preschooler, my soul needed calming: My parents were getting a divorce.

My mother met my father when she was seventeen and he was twenty-nine. She was a guest at a resort in the Catskills where he served as the entertainment director. Imagine *Dirty Dancing* but replace Patrick Swayze with Woody Allen and you're in the ballpark. He had already been married twice before, and she was obviously too young for him then, but I guess she went back, because two years later, when she was nineteen and he was thirty-one, they eloped and she became wife number three. And four years after that, they had me. When I was two, we moved from Queens, New York, to sunny California because my father, Stanley Myron Handelman, who'd been working as a stand-up comedian for years, was really starting to make it. He was a regular guest on *The Merv Griffin Show*, *The Ed Sullivan Show*, *The Flip Wilson Show*, *The Dean Martin Show*, *The Smothers Brothers Comedy Hour*, and *The Tonight Show*.

Whenever my father was on TV, my mother would let me stay up late to watch. I'd sit cross-legged directly in front of the twenty-three-inch screen with the rabbit ears and wave madly at the television, trying to get his attention. "Hi Daddy! Hi Daddy! Hi! Daddy!" I'd yell. But he never acknowledged me, even though he seemed to be looking straight at me. My mom said he couldn't see me, but that seemed impossible. I was right there.

As my father's star rose, he traveled back and forth to Vegas, first to open for Frank Sinatra and eventually to headline Caesars Palace. He said everyone thought he would bomb because the comedy in vogue was more in line with Don Rickles's rapid-fire bada-boom style, not my father's subtle, deadpan, silly delivery. But he killed it that night and continued to be successful for many years to follow.

My mother was also funny and bright. Once Rodney Dangerfield was at our house writing jokes with my dad. Rodney was trying to figure out an opening line for his appearance that night on *The Tonight Show* and my mom tossed out a line from the bathroom while she was peeing. Rodney didn't acknowledge her at the time or anytime after but he used the joke that night and it got a huge laugh. I think she was always a little bitter about that. I would be too.

My mother has said that although she appreciated comedy, show biz life was not for her. She wanted to lounge around the house with no makeup on in her underwear, not host cocktail parties for Hollywood phonies. I'm not sure why she and my father split up—I later heard rumors of a cocktail waitress—but I suspect that my mother, with dreams and aspirations of her own, didn't relish her role as a background player to a man who always had to be the star of the show. While I was still in nursery school, the final curtain came down on their marriage.

After the divorce, like a lot of kids, I had big emotions that had nowhere to go. We were still a couple of years away from Marlo Thomas's *Free to Be You and Me*, where kids were told their feelings were valid and Rosey Grier sang that it's all right to cry. Sometimes, when the angst got to be too much, I took it out on my stuffed animals—one night I literally let out primal screams while tearing my Flip Wilson doll limb from limb, until Flip was a pile of stuffing and I fell asleep, completely spent, clutching his one tiny amputated leg, which was all that was left of him.

My father lived his dream by renting a house out in Malibu with its own private beach so he could roll joints surrounded by hippies, celebrities, and surfers, while my mother and I lived in a one-bedroom apartment in a not-so-nice area of Hollywood, which, considering the fact that no parts of Hollywood could actually be considered nice is really saying something.

My soon-to-be stepfather moved in with us a few months later. Up until that point, he'd been my dad's best friend and had lived in our guesthouse. So that was awkward. I never really got the full story, because my mother was a classic under-sharer, but you do the math.

At first, every few Sundays I would throw on a romper sewn by my mom from a Simplicity sewing pattern, which I tied around the waist with a delicate velvet rope, and either my father would pick me up or I'd be driven to his house, where I would play on the beach or swim in the waves with a famous neighbor or one of my dad's random new girlfriends. I was fairly brave and would often swim out into the surf, where sometimes I'd get caught in a breaker and tumble head over feet, petrified because I couldn't breathe. But eventually I'd pop up, hair tangled in seaweed, the crotch of my bathing suit packed full of wet sand, eager to go out and do it again.

At night he would take me to dinner at restaurants that served tons of warm bread and butter and my favorite dish: fried shrimp. I would stuff myself, eating every bite of the crispy, greasy, hot shrimp, including the tail, because I couldn't seem to get enough food or enough of my dad. He'd let me top off my meal with a huge hot fudge sundae and marvel that I could eat every bite. There are kids who will eat four bites of dessert and forget about it; some of those kids grow up to be adults who are not my kind of people.

Many times when I was out and about with my dad he'd be approached by people who recognized him and wanted to meet him and steal some of his time. "Hey, are you that comedian?" they'd say. "Hang on, I'm bringing my wife over here. She loves you on *Ed Sullivan*." And with that, my father would find himself surrounded by fans, enjoying the adoration he'd always suspected he deserved. Sometimes I would be introduced and feel special, but other times he seemed to forget I was there.

There were also a lot of times my father was late and even more times he didn't show up at all. I'd wait for him in front of our upper duplex's bay window, which looked out onto the street, watching every car turn the corner, hoping it was his. As it got later, my anxiety would climb higher. Blue car, nope; red car, nope; beige car . . . oh, it's him! Wait, wrong beige car. My mom would try calling him and sometimes he'd answer and say he had a headache and wasn't going to make it, but other times he wouldn't pick up. After an hour and still no dad, we were left to simply assume he wouldn't be coming. My mother may have felt bad for me, but since he refused to pay any child support despite making boatloads of money, she had very low expectations.

By the time I was six, I'd started to feel more anxious when he *did* show up. Sometimes our visits were cut short because I'd be "acting up," he told my mom, so he'd drop me back off thirty minutes after picking me up. This was fine with me. Sometimes he wanted to take me to Disneyland and I'd ask to bring a friend because I needed a buffer between my increasingly absent dad and my rising angry feelings.

The high point of any trip to Disneyland with my father was our trip to the Candy Palace on Main Street, where, possibly out of guilt, he would buy me and my friend a big bag of candy; sometimes saltwater taffy, sometimes lemon drops coated with granulated sugar, and sometimes brightly colored rock candy on a stick. But eventually, even the promise of the Matterhorn and sugar wasn't enough for me to deal with the awkwardness and anxiety of a distant dad, and I'd ask if I could just stay home with my mom.

By the time I was nine or ten, our outings were much less frequent—we often went many months between visits—but when I did see him, my anxiety was even more magnified. His star, which had shot up when I was little, somehow never shined quite as brightly as we'd all expected, and by the time I was nine, it was starting to dim altogether. The development deals never turned into anything, the TV spots dried up, and he began teaching comedy. He'd moved from his sweet Malibu rental to a one-bedroom apartment in a decidedly less cool part of town. It wasn't the lifestyle to which he'd grown accustomed: There was no doorman or valet; in fact, the amenities were limited to a parking spot and laundry. Now when he claimed he had no money to pay child support, my mother believed him.

Sometimes I would have to go to his place for a visit. We'd long since stopped going out to nice restaurants and there wasn't much food in his fridge but he'd offer me a glass of OJ and ask me to sit while he played jazz piano for me. "Heya Stef, do you want to hear me play?" I really didn't, to be honest. As a preteen, I wasn't much of a jazz fan. Come to think of it, as an adult, I'm not much of a jazz fan, at least not the improvisational, meandering, no-lyrics-having variety. I like my songs to have a specific beginning, middle, and end, with no directionless jamming. But my father wasn't interested in my honesty, and since he wasn't making television appearances, he was starved for an audience, so I had to say yes.

I would perch on an uncomfortable chair in front of his piano bench so he could watch me listen and I would try to make interested faces. But how do you look "interested" in someone playing the piano? It requires a lot of face acting, plus you have to engage your head and neck a little with some bobbing but not too much bobbing, or you could overdo it and seem like you were being sarcastic. It was a lot for a kid with undiagnosed ADHD.

During these visits and subsequent lunches, I noticed that my father took a lot of pills. He said they were for migraines, but I didn't love how he seemed to act about twenty minutes after he'd take one. I also understood migraines; I'd gotten them for years already at this point. I knew that when I had a headache I was given two Bayer aspirins and hoped for the best. Even if it didn't work, I had to wait four hours to take more. I certainly didn't carry around a bottle of aspirin and chew a few up every so often and then start talking like my words had been thrown in a blender and set to whip.

Sometimes I'd ask him about it. "Why do you take so many of those pills?" I'd say, casually, with a mouth full of grilled cheese.

"It's for my headaches."

"Why can't you take aspirin?" I'd ask, as if I was trying to be helpful, but I was really annoyed.

"These pills are the only things that work for me, Stef. I need 'em." And with that, case closed. You didn't argue with my father, because when he was angry, it was like watching a total eclipse of the sun. His face would go from bright and animated to dark and shut down. It wasn't energy you wanted to be around.

Back at home, my mom, who'd had my baby brother with my stepfather when I was seven, had just given birth to my baby sister. My mother seemed incredibly happy with my stepfather, and now, with the addition of a boy and a girl, they felt like one happy family. But rather than feeling a part of it, I felt apart. My mother didn't speak to my father anymore at all, and I was finding it more and more difficult to maintain a relationship with him. But I also didn't understand my place in this other, new family.

If a therapist were questioning me right now, I might make the connection that it was around this time that my candy addiction began to pick up steam. But who can really tell? Maybe I was simply born this way. All I know is that at some point my mother became more into health foods and I became acutely aware that it was up to me to secure my next hit of sugar.

Enter my best friend, Debbie. My stepfather was close with Debbie's mom, and Debbie and I took turns sleeping at each other's houses on weekends. Debbie lived with her mom and her mom's boyfriend, who was a famous jazz producer and ran a comedy record label in the seventies. They lived in a humongous house in the Hollywood Hills with its own parking lot, sauna, and maid's apartment. I want to say the Jackson 5 had lived there at one point, but I could be wrong. That's what the disclaimer at the beginning of this book is for. Anyway, when Debbie and I slept there, we had access to ice cream, candy, and any snack we could dream up served by maids dressed in black and white. Plus, they threw lavish parties, so we would sneak around eating desserts off of trays and helping ourselves to little sips of champagne left unattended.

Debbie's house was the first of our friends' houses to have cable TV, most notably the Z channel, where we could watch R-rated movies like *Blazing Saddles* and *Airport 1975*, movies that featured lots of swearing and sometimes boobs—once we even had a rare bush sighting! These were decadent times, and the jazz producer seemed to have an endless supply of cash, so sometimes, when it was Debbie's turn to sleep at my place, she would sneak into his closet and steal a fifty-dollar bill from the pocket of his suit jacket. Debbie and I would take the smuggled cash, walk four neighborhood blocks, cross one major street, and head into Montgomery Ward—a kind of precursor to Target—where we would buy bags full of Brach's penny candy. The Royals were my favorite in orange, maple, chocolate, and raspberry but I also loved those square Neapolitan coconut chews—yeah, I'm the one.

Fifty bucks buys a shitload of candy, so with our leftover cash we'd buy as many Wacky Packages as we could afford. Wacky Packages were like baseball cards or Garbage Pail Kids cards for you eighties babies. The idea was to collect an entire series, so the more you could buy, the better your chances of completing the collection. Each pack cost about five cents and contained a few stickers that made fun of products—for instance, they had Cup-a-Slop instead of Cup-a-Soup or Ratz instead of Ritz; you get the picture—a cardboard puzzle piece, and a slab of bright pink bubble gum. So every other Saturday, Debbie and I ate our way through bags of candy and piece after piece of bubble gum. No piece of gum got more than twenty seconds of chewing time before we decided to replace it with a newer, sweeter piece. There was something that felt magical about having more candy than I needed, something soothing about feeling like I'd never run out. Life felt briefly manageable.

But when I turned twelve, my mother and stepfather decided to leave Los Angeles and start over somewhere else. That somewhere else turned out to be Spokane, Washington. In answer to your question, no, we didn't have family there. There was nothing there, no good reason to move. I wouldn't see my father again until I was sixteen—not that he seemed to mind.

We loaded up our used station wagon with camping gear in order to drive from Los Angeles to Washington, and my mother, stepfather, three-year-old sister, and five-year-old brother pulled away forever from my father, my friends, my home, my school, and everything I'd ever known. I felt like I was being kidnapped.

We arrived in Spokane three weeks before the moving van arrived with our furniture, so we were forced to go to bed in sleeping bags laid out on maroon shag carpet in the living room of an empty house. I started having nightmares every night—dreams of being eaten alive by giant spiders, or being attacked by masked robbers. I had one dream that I jumped off of a diving board into an empty pool and died. I could see myself from up above, watched the ambulance come and put me in a body bag and zip it up. This was way before I watched my first episode of *Forensic Files* or listened to a true-crime podcast, so it was all created in my anxious imagination. Luckily, my parents were sensitive to what was going on with me and got me right into some therapy to help me cope.

I'm kidding. I just dealt.

Twelve was also the age at which I started having what we now would refer to as disordered eating but at the time I considered dieting. I didn't need to lose weight; back in LA I'd been doing gymnastics three times a week for years. And wanting to control my food wasn't a learned behavior either, because, unlike a lot of my friends' parents, my mother was a unicorn—not obsessed with dieting or weight loss, never talked about calories or fat, just about health and the virtue of going for a walk; she was an early adapter of carob and wheat germ. She was also a proud feminist with no shame about her cellulite or ample thighs and never pointed out a thing wrong with my body.

I began with eating only Saltine crackers and drinking lemonade for about four days straight until I got really hungry, walked to 7-Eleven, and binged on three Hershey bars and a Blow Pop, thus kicking off many years of all-or-nothing, black-and-white eating. I was being good or I was bad. But I had no control.

My parents kept ice cream in the house in half-gallon containers—Jamoca almond fudge or rocky road. My brother and sister and I were each allowed a small serving in a little white coffee cup, a perfectly reasonable amount for a perfectly reasonable person. My parents would take their perfectly sized servings into their room and sit on their bed watching TV and having "their" time while my siblings and I would eat our ice cream at the kitchen table and then go to our rooms—theirs next to each other on the same floor as my parents and mine in the basement.

And then the obsession would take over. You see, I needed just one more bite of ice cream. Just one. So I'd sneak upstairs, quietly slide open the silverware drawer, grab a spoon—not a teaspoon, the bigger spoon, the tablespoon—open the freezer, take out the ice cream, and scoop myself just one more big bite. *That should do it*, I'd think, and I'd go back downstairs and try to take my mind off of dessert. But I needed a little bit more, so I'd creep back up the stairs and take one more bite, but I was careful to even out the ice cream in the container, smoothing it over with the back of the spoon so it didn't look obvious. Up and down the stairs I'd go, as the level in the container got lower and lower. The next time my mother went to get ice cream, she'd be furious, and she knew from experience exactly who was responsible.

Much like my later alcohol addiction, for a long time my sugar addiction was mostly a battle I fought internally until, ten years after Halloween-Pantry-Gate, my candy obsession actually got me fired from a job. I was babysitting two young girls and it must've been right around Easter, because these people had two full bags of those seasonal little chocolate eggs wrapped in brightly colored foil in their refrigerator. Why were they keeping them in the fridge? Did they not have air-conditioning? I don't know. What I do know is I could not stop eating them. I'd play with the girls for a few minutes but then hear the chocolate eggs calling to me from the fridge. "Just one more," they would say, in high-pitched chocolaty voices. So I'd go back into the kitchen, berating myself the entire time. *Stop. Don't do it!* I'd say inside my head while reaching for just five more and then just one more. Those eggs were so little, and I just couldn't seem to eat enough to satisfy myself. I knew what I was doing was wrong. I was embarrassed that I couldn't stop and petrified of the possible repercussions if I was found out. *What was wrong with me? Why was I like this?* I tried to hang out with my charges and focus on our Yahtzee game but I simply couldn't. The kids kept asking me where I was going. "The bathroom," I'd say, like it was none of their business—I'm in charge here. And so I kept going until I'd eaten through all of one bag, leaving only three quarters of the second bag in the fridge, which I'd half hidden behind a gallon of low-fat milk.

Naturally, the parents complained to my mother that I'd eaten all their kids' Easter candy. I tried to deny it, pleading with my mother to tell the parents that their kids ate it while I wasn't looking. But no one bought it, especially my mother, who was used to living with a lying sugar thief. I was never hired back.

By the time I was sixteen, my amateur attempts at dieting eventually morphed into a full-fledged cycle of binging and purging—also known as bulimia, but it's such a gross word. Let's just say that I binged large amounts of food and then felt a compulsion to get it out of my system so I wouldn't gain weight. I liked the feeling of letting myself lose control and eat everything I wanted all at once, but the second I was done, finally feeling full and sick after two pints of Cherry Garcia, Kraft mac and cheese, and whatever was soft and could be brought back up easily, I would be overcome with an even more powerful urge to regain control.

In case you are thinking, *Genius! I hadn't thought of that, but it makes sense! I might give it a go!*, please don't. First of all, it doesn't work. Second of all, it's a trap. Once you're ensnared in the binge-purge cycle, it's next to impossible to stop. Like drinking, it's addictive because the act of eating all the food releases dopamine, and once the food is gone, the dopamine levels drop and you're back to needing to do it again to raise the levels back up. I treated my anxiety with food, and then I treated the anxiety of having eaten so much food with purging. Like with alcohol, after a particularly gnarly binge I'd promise myself, *Never again*, but by the following day, the thought of *just one more time* would start rattling around my head like a ghost in the attic—getting louder and more insistent until I couldn't stand it anymore and the only way to get some goddamned quiet in my brain would be to head out in search of snacks for my next binge.

Some alkies go to several liquor stores to load up on their supply so it doesn't seem like they're buying so much. With bulimia, I would do that same thing, but with different grocery stores to gather my donuts or ice cream or cheese. I'd load my cart with cheap snacks and head to the cashier, where I'd have to make a choice: either avoid eye contact altogether, having to imagine the employee's grimace as they scanned the conveyor belt and saw all those calories or . . . get ahead of it by facing the cashier with confidence, letting them know, *I'm just grabbing some snacks for the party I'm having later*!

The thing about bulimia, as opposed to alcohol addiction, is it's pretty obvious to yourself if you have it. You're either throwing up every day on purpose or you're not. And if you are, you're walking around with a painful secret, a life that has become ritualized and small.

The obviousness of my problem was what enabled me to seek help with my food issues later in life, long before I dealt with the drinking. I started with talk therapy around the age of twenty and advanced to a few meetings designed for food addiction, read dozens of self-help books, and was eventually able to leave bulimia behind for good. Of course, nature abhors a vacuum, and without the anxiety-quelling assist of a solid binge and purge, I eventually leaned harder into alcohol.

4. I Remember
My First Beer

I drank for the first time at the tender age of fourteen, as a freshman in high school. It sounds young to me now considering that, as I write this, my twins are ninth graders themselves, but at the time, I would've told you I was late to the party. My best friend, Jamie, and I were obsessed with two boys, both named Brett, who were seniors. Just like in every John Hughes movie, the Bretts didn't know we were alive. And since I never love anything with half-assed effort, I made it my business to get my Brett's attention—hanging near his locker, passing him carefully crafted notes, focusing all my psychic energy on getting him to think about me while lying in my bed at night listening to REO Speedwagon's "Keep On Loving You."

Jamie did the same with her Brett, and with probably the same intensity, since—spoiler alert—she ended up with addiction issues as well. Whatever witchcraft we did worked, because one night, the Bretts picked us up in my Brett's little yellow VW Rabbit and took us to a drive-in to see *Stripes*. But first, we stopped at a liquor store, where the guys somehow procured us two six-packs of Olympia beer.

Sitting in the backseat of the car, Brett right next to me smelling of Pierre Cardin, sipping my first beer, I was already feeling some things I'd never felt before, and those things were scaring the shit out of me. I'd never kissed anyone, but it felt inevitable it would be happening. Tonight.

The Bretts went to buy popcorn while Jamie and I sipped from our cans, the Olympia label sneakily hidden by our foam beer koozies, in case any nosy car neighbors noticed our underage drinking. The first few swallows tasted pretty nasty—which is why I'd never had more than a sip here and there of my parents' beer—but I noted that it got better once you were about half a can down. When the Bretts returned, it seemed obvious they had strategized, because within minutes, they had each draped an arm around our respective shoulders.

This shit was on like *Donkey Kong*.

As I sat there in the car feeling paralyzed by excitement, fear, and self-consciousness, the beer slowly brought on a less familiar but welcome sensation. I began to feel buzzy, warm, and settled. It was as if my body's internal alarm systems, which had been overactive as far back as I could remember, somehow lowered their defenses just a bit. I was still very nervous, but somehow it all seemed slightly more manageable.

Brett's face was getting closer to mine and my heart was beating like a ferret that just realized it was prey. I had to stop him because . . . I didn't know how to kiss. I could have been twelve beers in and I still would've felt stupid and inexperienced. I was just built that way. I had no idea what else to do but tell him. Thank God my buzz made me brave. "You're probably wondering why I'm not kissing you," I whispered. I didn't exactly want the entire VW to know my business.

"Yeah, I kind of was," he said, but nice and patient, like a favorite camp counselor who plays guitar.

"I've never done it before and I don't know how," I said. And I cringed so hard I can still feel it now, forty-plus years later.

"It's okay. I can teach you." With those words, my life went from black-and-white to color, just like in *The Wizard of Oz*. He started me off with the peck. "The way you kiss your grandma," he told me, as he gently pecked me on the mouth with semi-pursed lips. "Next we move on to the medium, 'I like you' kiss," and he laid one on my lips with his soft, smooth, but way more confident lips. This man was definitely not a virgin. "And now, the granddaddy of all kisses, the French. We employ a bit of tongue, a soupçon. I'll show you." And then I got kissed for real. At this point I was three beers in, feeling like I finally understood what every soft hit of the eighties was really about.

The second time I drank, a few weeks later, ended with me throwing up violently on a stranger's porch after a night of drinking grain alcohol punch from red Solo cups (we called it spody-ody and its appearance at a party would always be greeted with whoops of "spody-ody!"). I woke up in my bed fully dressed right down to my jelly shoes with a scorching hangover and a spotty memory of what had happened the night before. Jamie was in my bed beside me, crying because her ankle was swollen as if someone had blown it up like a balloon. She didn't go to the doctor for three days because we didn't want anyone to know what had happened. But rather than learn my lesson from the second experience, I was off to the races in an effort to recapture the magic of the first experience.

One night soon after, Jamie and I were alone in my kitchen and decided to make some mixed drinks with vodka we found in the liquor cabinet. My parents mainly drank Carlo Rossi Chablis out of four-liter glass bottles they kept in the fridge, but there were plenty of bottles of hard liquor in the cabinet growing dusty waiting for company to come over. We pulled out the Smirnoff vodka figuring we could most easily mask the taste of it with the only mixer we had on hand, pink lemonade. We called our concoctions Pink Indians, named for . . . I don't fucking know! We were fourteen!

The next thing I remember is being at the movie *Heavy Metal*, coming in and out of consciousness and then somehow being back home puking, leading into my next of a long series of horrendous hangovers.

By the time I was fifteen, I was drinking every weekend, often hanging out at local parks and campgrounds attending "choir practice," which was our code name for keg parties, with—at least it seemed at the time—the majority of my high school. I couldn't tell you how these kegs were procured, only that they showed up and were hoisted off the beds of pickup trucks, positioned under a tree, and drained by the end of the night. We got rides from older kids and sometimes walked home, drunk and stumbly.

Sometimes parties and hangouts happened after curfew. Jamie and I would come back to my house by midnight and then wait for the sounds of my parents having sex to carry through my heating vent. Once they got loud enough, we'd sneak out of my basement bedroom window. One night, parked in an older Chevy Malibu at three a.m., drinking cans of Bud, a police officer knocked on the window with his flashlight, scaring the shit out of us. I silently prayed he wouldn't force us into his cruiser to drive us home, possibly putting an end to my extended late nights and tipping off my parents to my drinking once and for all, but he only poured out the remainder of our beer and told us to go home.

At this point you must be wondering, "How did your parents not know?" No clue. You'd think my parents would have caught on, considering the fact that every single Sunday morning I was unable to go to Hebrew school due to a sudden-onset stomach virus or migraine headache. You'd have figured at the very least I'd be brought to the doctor to check on my weekly health issues. Once in a while I would be accused of faking my symptoms and, afraid I'd never learn Hebrew, my mom would force me to go to our temple, where I'd sit, nauseous and sweating, rushing in and out of the bathroom to puke. But not even the rabbi questioned what was going on with me.

I spent a lot of time at Jamie's house. She lived almost directly across the street, and her mom was someone I considered a safe person. My mother was moody and inconsistent, one day nurturing but the next flying into a rage. One night, in a fit of anger that could have been over homework or coming home five minutes late, she called me a selfish bitch and threw a large mason jar she used for canning jam at my head. I ducked and it missed my face but shattered against the wood-paneled wall, raining glass over me. I ran crying to Jamie's house, where, for the next two hours, I sat on their blue shag rug sobbing while Jamie's mom sat behind me in a chair, meticulously picking shards of glass out of my hair.

If my relationship with my mom was tense, my relationship with my stepfather was downright rocky. But by the time I got to high school, it had deteriorated to an almost unlivable situation. My stepfather was a gifted photographer but unfortunately found it impossible to hold a job where he had to work for someone else, so he was usually at home, in close proximity to me, while my mother was at work. Since he didn't care for me, my stepfather mostly acted like I didn't exist, finding any excuse to give me the silent treatment. I'd walk into the kitchen in the morning while he was making omelets for my mother, brother, and sister, and he'd straight up pretend I wasn't there. This could go on for days, but sometimes it went on for months at a time. When he *was* speaking to me, he picked fights over anything and everything—the pronunciation of the president's name, whether a tomato is a fruit or vegetable, whether 54 degrees is cold outside—not stopping until he got a rise out of me, pushing relentlessly until I cried, which made me wish he'd go back to not speaking to me.

A few of my therapists over the years had their theories: Maybe I was a constant reminder of my mother's previous life; maybe once he had his own kids with my mom he didn't see me as part of his real family. All I know is that he had a chip on his shoulder as heavy as a boulder, and eventually, he passed that chip down to me, and I carried it well into adulthood.

Looking back on things, my stepfather definitely had his own demons to contend with, but at the time, all I knew was I didn't fit in with my family and often felt as if I was floating around like an angry ghost.

And then, the spring before I turned sixteen, I found out we were moving again. It all started when I steamed open a legal-sized envelope addressed to my mother from Baystate Medical Center in Springfield, Massachusetts. My mom taught nursing at a school in Spokane and she complained about her job a lot, so a letter from a medical center was highly suspicious, which is why I intercepted it. And I was right: It was a job offer. After our move from California before seventh grade, my mother had promised me we would stay put until I finished high school, but now, while I was still a sophomore, she'd been actively applying for jobs and apparently had landed one.

I carefully resealed the letter and silently prayed I wouldn't hear more about it, that she was just putting out feelers for the future. But

I wasn't surprised when the following week my mother announced we were moving.

I sobbed and tried pleading with her: *"We've only been in Spokane for four years! I have a best friend! I'm in tenth grade! No one moves in the middle of high school!"* But my mother was unaffected. It was a done deal. Jamie's mother offered to let me live with them so I could finish high school, even speaking to my mother about it. But I wasn't allowed to stay.

In Springfield, my drinking and drug use escalated, starting that very summer. We arrived in the new city and stayed with an old friend of my mother's while my parents went house hunting. This friend had a son named Josh, who was a year or two older, and he was forced to let me tag along with him and a few of his friends. Our first outing was to a bar called Ichabod's. In Spokane, underage drinking in parks was the thing; in Springfield, kids drank in bars. Once Josh's mom's Toyota was parked in the lot and we were piling out, it occurred to me that I wasn't twenty-one, the legal drinking age in Massachusetts. "How am I going to get in?" I asked, hoping someone had a plan. I was already way too excited. "I'm only sixteen." *Just turned*, I didn't add.

"They don't check IDs," Josh said, like this was the most normal thing in the world and pretty ridiculous that I would even bring it up. Well, okay then.

Sure enough, we walked right past the tall bouncer at the door, slid into a high-backed wooden booth, and, just like that, I ordered my first Heineken in a bar.

A week later, I had another first: I actually got stoned from smoking pot. The Ichabod's gang was hanging out in Josh's garage, and his cute friend Aaron was working out the beginning riff to Pink Floyd's "Wish You Were Here" on guitar while I listened, thrilled to be included. Naturally, a joint was passed around, and when it reached me, I took it without hesitation. I'd tried pot many times before. The first time had been when Jamie and I went into my parents' bedroom and stole some of my stepfather's homegrown weed, which he thought he kept "hidden" in aluminum film canisters. It was the worst-kept secret in our house, since to my great embarrassment my parents grew pot right in our breakfast room. Rows and rows of cannabis plants lined a wall next to the staircase that led to our basement—and, subsequently, my bedroom—so all my friends had to walk by this marijuana mecca anytime they came over. I tried to pass them off as Japanese maples, which were all the rage in the eighties, but only because they looked exactly like pot plants. I wasn't fooling anyone.

Jamie and I found some Zig-Zag rolling papers right next to the pot and we attempted to create a couple of joints the way I'd seen my parents do it a million times. The problem was, the homegrown shit was dry and crumbly like oregano, and, come to think of it, it didn't smell like much either. My stepfather would never have made it in the serious drug trade. We took our DIY doobies into my backyard and lit up, intent on getting giggly and mellow, the experience every Cheech and Chong movie promised.

"Do you feel anything?" Jamie asked, after she'd finished coughing.

"My throat burns, but other than that, no." We were sort of laughing a lot, but more because the situation was kind of hilarious, not because we were high. I chalked it up to bad weed and left my parents' stash alone after that.

The next few times I tried pot, it was out of a bong, and although I coughed a ton, I never felt any real effect. So back in Josh's garage,

I was confident I was just immune to the effects of marijuana, and I took a long hit so everyone would see I knew what I was doing, which caused me to cough violently.

"Ever had indica?" Aaron asked, between guitar strums. He had a spare guitar pick in his teeth, so I wasn't 100 percent sure what he said.

"Of course," I said confidently, even though I'd never heard of it.

"It's good shit." Aaron seemed to have been playing that same "Wish You Were Here" riff forever, but I wasn't complaining, because it sounded amazing; possibly better than the album. Next thing I knew, we were squeezed into a booth at Friendly's ice cream, sharing a mint cookie crunch sundae, which was the best thing I'd ever tasted up until that point. I could make out every ingredient as if the flavor was coming at me in stereo, separate but blending beautifully, the fudge a magnificent thick condensed foil to the airy lightness of the whipped cream.

And then I was laughing and laughing and oh God I couldn't stop laughing, but then out of nowhere, I could no longer feel my legs; not like they were numb, more like they didn't exist, had never existed, like I was literally a torso with arms attempting to balance on my vinyl seat. I was so fucking high and I couldn't wait to do it again.

But the very next time I got stoned, I spent most of the experience wishing I weren't so stoned, feeling paranoid that everyone knew I was stoned and worrying that I might be permanently stoned. I'd heard of people who dropped acid and never rejoined reality. Could that happen with pot? If so, it would definitely happen to me. Was there anything I could do to hasten a comedown? I'd once heard that the potassium in bananas can make you feel less high but I didn't have a banana. Eventually I had to settle for some Hostess mini powdered sugar donuts and wait it out. For me, getting high was a lot like when

I go on CraZanity at Six Flags Magic Mountain: It always seems like a great idea when I'm in line, but once I'm swinging pendulum style 170 feet up I remember how much I dislike the feeling. But by the time I have that realization, the ride hasn't even swung to its highest point yet, so I have to just close my eyes and pray that I live through it. And then the next time I'm at Magic Mountain I do it again.

My first friend at my new Springfield high school was a girl named Abby whom I'd met over the summer at the Jewish Community Center. I was happy to know at least one person and to have someone to meet up with at my locker the first day of school, but Abby didn't drink or smoke pot and seemed to have no dark, chaotic feelings she needed to numb with substances, so I knew I'd have to expand my horizons very quickly and find friends with common interests.

Somehow I found my way to a small group of girls who became my party buddies and best friends. Similar to Spokane, Springfield didn't have much to offer teenagers in the way of entertainment besides drinking. When we weren't going downtown to bars like the Keg Room, Ichabod's, and Bar Association—cutely named for its proximity to the courthouse—our ritual was to go to a nearby liquor store, stand outside, and ask guys who looked like they'd recently turned twenty-one to buy us booze. If we were successful (which we mostly were), we'd then walk approximately a mile and a half from my house down Sumner Avenue to a parking lot where we would hang out and drink. Our go-to was beer, but sometimes we were able to procure something a little more fancy. For a while my thing was a small bottle of DeKuyper 100-proof peppermint schnapps, which I'd pair with a can of grape soda, alternating sips of the schnapps with sips of the soda to help it go down easier, until the time I got so sick from that combination I couldn't brush my teeth with mint tooth-paste for a month.

I honestly couldn't tell you at this point if I drank more or less than anyone else I knew. It was just what everyone did, at least the people in my group. Among my crew, I blended. I wasn't the "prob-lem" friend, the girl it took two people to carry out of a party, one holding her arms and one her legs. We all knew that girl. That was the bar I measured myself against; that's how I knew that I wasn't out of control. I told myself I was having fun, despite the regret I would feel when I woke up in the morning with a vague memory that I'd made out with three different guys throughout the night.

The school part of high school was a shit show for me. Although I'd been a straight-A student through junior high (yes, it's now called middle school, but I didn't go to middle school, I went to junior high, so stop correcting me in your head), it was only because I was coasting on my elementary school knowledge. I won an eighth-grade spelling bee, not because I was any sort of Scripps-level speller but because I was a voracious reader, and when I didn't know a word in my Nancy Drew Mystery, I would look it up in the dictionary, and also, *no one* at my new school knew how to spell. But by the time I hit high school, I couldn't float by on my God-given smarts anymore, and I was also expected to do homework and pay attention in class. Once it became challenging to get good grades, I simply gave up. This was especially true in math. I had always struggled to understand any math concepts as early as I could remember, but once I hit geometry, I may as well have been dropped on Mars and expected to converse with extraterrestrials. It seemed so impossible that I sort of assumed everyone who said they understood it was lying. I would sit in class, feeling adrift while the teacher explained some concept and I would feel the pressure rise, wanting to raise my hand and say, "I don't get it!" But I'd look around, hoping everyone would look as lost as I felt, but no one did. So I kept my confusion to myself and pretended like there was no issue. And when it was time to take a test, I would defiantly leave the entire paper blank. *Fuck all this*, I'd think. *I don't care.*

My report cards were littered with comments like, "Not working to potential," and, "Has trouble staying on task." When my mom would scream at me about my grades, take away privileges, and threaten consequences, I'd promise to try harder and tell her the next semester would be different, but just like with drinking, willpower wasn't going to fix this problem.

At this point, my alcohol consumption was mostly limited to weekends, although there were times I would skip entire days of school and my friends and I would drink at a friend's house, someone with two working parents. I loved those days. We'd catch a buzz and then take turns calling the school, impersonating our parents, letting the office know "my daughter" is home with a sore throat and fever. I did get busted for this one time when the school administrator who answered the phone was the mom of one of my friends. She recognized my voice right away. "Is this Stefanie?" she asked, after I had *very clearly* said I was my mother. I was completely caught off guard.

"Huh? No! This is her mother, Rita." And then I abruptly hung up. I got grounded for skipping school but not for drinking. And although my grades were terrible and I skipped a lot of school, I still wasn't drinking much more than my friends. I wasn't hiding bottles of vodka in my locker or dealing pot from my Nissan 200SX in the school parking lot, like that burnout Skinny Rob. Possibly because I didn't have a car or any real drug connections, but still. I wasn't like after-school-special bad. I'd seen that seventies movie *Sarah T.—Portrait of a Teenage Alcoholic*. In that movie, Linda Blair stars as fifteen-year-old Sarah, who, possibly due to her parents' divorce, starts drinking every day, waters down the scotch in her parents' liquor cabinet, drinks at school, forges notes from her mom, has slipping grades, etc. This all culminates in Sarah getting drunk and riding her beloved horse, Daisy, into traffic. Sarah ends up in the hospital and her poor horse has to be shot. There were a few obvious things I had in common with Sarah (divorce, grades, forging notes), but she'd ridden a horse into traffic! Who does that?

Still, I wanted to make absolutely sure I wasn't dependent on alcohol to have a good time. So in eleventh grade, I had another first: my first attempt to quit drinking. I decided that I was going to try for complete abstinence. Surely I could still have fun without it! I just needed to convince my friends since it would be very challenging to be the only one, and I figured this group of lushes could all use the test as well. As it turned out, not one of my friends was interested in this experiment.

"Why?" my friend Amy asked, truly shocked that I would even suggest something so ridiculous.

"Because I just worry that we drink so much every single weekend. I want to see if I can function without drinking."

"You're not going to start now, are you? We're going to the Keg Room this weekend. What are you going to do there, *not drink?*"

Amy had a point. I couldn't go to bars. How would I talk to anyone? How would I dance? I'd have to find alternative activities. I enlisted the help of my Jewish Community Center friend, Abby, who was now in my math class. Even though my attendance in math was spotty at best, and I'd sort of blown her off after that first week of school, Abby was still sweet to me, so I told her about my plan to quit drinking and my worry that I couldn't have fun without alcohol. Since she already didn't drink, she was game.

That Friday night, Operation Find Other Shit to Do Besides Drink was underway. Abby and I made a plan to attend our school's home football game. I had less than no school spirit, no understanding of or interest in football; in fact, I'd resented the sport ever since I'd been forced to miss my beloved *Little House on the Prairie* when my stepfather commandeered our one TV for his *Monday Night Football*. But there was really no alternative activity we could think of so while my friends got hammered downtown, Abby and I sat in the bleachers screaming, "Defense!" and "Go Bulldogs!"

My sobriety experiment lasted maybe three weeks. It wasn't that I *couldn't* refrain from drinking—obviously I'd just proven to myself I could—it was just that not drinking was boring. If I was sentenced to another year of high school and one more year living in my tense home, I wasn't going to survive it by going to football games and drinking soda. By the way, I don't know what became of Abby, but I'm assuming she'll never need to write a book like this. Hi, Abby!

Another major problem with not drinking was that without a buzz, I felt stiff and awkward around boys. When I was sober, I couldn't imagine kissing anyone—the idea of a stranger's tongue in my mouth seemed weird and unappealing. Worse yet was the thought of allowing someone to touch my body. Sober, I was prude; a few beers in and I could find a totem pole sexy. I loved being drunk and making out. I made out with boys I'd just met and with boys I'd been friends with but suddenly saw in a different light after a few beers. The problem was, I had no follow-through. I couldn't keep the attraction going once I was sober. I'd fall asleep in love and wake up devoid of any feelings. If the guy called me the next day, he'd be confused by my cold response and wonder what had happened to the girl who'd seemed smitten only twelve hours before. It made no sense, even to me. I wanted a boyfriend so badly, I wanted to feel that connection. I thought a boyfriend could fix the loneliness I felt all the time, but once the feelings went away, I couldn't will them back no matter how hard I tried. I had no idea what was wrong with me. I just figured I was defective. At least when I was drinking, I could feel something, even if it didn't last.

My senior year of high school brought another first: my first job. My mother forced me to seek employment; possibly to teach me responsibility, possibly to keep me busy, but probably to keep me out of the house. We'll never know, but that's how I ended up at Burger King. As you can probably imagine, a job in fast food wasn't the best choice for a teenager with a chip on her shoulder. I quickly rose through the ranks, starting on the grill, then being promoted to fries, and eventually being put on the cash register. But once I was on the register, customer service became my undoing because of that whole "not being able to hide my expression" thing I've told you about. It was obvious I didn't agree that everyone should automatically "have it your way," especially if they were going to be an asshole about it. My feeling was, a Whopper with cheese comes with cheese. It's in the name. If you didn't want cheese on your Whopper, then you should have made that clear and not just brought it back up to the counter to say, "There's cheese on this," like it's my fault.

After I was suspended from Burger King for two weeks, I decided it was best to just quit, and I moved on to waiting tables, which became one of my many hustles until I was twenty-eight. Like my teachers all said, I wasn't working to my potential. By the time I barely graduated from high school, I knew three things: College wasn't for me, I needed to get the hell out of Springfield, and quitting drinking was not an option. So at nineteen, I packed up the yellow Mazda GLC I'd bought for a thousand dollars, its floorboards rusted through from shitty Massachusetts weather, and headed west, back to Los Angeles, where it was warm and familiar. I didn't know exactly what I would do but, fuck it, I'd figure it out.

5. I Drink Because I'm a Comic

I was twenty-two years old and six rum and Cokes to the wind the first time I tried stand-up comedy. I'd known I wanted to be a comedian for at least three years by that point—but maybe even since I was a teenager sneaking into bars in Springfield to watch touring comics. It's even possible the seed was planted when I was that little girl sitting cross-legged on the floor watching my father on TV. I'd acknowledged to myself that I dreamed of doing stand-up—I even thought I could possibly be good at it—but it remained a thought bubble in my brain because I was too scared to admit it to anyone else. What if I tried it and I wasn't good? I knew that would be devastating.

As a half measure, I decided to try and join an improv theater called the LA Connection after I saw in *Backstage* magazine they were having auditions. I wasn't ready to try being funny all by myself, but being funny in a group sounded almost doable. It was worth a try since I was twenty years old, hadn't gone to college, and was stuck waiting tables. I needed to do something.

I showed up for the audition fairly terrified, a feeling I despised and normally tried to avoid at all costs. I'd never even attended an improv show and felt consumed with rabid imposter syndrome: Who was I to think I was funny? I mean, sure, my friends thought I was funny, but that didn't mean the world at large would agree. By the way, my imposter syndrome has never gone away. I'm having it right now while working on this very chapter. Inside my brain there's an argument going on that feels like two lawyers fighting in court. *Objection! Relevance? Why is she talking about her experience doing improv? Who cares? What does it even have to do with giving up drinking?*

Your Honor, I'd argue it relates to her low self-worth along with her grandiosity—the "piece of shit the world revolves around" mentality— textbook alcoholic thinking! Objection overruled: You may proceed, but please try to make it interesting.

Anyway . . . I fought the anxiety and stumbled through the audition (a scene with the suggestions of a household appliance and an animal you wouldn't typically have as a pet) despite feeling as if everyone else auditioning had at least some idea what they were doing. Driving home, I was happy I'd done it but not at all hopeful I'd get the gig.

But the call came in a few days later letting me know they wanted me for their Sunday group! Relief flooded through my system. I hadn't realized until that very moment how stalled I'd felt, how paralyzed. Up until then, I'd worried it could have been a mistake to turn down my spot at UMass, especially since they'd accepted me with a 2.3 GPA. My mother had even paid a nonrefundable deposit! Instead, I'd decided to just drive to LA and figure it out? What had I been thinking?

But now I'd taken this huge risk and it had paid off—in dividends! *I was going to be paid for my natural wit.* Who needed college? And screw waitressing! Let other people waste their time marrying ketchup bottles at shitty restaurants; I was going to be an improv star! See you on *SNL*, bitches!

But it turned out anyone who auditioned at LA Connection was invited to do improv. It was a class. I'd auditioned to pay *them* money. And to add insult to injury, the Sunday group was for the barest beginners. I signed up anyway, but it quickly became apparent I was terrible at improv. I just wanted to say funny things, not wear crazy wigs and top hats or learn to move in slow motion or pretend to joust. I tried for months and struggled through a few live shows, knowing this wasn't my jam but not wanting to admit defeat. One night, after arguing with a fellow performer because he wanted us to add an Irish brogue and a limp to play two monks robbing a bank and I . . . *didn't want to do that*, my improv teacher sided with him and said to me, "Your problem is when you're onstage you're always you. You need to learn to do characters and accents." What I heard was, "These try-hards are holding you back, you should do stand-up."

One of the reasons I'd moved back to Los Angeles was to find my stand-up comedian father. Despite the fact that I hadn't spoken to Stanley in years—he'd made very few attempts to contact me—I had held on to some fantasy that if I just moved to LA, he would be thrilled to see me and want to make up for lost time. Yeah, I'd watched a lot of ABC made-for-TV movies. Maybe, just maybe, I didn't fit with my family because I was an artist—maybe show business was in my blood—maybe if I found my dad, I would also find my place in the world.

I surprised him at a Culver City jazz club called the Alleycat Bistro, where the *LA Weekly* listings showed he was doing stand-up. I didn't have his phone number or address, so this was the best I could do. I snuck in and watched him perform from the back of the room, not wanting to take the chance of him recognizing me in the audience and ruining his flow.

The audience loved him. He was such a natural, holding his place on the stage, delivering subtle jokes, taking his time between punch lines, not afraid to do a really long setup, gleefully watching the crowd squirm, wondering where he was going with this and then BOOM, the ridiculous twist they didn't see coming made up for all the waiting. This was my dad! I wanted to be like him. I had to be like him.

When his set ended, I lined up with other audience members along the back of the showroom wall so I could be sure to stop him as he passed by.

Of course I was trembling with nerves by the time I spotted him making his way toward us with his trademark newsboy cap and glasses. His posture was slightly more stooped, but his face hadn't changed much from the last time I'd seen him years before. For some reason I felt like a lot was on the line—as if my future hung in the balance.

"Hi. You were great!" I said. My eyes met his purposefully and I stood there waiting for his acknowledgment, waiting to matter.

"Thank you very much! I really appreciate it." No spark of recognition. There was that familiar ghost feeling again. He was about to move on and shake hands with the next person.

"It's me, Stefanie." I took a beat, generously allowing him to catch up, but he didn't. "Your daughter?" I added. His face slowly changed from that of the showman greeting a fan into an expression of surprise.

"Oh! Heya, Stef! Wow. It's so good to see you! I didn't recognize you! I'm tickled that you're here!" I decided to give him the benefit of the doubt. To be fair, he hadn't been expecting me and it was out of context. I gave him a hug, because when in doubt, I'm a hugger. "Come and sit down. Let's get something to eat," he said. I followed him to an area in the back of the club with bar tables and chairs, where we ordered a few appetizers. But before the guacamole even arrived, he pulled a prescription bottle out of his jacket pocket and opened it without looking at it, as if it was second nature. He popped a few pills, never taking his eyes off of me. And then he went over his whole set, pointing out every big laugh he'd gotten and complaining about a few jokes that should have killed. The audience wasn't that smart, he told me. And when the check came, he asked if I could possibly cover it because he didn't have his wallet.

My reunion was disappointing, falling short of my fantasy that he'd somehow magically become capable of being a real dad. But seeing him perform, watching him get that love and validation from the crowd, did make me want to hang out in his stand-up comedy/acting class. He could at least offer me that.

For the next few years I did temp work, cocktail waitressed in comedy clubs, and watched open-mic nights while attempting to write jokes and work up the confidence to perform them.

It took me three years after reuniting with my father and two years after my plan B of improv not working out to actually try stand-up. But finally, with the help of a lot of liquid courage, I got up the nerve to sign up for an open-mic night. I had two minutes of material (I know, because I timed myself over and over in front of the mirror) about my boobs and trying to pick up guys at the gym. I was no George Carlin, but, thankfully, it went well. I made a small group of UCLA frat boys, two waitresses, and the bartenders laugh, a sound almost as addictive as cocaine. And with that, I decided I was a comedian.

I enjoyed everything about being a comedian except the whole "performing" part: I loved the feeling I got in my gut when I knew I'd written a funny punch line; I loved the camaraderie with the other comics: writing jokes at Denny's, hanging out in the back of the room laughing loudly at our friends' jokes and openly judging the bad ones. I lived for that feeling of belonging, but I hated going onstage.

So you had a little stage fright, you're probably thinking. *Didn't Dustin Hoffman throw up before every stage performance?* I just Googled that, and while he does have horrible stage fright, I couldn't get confirmation on the puking thing. But it turns out that Barbra Streisand also has terrible stage fright. I read she got so nervous at a show in 1966 she forgot the lyrics to one of her songs and didn't perform live for twenty-seven years! And when she did start performing again, she always had a teleprompter in case she forgot something.

For all my years doing stand-up, a lot of my anxiety centered on forgetting my jokes. But since I was performing in dive bars and not playing Madison Square Garden like Babs, no one was lugging in a teleprompter for me.

For years, I did mostly open-mic nights to get better at performing. I booked a few gigs here and there at pubs or coffee shops that paid twenty-five dollars plus a beer, but whether I was being paid or doing it for free, the thing that never changed was I hated going onstage. Sometimes the fear would hit the minute I woke up on the day of the show, knowing I had to perform that night, but mostly it happened while I was waiting to go on. My inner critic would start in on me: *Why did you sign up to do this? The audience is going to hate you. They really liked the juggler they saw tonight, so they definitely won't get you. You're too dressed up; you only do well when you're not wearing any makeup. You're not funny. Who do you think you are, calling yourself a comedian? You're just not a natural at this!* I'd watch the more well-known comedians perform and think, *I'll never be that good.*

But as much as I hated performing, I still wanted to be a stand-up.

Having a great show was the highest high; hearing applause for a joke that I'd thought of in my head that afternoon and making a group of strangers all laugh in unison, agreeing that I was funny, that I was worthwhile, that they approved of me, felt like the validation I'd been seeking my entire life, and I couldn't get enough of it. But I was like a broken cup; I'd have a killer set, but all the good feelings would slowly leak out, leaving me empty until I did it again.

As amazing as having a good set made me feel was how awful I felt when I bombed—it's an entire room full of people letting you know with their silence that at best you're unfunny, at worst you're worthless. When I bombed, I needed an alcohol lobotomy. But I also needed to drink to buffer the anticipation of possibly bombing. Pretty soon I just needed to drink, period. I always went onstage with at least one drink in me, but sometimes it took much more.

A few years into my stand-up career, I was booked back to perform at a club in San Diego. The difference this time was that the club was doing a TV taping for a show called *Comedy on the Road*. I wasn't going to be on the actual TV show, but I would be tasked with doing ten minutes for the audience to warm them up before the actual taping began. Sounds kind of simple and low-pressure, right? Yeah, no. First of all, the place was lit up like Times Square for the taping, and there were cameras everywhere. Intellectually, I understood that the cameras weren't there for me and I wasn't on the show, but my limbic system hadn't gotten the memo and instead told me I was about to debut on Broadway. As I paced around before the show, I couldn't quite catch my breath or think clearly, like I'd just gone jogging eleven thousand feet above sea level. There was no way I would be able to remember my first line, let alone all the jokes in my act, feeling like I had altitude sickness.

I desperately needed a drink.

But I didn't want to be seen drinking either, because that would seem unprofessional, and, in my mind, this was a *very professional situation*. And then the thought that this was a very professional situation made me feel like I was going to pass out.

Luckily, I didn't have to go on for another twenty minutes so I found a back bar away from production and I asked for a Coors Light. I really wanted a shot of tequila but didn't want to seem like some kind of boozehound, so I chose the Coors Light, which seemed casual, like I was chilling on a fishing boat, not trying to stop a panic attack. But one Coors Light didn't help at all, so I had six more in the next fifteen minutes. I kept waiting to feel calmer, more in control. I repeated my opening line to myself over and over to make sure I could still remember.

When I was told to take the stage, instead of the lights dimming, which would signal to the audience that the show was starting, the production lights stayed bright, so the audience kept right on chatting. My first joke barely got a laugh, and then my second joke got no response. And I was still nervous—actually more so. Usually my nerves would dissipate a bit after the first joke got a laugh, but there were also times when my nerves never went away. It was a crapshoot, and I'd just crapped out.

And then the worst happened: I pulled a Streisand and forgot how my joke went in the middle. I started the joke but the punch line wasn't coming, so I stuttered and stalled. Someone in the front row let out an audible sigh, as if the lack of laughs wasn't enough to let me know I should get out of the business. I struggled through nine more minutes of this torture until I was mercifully given the signal to get offstage.

I've bombed a lot of times, but this one sticks out in my mind because it was the first time alcohol didn't help. It was as if it had lost its magic effect and couldn't be depended on to help save me from the pain of rejection. There was now no guaranteed reprieve from nerves. But it didn't stop me from trying. What was the alternative?

When I got booked to do my first TV gig, *Star Search*, the excitement was short-lived. Getting a gig is one thing. Everyone likes the feeling of winning. Everyone wants to hear yes. But what if you have success? What if you get the guy or the job or the part? There's the initial rush of triumph—your blood is flowing, everything is falling into place! You're in perfect synergy with the universe! And why? Because you set the stage for success! You set goals! You took a risk! You incorporated at least one Habit of Highly Effective People. But hold on, not so fast. Because you can't live on that high feeling; that rush ain't gonna pay your bills. Now you have to actually put in the work: you have to *do* the job you got yourself into, you have *be* in the relationship you went after. I don't think I'm alone in experiencing the crash and the anxiety that kicks in when the adrenaline from all that winning reverts back to normal "lying on the couch" levels.

Now that I would be appearing on television, the goal I'd set for myself, I would need to make sure I could remember my jokes and ensure I didn't get that high-altitude feeling again. A TV gig was my big break, the thing that would take me from shitty bars to headlining clubs, allowing myself to prove to everyone else that I belonged. I couldn't afford to fuck this up.

I asked a fellow comedian for advice and she said, "Just grab one of those minibar airline bottles of tequila from your hotel, bring it with you to your dressing room, and drink it about ten minutes before you go on." It was ridiculous advice, obviously. I wasn't going to drink tequila. But I did smuggle a beer into my purse. Unfortunately, we were stuck in our trailer for hours before showtime, so by the time I was ready to guzzle my Budweiser, it was the temperature of pee. But I didn't care. I needed my medicine. I was positive I couldn't perform without it. (I kind of want to just move on from this part, but I feel like you would want to know that I lost *Star Search*. Ed McMahon announced in his booming TV voice that "Stefanie Wilder receives two and three quarter stars and her competitor, Keith Michael Ashton, receives three and a half stars." Keith deserved it. Good for him.)

Right about now, or even many paragraphs back, you might be wondering why I didn't just quit doing stand-up at this point. It would seem like if I had to drink every time I performed, if it never came easily, I would have let it go by now. I don't know why I held on so long, but I think it's because I'd invested so much of myself into it. It felt primal. It was in my blood. But it was like a toxic relationship, I just couldn't seem to break away without something to replace it. And despite *Star Search* not leading to anything, I didn't quit.

But luckily, a few years into my not-really-going-anywhere stand-up career, I got my first job writing for television, and it changed everything. Although I wasn't writing on sitcoms like *Friends*, more like game shows, I knew right away that this was what I should have been doing all along. I got to write the jokes, which had been my favorite part of stand-up, but I didn't have to perform them! Some other sucker had to stand out on that stage, in front of those lights and cameras and live or die based on something *I'd* typed onto a computer while wearing sweatpants and eating Red Vines. It was the best of both worlds—so I gave up the dream of making it as a stand-up. I still performed sporadically and I still hated it every single time.

Eventually, once I had twins, I stopped performing stand-up completely. It didn't feel like failure; it felt like freedom. The best part was, without the pressure of going onstage, I no longer had to drink every night. Problem solved, right? It turns out you can take the girl out of the drinking world, but you can't take the urge to drink out of the girl. I didn't know it yet, but I was just looking for another reason.

6. Let's Play Twenty Questions

The first time I went to a twelve-step meeting, I wasn't sober or even sober-curious. It was pretty clear to me that I didn't have an actual problem with substances, because I had someone to directly compare myself to: my good friend Landry. I met Landry doing stand-up in LA, and I was immediately drawn to his boisterous energy. He was a tennis-playing WASP from Florida who was tall, dark, and Irish and so incredibly goofy and hilarious. We were attracted to each other like magnets, and before long, we found ourselves making out in one of our cars after gigs on a regular basis. Within a week or two, this became something akin to dating—but not quite.

In many ways he felt like boyfriend material: He was cute and sweet and down-to-earth and generous to a fault, but I had nagging doubts about the way he drank. We both loved our cocktails, but Landry had some classic signs of someone who actually had an issue: After only two drinks, his personality changed. It was almost fascinating to see, like those little Magic Grow capsules where one minute it's a tiny blue sponge but you drop it into water and the next minute it's a dinosaur. Before he'd even sipped from his second Stoli cranberry, his laugh would get louder, his movements slower, and his words would lose their crispness. I'd think, *How is it even possible he's already slurring?* But there were other signs as well, more obvious signs, billboards: Once he started drinking, it was almost impossible to get him to stop, and his drinking sometimes led to buying crack.

Our evenings would start out innocently enough with a few beers before performing at whatever club booked us that night. We'd then head to a dive and have a few more. Often I'd lose track of how much I was drinking and end up puking once I was in the comfort of my own apartment. But Landry's evenings apparently continued once the rest of us had gone home, and we'd hear about it the next day. Once he went out on his own and got so drunk at a dive bar in Hollywood that he couldn't drive home, so he fell asleep in his car—only it wasn't actually his car. Not being able to find his Audi, he'd walked up the street pulling on door handles until he hit upon an unlocked Acura, climbed in, and passed out. When the actual owner found what he thought was a vagrant sleeping in his car, he called the cops, and poor Landry was arrested and taken to jail. The very next day, he was out of the pokey and on the stand-up stage like nothing had happened. He was like a young John Belushi—destined for either *Saturday Night Live* or to crash and burn in spectacular fashion.

I really wanted to see him clean up his act but I wasn't the best influence myself. One day, possibly after reading a Jay McInerney book where the characters did a shitload of illegal drugs and made it seem glamorous, I realized that I'd never tried heroin, and though I'd never tried anything harder than cocaine, heroin seemed like something a person should do at least once in their life, so I called Landry.

"I think I want to try smoking heroin," I told him.

"Oh, you want to chase the dragon."

"Yeah, I guess," I said. I definitely wasn't looking to inject it—that was for drug addicts! I was too classy!

"We'll need some black tar. I know a guy." Landry always knew a guy. "I'll be right over." So he rolled up to my apartment, and on a beautiful Sunday afternoon we drove seventeen miles down to a shady neighborhood, picked up a little tinfoil package of heroin, and brought it back to my place. The heroin itself looked like one of those black-snake firework pellets you get as a kid for the Fourth of July that you light and it pushes out a dark column of ash.

Landry lit the underside of the tinfoil, and then he pulled a four-inch-long red straw out of thin air, as if he was doing a close-up magic trick, and handed it to me. "Ladies first." Landry was nothing if not chivalrous.

I leaned down and tried to breathe the fumes directly into my lungs. I wasn't nervous or excited, really. This just felt like something to do. I waited to feel something, a rush, I guess. I wanted to feel it. I really liked painkillers like Vicodin, and wasn't heroin the granddaddy of painkillers?

Landry had taken a few pulls from the straw too, and he looked up at me expectantly. "Are you fucked up?"

"No. I feel the same. What about you?"

"Nothing. Nada. Maybe it's not good stuff."

I figured it could be for the best. I was almost thirty. Who starts doing heroin at almost middle age? Suddenly I felt relieved, like I'd driven through an intersection two seconds before a semi-truck ran the red light. What had I been thinking?

I didn't know if Landry had ever smoked heroin before, and I was afraid to ask. But when he decided to get sober not too long after, I thought it was a great idea, which was how I found myself attending a meeting with him. Even though we weren't dating, I could still be a supportive friend.

The meeting was held at a church in Santa Monica, and as we walked up, I noticed a whole crowd of surprisingly youngish people outside smoking cigarettes like it was a hip club and not a place where drinking habits came to die. The thing that was incredibly annoying was just how overly invested these alcoholics seemed in *my* drinking. Everyone I was introduced to by Landry immediately addressed me with, "Welcome, how long have you been sober?"

I'd answer, "I'm not sober but I don't have a problem with alcohol." And then I'd quickly follow it up with, "Not that there's anything wrong with it. I'm here to support my friend." But it was like I was speaking a foreign language, because almost every single person told me to keep coming back.

Keep coming back? Why? I for sure didn't have a drinking problem. It was a little irritating that people assumed I was there to get sober— I guess guilt by association. I wished they could see me the way I saw myself: as a helper, someone who, despite not being afflicted with this particular problem, wasn't judgmental at all. In fact, I was genuinely so glad these people were here, because my friend needed help.

One dude, who smelled like he'd just smoked a carton of Pall Malls, handed me a pamphlet titled "The 20 Questions" and told me to have a look. I thought I'd rather not, but I didn't want to seem defensive, so I said thank you, popped it in my bag, and went to sit in the back of the room to give my friend a little space to work on his sobriety. And while I was just sitting there, since I had sixty minutes to kill, I figured I could use a little reading material, so I opened up the pamphlet and saw it said, "Are you an alcoholic?" which was followed by twenty questions. Ugh. These people were so pushy!

Of course I knew that I drank too much. I was forever trying to cut down or making promises to quit after a rough night, and many of my journal entries ended with "I'm so druuunk"—but alcoholic? No. The word "alcoholic" is so loaded—and not in a good way, like potato skins or a new Lexus; more in a shameful way. The word immediately paints a picture in your mind of a permanent affliction, one that requires a life of these types of meetings. The worst part is, if you're an alcoholic, you can't drink. Yeah, let that soak in. Once you acknowledge that you have a drinking problem, it follows that in order to not have a drinking problem, you need to stop drinking. I felt so sorry for these people that they'd let things get so out of hand that now they couldn't ever drink again.

On the off-off chance that I was in denial, I decided to go ahead and take the quiz. Two little boxes followed each question: *Check yes or no*. I pulled a pen out of my bag. I was going to take this seriously.

Question 1. Do you lose time from work due to drinking? Well, that was an easy no. I'd gone to work with some nasty hangovers, but lose time? Nope. In fact, being a comedian, drinking is practically a job requirement. Although there was that one time my neighbor in the next apartment over offered me some pot brownies that she'd already sampled and determined to not be potent enough to have any effect. Not wanting to let a perfectly delicious brownie go to waste, I'd eaten three of them. Hours later, while driving to a comedy gig thirty miles away, I suddenly realized something was off: The steering wheel felt three times its normal size. Either I was shrinking or everything around me was expanding like in some kind of sci-fi movie. Then came a familiar floating feeling. What was happening? Was I sick? And then it hit me: I was stoned. And very quickly I was stoned and paranoid. I pulled over and forced my friend to take the wheel and drive us straight back home, because I could definitely perform drunk, but there was no way I could do it high.

I had to call the booker of the gig and tell her I'd suddenly come down with the stomach flu and couldn't perform, which was actually a performance in itself! I then called my neighbor, who was by now stoned out of her tree. She was so stoned, in fact, that she was still high the next morning and couldn't go in for her waitressing shift. So I guess we both lost time from work. But I had no idea those brownies would get me high. It's all about intention. So still no.

Question 2. Is drinking making your home life unhappy? Okay, this one was obviously aimed at people who had their shit together enough to have a home life—people who were married with kids—men who came home from their corporate job, swilled eight martinis, and yelled at their wives. I lived in an apartment with a roommate I never saw, and I wouldn't exactly have called my apartment a home considering I was still sleeping on my ex-boyfriend's futon that he'd left behind after breaking up with me and I didn't even own a dish-drying rack. In fact, a German guy who was going to school for architecture but lived in a youth hostel, where he shared a bathroom with seventeen other people, once told me he couldn't date me because my apartment was aesthetically displeasing. So, again, no.

Question 3. Do you drink because you are shy with other people? "Shy" is definitely not an adjective people would use to describe me—"attention whore," maybe; "drama queen," possibly; I preferred "outgoing." So no.

Question 4. Is your drinking affecting your reputation? Hmm . . . was drinking affecting my rep? Was I known around town as someone who drinks too much? I certainly didn't think so. I blended into my crowd of friends, who all seemingly drank like I did. Except for Landry, of course, which was why I was here. I drank at appropriate places like parties or bars or comedy clubs. I certainly wasn't the type of drinker who made big scenes. I couldn't imagine anyone ever thought, *Let's not invite Stefanie because she has a reputation of getting too hammered.* I wasn't that girl getting carried out of the Roxy and folded into a cab after partying on the Sunset Strip. I experienced the worst of my drunkenness at home, puking all alone in the privacy of my own bathroom—so no, reputation intact.

Question 5. *Have you ever felt remorse after drinking?* Well, duh, tons of times. But that question is so general. Wouldn't anyone answer yes to that? There were countless mornings I'd woken up deathly hungover with almost no memory of what had happened the night before. But nothing catastrophic ever happened. So, yes, but with the caveat that so does everyone else.

Question 6. *Have you gotten into financial difficulties as a result of drinking?* No. Boom. I've gotten into financial difficulties from being irresponsible—like the time I didn't realize I was supposed to pay taxes on the car I won on *Hollywood Squares.* But who the hell knew there was even such a thing as "gift tax"? I've also gotten into financial trouble for being chronically underemployed, but that's called "being an artist," not "alcoholism." So no. Final answer.

Question 7. *Do you turn to lower companions and an inferior environment when drinking?* What kind of a question was this? Like, do I end my evenings crowded around a bonfire in a homeless encampment surrounded by crackheads? No. This was getting stupid.

Question 8. *Does your drinking make you careless of your family's welfare?* Again, this is something for people who are married with kids. Moving on.

Question 9. *Has your ambition decreased since drinking?* Au contraire, mon frère! When I'm sober, I am not the most motivated person and I'm easily discouraged, but get a few drinks in me and I'm an idea machine, energized and excited. I'll come up with a sitcom or a business or a brand-new career direction. Unfortunately, I just lack follow-through when sober. So that's a big NO.

Question 10. Do you crave a drink at a definite time daily? That was an easy no because I didn't *crave* drinks ever. Drinking just usually seemed like a good idea. If I was out at night and someone was buying drinks, who was I to say no? Sometimes drinking opportunities came up even after I had tried to swear off drinking for a while and I would cave and rationalize that this was a special occasion or "just this once," but that could happen anytime. I definitely didn't crave a drink at a definite time daily.

Wow, the nos were really adding up. I was feeling pretty good about this quiz. I could probably teach these people a thing or two about responsible drinking.

Question 11. Do you want a drink the next morning? Absolutely not. Nothing sounded less appealing than a drink in the morning, especially if I was hungover from the night before. Of course, having a Bloody Mary or mimosa at brunch certainly didn't count as wanting a drink the next morning, right? An eleven a.m. buzz was a really nice feeling but certainly not something I did regularly. That was reserved for baby showers or other places I didn't want to be.

Question 12. Does drinking cause you to have difficulty sleeping? Not even! If anything, it helps me sleep! Damn! I had to hand it to myself; I was going to ace this thing for sure.

Question 13. Has your efficiency decreased since drinking? What did that even mean? It made me think of someone who works in a factory line putting caps on shampoo bottles. They are so miserable at their job (and who wouldn't be?), that at their noon break they sneak a little liquid lunch, and when they get back to the line, the machine measures them putting approximately eight fewer caps on bottles per hour. Obviously this had nothing to do with my life. Hard no.

Question 14. Is drinking jeopardizing your job or business? No. But I definitely had a couple of close calls. Back when I was a cocktail waitress, a long, long time ago, we would do shots of Jägermeister while standing at the bar waiting to load our trays with cocktails and beers for our tables. Although slinging drinks was a job that put quick cash in my pocket, it was also one that required putting up with drunk people, and that required being drunk or at least dulled to a degree that could blot out the loud music, comments about my tits, and the low self-esteem that came with the doubt I'd ever have a job not in the service industry. Usually I was fairly good at gauging how many drinks I'd had, rationing them out to keep me just above buzzed for a whole six-hour shift. But one night I must've seriously miscalculated, and by the time the lights went on and it was time to count my cash and add up my checks, I was too out of it. My friend Trina sat me in a booth far away from the other employees and covered for me, doing my checks and finishing my side work. In the end, our boss somehow was none the wiser and my only punishment was I had to continue working there for another year.

Question 15. Do you drink to escape from worries or troubles? Another easy no. I wasn't someone who drank *at* a problem. Drinking was fun. I drank to celebrate! To have a good time or to turn a potential good time into a better time. My issue was strictly that I wasn't great at knowing my limits, not that I was holed up in my apartment drinking away my latest breakup.

This quiz was starting to bum me out. I knew there were people who drank like this: spending all their time in the neighborhood dive complaining about their wife or boss or neighbor, and I felt for those people and really and truly hoped they found their way to this meeting. But this was definitely not me.

Question 16. *Do you drink alone?* No. Well, once in a blue moon I'll have a beer while I'm putting on makeup getting ready for a date. That obviously doesn't count, because everyone does that. It's not the sad, crying, sitting on the floor, listening to *Madame Butterfly*, turning the light switch off and on à la Glenn Close in *Fatal Attraction* drinking alone; it's the good kind of drinking alone.

Question 17. *Have you ever had a complete loss of memory as a result of drinking?* Okay, yes. *A lot* of times. Starting with the second time I ever drank, I couldn't remember much of it the next day. But here's the thing: I think some people's bodies just metabolize alcohol differently. Isn't that possible? Alcohol is a chemical and it probably has a chemical reaction with some people's brains, causing them to lose time. This, I'm fairly sure, is absolutely common; it's just science. But the answer is yes.

Question 18. *Has your physician ever treated you for drinking?* Of course not. My drinking is none of his business.

Question 19. *Do you drink to build up your self-confidence?* I had to think about this one for a minute. I didn't drink at parties because I was shy, or because I was insecure, but I definitely drank before going onstage. I had to. I needed to drink to deal with my intense stage fright and to, yes, boost my confidence. Hell, I'd drink before a job interview if it was slightly less frowned upon. It seemed to me that performing was an extenuating circumstance, and I didn't think that counted toward drinking to overall build up my confidence. I think anyone could understand my thinking here. In general, drinking was strictly for fun, but if I had to perform, it was a useful and indispensable tool. I knew

I couldn't perform without it. So yes and no? I gave myself half a yes. But I could certainly afford it given my long streak of nos.

Question 20. Have you ever been to a hospital or institution on account of drinking? Absolutely 100 percent no. I couldn't even believe this was on the quiz. If you've been institutionalized due to your drinking, do you really need this glorified *Cosmo* quiz to convince you that you have a serious problem? I hoped not.

Okay, kids, pencils down. Time to look over my answers. I had a grand total of two and a half yeses. Pretty impressive, I was sure. But then my eyes scanned down the page and took in some disconcerting information: *If you answered YES to any **one** of the questions, there is a definite warning that **you may be an alcoholic**.* Dude, what? But there was worse news ahead: *If you answered YES to any **two**, the chances are that **you are an alcoholic**.*

This was pure insanity. These people just wanted everyone to be an alcoholic; misery loves company and all that. Well, I guess I'd fallen right into their trap. They want me to think that because I've had a few blackouts I'm suddenly a full-blown alcoholic? Because I needed some liquid courage to perform onstage, now I needed help? Had the person who had come up with these questions ever tried stand-up? Were there even stand-up comedians in the thirties, when this quiz was invented? Public speaking was the number one fear according to what I'd heard somewhere. Fear of dying was all the way down at number ten! I should probably go back and switch that yes to a no. But that would still leave me with two yeses, which, according to these assholes, still made me a problem drinker.

I seriously doubted that anyone could have passed this test the way it was written. Their view of alcoholism was way too narrow and strict—everyone would be an alcoholic according to these impossible standards. Everyone drinks and if you drink, you're bound to say yes to at least one question! I wasn't going to let this bring me down. In fact, it was kind of laughable.

I wanted to leave, to get up and storm out, but the damn meeting still had a solid half hour to go. I sat there hoping someone else would get up and leave so that I could just follow right behind them as if I was worried about them and just wanted to make sure they were okay. But if I were to leave on my own, people might assume *I* was the one who was freaked out and someone might follow *me* to make sure *I* was okay, which would be horrifying. So I sat there clapping in the appropriate places until it was all over, but I swore to myself that next time, as much as I loved Landry and wanted him to get better, he was on his own.

7. DUI (Dating Under the Influence)

I can probably count on one hand the number of times I had sober sex before I actually quit drinking and yes, that's including the night I lost my virginity. The first time I had sex I was a senior in high school and it was with my steady boyfriend, Michael, who named his penis "Ralph." We were in love, and after many super-deep conversations about the implications of physical intimacy, we both felt mature enough and ready for this next step in our relationship. Oh wait, that's the plot of Judy Blume's book *Forever* . . . Never mind.

My first time wasn't the stuff of Judy Blume books or John Hughes movies. I was nineteen years old, coked up, and very, very drunk. Even though at nineteen I was already living on my own in Los Angeles with all the trappings of adult life—two shitty minimum-wage jobs; a shitty car; a weird, shitty-smelling apartment—I was still young in one very important way: I was a virgin. I couldn't say I was a virgin for religious reasons—or even moral ones; I was just chicken-shit. My sexual experience was limited to heavy making out, letting guys touch my boobs, feeling an erection through the safety of jeans, allowing a hand to wander into my underwear and the occasional finger or two to slip inside me, and a couple of failed attempts at a hand job. I found the prospect of actually having sexual intercourse (sorry for even using that term, ewww) terrifying and unnatural somehow.

I wasn't gay, I knew that; I was boy crazy, easily obsessed, but I couldn't handle it when the feeling was mutual. I was much more comfortable pining for guys who didn't call me back so I could love them from afar and never have to see their penis. But at nineteen, still having my V-card was just getting weird.

So when I found myself drunk and high in my bed with Art, it seemed as good a time as any. I met Art at a bar called the Seven Seas, which my roommate, Beth, and I lovingly referred to as the Seven Diseases because it was on Hollywood Boulevard, a location that didn't really attract life's winners—more like heroin addicts, people looking for a check-cashing place, and tourists—but it was walking distance from my first apartment in Hollywood and they didn't ask for ID.

Beth and I had a system: We'd pregame with a beer or two back at our apartment, just enough alcohol to make us feel less desperate for drinks we couldn't afford; then we'd position ourselves at a little cocktail table, making eye contact with random guys until one of them offered to buy us a drink. Sometimes, toward the end of the night, we'd make out with these guys in the alley behind the bar because we were classy ladies and didn't just want to bring them back to our apartment!

But one night we met Art and his friend . . . let's call him Leo (I'm lucky I remember Art's name, so I'm not even going to pretend to remember his friend's name). After dancing with them to Depeche Mode and letting them buy us several shots of Jack, we made an exception to our rule and decided to forgo the alley and let Art and his friend come back home with us. They seemed really sweet. Also, they had coke.

They say you never forget your first, but all I can tell you about Art is that he was cute. I mean, he wasn't blond and he wasn't a redhead, so I guess by process of elimination he must've had dark hair. That's it. If he were a serial killer I'd managed to escape from and I had to describe him to a police sketch artist, I'm afraid he'd still be at large.

That first night Art came back to our apartment after drinking all evening, we did some lines of coke, and then Art and I went into my bedroom and fooled around. This was where I shined: I loved the feeling of hard-core sucking face with someone new and foreign to me; I was in audition mode, hoping to be found sexy, fun, and not too fat. I would allow myself to only get so worked up, though. I felt my nether regions pulsate from a tongue in my ear; I wanted hands on me, stroking my breasts and working their way slowly down. I would breathe harder and close my eyes, letting myself get lost in the moment. But when a guy took my excitement as a green light to try to take my pants off, I would shut it down. Even with plenty of alcohol on board, when fooling around escaped the boundaries of my comfort zone, I panicked.

I'd been this way all through high school, which I tried to convince myself wasn't weird. I was young! I just wasn't ready! But as my friends progressed sexually, I stayed scared. In high school, girls' levels of experience ran the gamut: Some had gone all the way by eighth grade and by sophomore year could teach a class in human sexuality, while others, like me and my bestie, Amy, were saving ourselves for a committed relationship. But then Amy caved.

Senior year, Amy was regularly making out with a guy named Sam—just making out, nothing serious. One night while we were all out at a bar, Amy and Sam went out to his car and when they came back an hour later, Amy was red-faced, with disheveled hair. She pulled me into the ladies' room to tell me that Sam had gone down on her. She looked really pleased with herself, but I was scandalized. She'd let him put his mouth on her privates? I'd thought we were both freaked out about the prospect of sex. "We didn't have sex though," Amy said, like she was reading my mind. *Well, pretty close,* I thought. It felt like she'd broken some unspoken pact, leaving me behind on the island of inexperience.

And then, in her first semester of college, Amy lost it to a guy who lived on the same floor of her dorm. She wrote me a letter telling me all about it, because I'd moved to LA, but before she could mail the letter, she was killed by a drunk driver while crossing the street. Her mom gave me the letter at her funeral, and even through my grief and tears, when I read that she didn't die a virgin, I had to smile, because fucking YOLO! Amy had definitely lived more life than I had in her short years here, and I became more determined to not be so scared.

I stopped Art that first night somewhere around third base. But the following weekend I brought him back home again, and after more drinking and more lines I let him take my clothes off, and when he took his clothes off, I didn't say no. I used my drunken state as a buffer to do the thing I wanted not so much to *do* as to *get done*. It hurt. I remember thinking, *Is sex supposed to feel like I'm getting knifed in the vag?* But I didn't mind, because I saw myself from above and I was proud of me. Yes, I was drunk, and yes, I was coked out, but I knew what was happening: I was facing my fears.

There was blood on the sheets when it was over. "Oh! You got your period!" Art said. He seemed grossed out. I knew for a fact that wasn't my period though.

"I was a virgin," I said. Art had the nerve to laugh.

"Not a chance." He had pulled his boxers back on and was reaching for his Levi's. It sure didn't seem like he was staying over. "You have any beer left?"

"I don't," I said. Even though I did. "I really was a virgin."

"Nobody bleeds like that the first time." What was this guy, a gynecologist? He left a few minutes later and I was relieved. He'd served his purpose. I was drunk and devirginized, and now I just wanted to go to sleep.

He called me a time or two afterward, but I didn't want to see him. I definitely didn't want to have sex with him again. I didn't want to have sex with anyone, for that matter, and I didn't for an entire year.

Then, when I was twenty, I met Jimmy at a Halloween party. Now something to know about me is I didn't like Halloween. I didn't like the pressure of figuring out whether to be a sexy kitty or a slutty nurse, and I didn't like flirting with guys at a party who are wearing a costume because it's like interacting with Goofy at Disneyland: It could be a hot guy in that costume or it could be the lunch lady from junior high. But Jimmy was dressed up as a baseball player, which was a pretty simple costume, involving only a baseball jersey, a bat, and a hat, and did not include a mask of any kind, so when he asked for my number, I felt comfortable that he wouldn't show up on our date out of costume looking less Ozzie Smith and more Ozzy Osbourne. But just in case, I told him we'd have to double date.

I dragged along a blond restaurant coworker of mine named Jena, and we met up with Jimmy at his friend Paul's house, where we started drinking immediately. Paul was thirty—much older than us, with laugh lines and feathered hair, and he worked for a record company, which was really cool. Sadly, Jena didn't seem attracted to him at all. I figured this out because from the second we sat down on the couch, she started overtly flirting with Jimmy, which I tried to ignore. Jimmy's claim to fame was that his recent ex-girlfriend was Susanna Hoffs from the Bangles and seeing as this was the eighties, Jimmy was hot by association. After we were already pretty buzzed, we walked to a Mexican restaurant up the street to drink flaming daiquiris and eat enchiladas verdes. As we got drunker, Jimmy started seeming dumber and Paul started seeming hilarious and intelligent. Pretty soon Paul and I were basically having our own conversation while Jena found reasons to touch Jimmy's leg.

As we were getting ready to leave, it seemed obvious something needed to be done, so I gestured for Jena to follow me to the bathroom. We stared at ourselves drunkenly in the mirror. "It's obvious you like Jimmy," I said. Jena looked worried. "It's fine. I like Paul better. Let's just swap."

When we got back to Paul's place, he and I went into his bedroom to make out and watch Sam Kinison host *SNL* while Jena had loud sex with Jimmy on Paul's living room sofa. Even though we'd only been together for two hours, my connection with Paul felt mutual and mature, and I was positive I'd like him even when I was sober. But when he called me the next day to ask me out on a proper date, I froze up once again.

But this time, rather than ghosting him, I decided to do the more vulnerable thing and be honest: I told him my history of getting scared and shutting down. To my utter shock, he completely understood. He said, "Let's just be friends then. Hey, friend, wanna go to the UCLA football game?"

With the pressure removed, I decided I liked him. But I was still anxious because he was thirty and I was twenty with next to no experience. But a few dates in, after drinking cocktails at a restaurant followed by a *lot* of wine at his place, he expertly moved me to the bedroom, laid me down on his I-have-a-real-job-and-therefore-nice-sheets bed, and while Rickie Lee Jones sang in the background, I finally learned all the things.

I wish I could say that he opened me up sexually, but this isn't *Fifty Shades*, it's a story about my alcoholism. For a brief time, I was excited to be in what I thought was a relationship. I was happy to like someone who I thought actually liked me. It felt like progress. The only problem was now that I was totally on board, his calls became sporadic. And one day after we woke up in his bed together, his phone rang . . . and rang . . . until his answering machine picked up and I heard, "Hey, babe, we have dinner with my parents tonight, so bring a couple bottles of cab. Six o'clock, okay? Call me."

After that experience, I had a slew of drunken one-night stands. It wasn't that I craved sex with no strings attached; it was that I couldn't seem to attach any strings. It was so puzzling: I wanted to find love, be in a relationship, but I returned to my old pattern of freezing up at the first indication that a guy was too into me.

I felt pressured and responsible, worried about being depended on. I'd be extremely interested in a seemingly good guy for a date or maybe two, flooded with intense feelings and possibility, and then wake up one morning and feel nothing. Nada. Zilch. Unless I caught a whiff of unavailability: Then I would pine, calling them "just one more time," even when it was clear they'd lost interest or hadn't been that interested in the first place. Getting approval from men who didn't give a shit about me lit up the dopamine receptors in my brain, so I went back time and time again looking for that hit like a lab mouse hoping for cheese and getting an electric shock instead. It truly felt like an addiction.

I sought therapy. I needed a relationship mechanic to check under my hood, determine the problem, and replace the broken part so I could drive into my future. Talk therapy helped me see how I was trying to win the approval of difficult men—like my father and stepfather. I also devoured self-help books like *Women Who Love Too Much* by Robin Norwood. *"Are you bored with 'nice guys' who are open, honest, and dependable?"* Check! *Therapist Robin Norwood describes loving too much as a pattern of thoughts and behavior, which certain women develop as a response to problems from childhood. This book takes a hard look at how powerfully addictive these unhealthy relationships are."* But although the therapy and books helped me spot patterns, I felt powerless to change them.

When I was twenty-six, I met Scott at a comedy club and I thought I broke my pattern. He wasn't a comedian, which was a plus. He was cute and tall and looked like Hugh Grant in *Four Weddings and a Funeral* and he was nice. In the first few months he did little things to make me feel seen and special—like bringing me a bag of butterscotch Jelly Bellies, which he knew was my favorite flavor. He told me he loved me after six weeks. It was the first time a man had ever said it to me, and that includes my father. I hadn't ever had a real boyfriend—not like this—one who actually loved me! I had thought I was defective, broken, possibly even unlovable, but now his proclamation erased all that and made me whole.

But being in a relationship didn't make me drink less. I got used to drinking to numb the anxiety that constantly thrummed below the surface telling me this man would realize he'd made a mistake sooner or later. I drank too much on camping trips, at dinners out and parties. I got drunk—always by accident. I still needed the veil of alcohol to feel comfortable and be intimate. He wanted to have a lot of sex, so I had to do a lot of drinking in order to play the role of someone spontaneous, someone who loved sex and didn't need to plan for it or shower first or psych herself up in her mind, someone who was always up for it—even when I wasn't, which was most of the time.

I didn't like being fully naked in front of him. From the front was okay, but I never wanted him to see my ass straight on, especially not in a fully lit room. I had too much cellulite, something that had haunted me since I'd discovered it while looking in my mirror in eighth grade. I'd been standing with my back to the mirror and twisting my head around to get a look when I found out my butt had little dimples. For a brief moment, I'd seen it almost as a curiosity, and I'd clenched and relaxed my ass, watching the dimples turn into craters on a moon—how interesting. But soon enough I had learned it was not socially acceptable, and I'd spent every day since then trying to figure out how to make sure my secret was never revealed.

I'd mastered the art of backing out of a room, figuring out complicated choreography of excusing myself from a man's bed to go pee in the middle of the night or, God forbid, in the stark light of morning. Scott didn't give me a reason to feel insecure, but I still felt like a glimpse of my imperfections could make this whole thing disappear into thin air.

Scott had imperfections too—which I tried not to notice—like major jealousy. If we were walking down the street and another man made eye contact with me, Scott would lose his shit and blame me for somehow giving off available vibes. He also didn't want me wearing tight shirts that showed I had breasts; again, he didn't want me to send the wrong message, so I wore loose T-shirts and stopped wearing makeup. My friends worried about Scott's controlling nature, but I wasn't having it. Scott had things from his past! He'd been cheated on! He was just insecure. So we moved in together. But strangely it wasn't the panacea I'd hoped it would be.

We started having big arguments. I felt bolder when I drank and more able to stand up for myself—or maybe alcohol just helped me access my anger. Our fights got loud and mean. After one really bad one, I called my friend Kristin, who'd been married for years. "Has Chris ever told you to shut the fuck up?" I sobbed, hoping against hope that swearing at your girlfriend was a normal part of arguments in an otherwise loving relationship.

"Never. I'd cut his fucking balls off if he spoke to me that way. Break up with him."

But I wasn't willing to admit defeat; this was the first man who'd ever loved me, and what if no one else ever would? If he wasn't treating me the way he'd treated me in the beginning, the fault must be mine. I was determined to try harder.

The most brutal part of this story is that *he* left *me*. He got distant, so I got clingy and desperate, and eventually he tearfully said he wasn't ready for marriage and he'd taken a job in Italy without telling me and I wasn't invited. Ciao.

I was devastated, but I was also twenty-seven. So I kept trying to find a nice guy. There was a Nice Guy at the restaurant where I waited tables who'd asked me out multiple times while I was with Scott. Now that I was free and single I decided to take him up on it. Why shouldn't I? He was cute, in a Nice Guy sort of way! And seemingly made a lot of money at whatever his job was! He was a good tipper! I deserved to be treated nicely!

We went to dinner at an Italian restaurant. Nice Guy ordered a bottle of Chianti—and we drank wine like normal people do. We talked and laughed and drained the first bottle, so I suggested we get another. *This is fun!* I thought. *See, I'm not unlovable! Other men want me! Look at us having great conversation! Maybe this is what I needed all along! A Nice Guy! Maybe we'll end up getting married! Wouldn't that be so funny? During our wedding toast, I'll be sure to thank Scott for breaking up with me!* "Thanks, Scott, you actually did me a favor. You're the reason I have such an amazing, happy, successful life! Too bad things didn't work out as well for you, but that's karma!"

The only other thing I remember about that night is being in Nice Guy's living room, drinking more wine, crying about Scott. And then apologizing for crying about Scott, while continuing to cry about Scott.

The next morning, to my relief, Nice Guy called me—but not to ask me out on a second date; he just wanted to make sure I was okay after the night before. I never heard from him again.

And so my pattern with men continued, and I did my best to ignore the role alcohol played. I drank on all early dates in an effort to cross the bridge from full-fledged strangers to possible partners but could never seem to get the balance right. I drank to try on the persona of a fun-loving, baggage-free, definitely not needy free spirit when really all I wanted to know was *where is this going?* And if it was going somewhere, I managed to slam on the brakes, preventing myself from ever reaching a destination.

At thirty-two, just when it started to seem that all hope was lost, I met Jon on America Online Instant Messenger. I was randomly checking out AOL profiles, looking for men who lived in my vicinity and then messing with them until I lost interest. Jon's profile said he worked in TV and enjoyed sleeping, so I sent him an IM: "Hi, I see you're in TV. I'm thinking about buying a new one and wondered if you have any tips?" He immediately shot back something smart-alecky to indicate he knew I was being funny, and from there I flirted and he entertained my playful comments without giving much back. I added him to my "buddy list" and hit him up the next night to chat again.

Before Jon moved from my AOL "buddy list" to my bed, I continued to go on dates but found problems with each of them: One guy was a member of a "smoked fish of the month" club; another accused a chef of purposely undercooking his chicken to give him salmonella. Sometimes I came home early from these dates, logged on to AOL, and chatted with Jon for hours, feeling strangely relieved and curious about whether this could work offline. This went on for a few months, but he never flirted or asked to exchange a photo or phone call. In fact, he seemed incredibly uninterested in our burgeoning love story. Eventually, I had to admit to myself that I'd never be open to anyone else until I met this stupid guy and figured out if he was my person whether he liked it or not. So I forced him to meet me at a Coffee Bean & Tea Leaf at nine a.m. on a Tuesday.

When I first laid eyes on him, I thought it must be the wrong guy. He'd said he'd have a red backpack with him and although there was a dark red JanSport backpack slung over his wooden chair, this guy looked like a twenty-year-old college student, not the thirty-five-year-old I'd been expecting. But it was Jon. He says my first words to him were, "You're just a baby."

I think I'd built him up so much in my mind, deciding that this was it—my older, nerdy, Jewish but somehow George Clooney-looking soul mate coming to sweep me off my feet—so much so that I was a little disappointed to meet a mere mortal. But he hadn't built anything up in his mind, assuming that since I was funny, I must look like a chain-smoking Fran Lebowitz, so he was pleasantly surprised.

We sat and had coffee and he reminded me that he was the same guy I'd spent months getting to know online, being myself with, because I had no other choice. He had a point: The hardest part, the getting-to-know-you part, was behind me. And then he asked me out for drinks and we lived happily ever after. Oh, and I never got drunk again. The end. Ha ha ha.

In reality, alcohol still featured prominently in our relationship from our first real post-coffee date. Intellectually, I knew I really liked Jon—that he was different from the rest—but opening up to love still scared the crap out of me, so I drank. I drank to tolerate the unknown, I drank to tolerate the insecure feeling that he might change his mind, and I drank to tolerate the too-secure feeling that he might want something from me that I couldn't deliver. I drank because at this point, drinking was just what I did. The first time we kissed, I was buzzed; the first time we slept together—drunk.

But we drank *together*, so my drinking never stood out to me except when I'd accidentally drink too much. This seemed to happen in circumstances where I was eager to please or fit in with his life—like the time we hung out with his best friend, Rick, and Rick's cool newish girlfriend, Maggie, at her spacious Silver Lake apartment. Her place was decorated in a very aspirational way: velvet Italian sofa; colorful prints probably by an independent artist she knew personally; the glass knobs on her cabinets from Restoration Hardware. We drank a delicious Chilean cabernet while we talked about her experience with Habitat for Humanity and the movie she'd just produced. She was lovely and fun and I wanted to impress. The wine continued to flow, and somehow, in the way things like this happen when I'm drinking, Rick's girlfriend and I offered to make out in exchange for La Perla lingerie. The La Perla was Maggie's idea, and even though my fanciest bra to that point (and this point) came from Victoria's Secret, a $240 bra seemed like just the thing I deserved for being so fun. I'd never kissed a woman before, but I was drunk on wine and the promise of high-end Italian underthings, so I went for it.

The next thing I remember clearly is puking on a sidewalk in front of Jon's green Acura. We couldn't take the freeway home because he needed to pull over every few miles so I could get out and throw up again. Eventually we made it back to his one-bedroom apartment, where I tried to get to the toilet but only made it as far as the bath mat when I threw up again. You'd think I would have been completely puked out, but it was like a July Fourth fireworks finale and my body purged everything left in me in one great burst.

I woke up the next morning, my head in a vise, sick to my stomach. I wasn't a cute nineteen-year-old sorority girl who hadn't quite learned her liquor limits; I was thirty-four. I cried because I was full of regret, embarrassed that once again, I hadn't meant to get drunk; I hadn't meant to lose control. I promised myself I wouldn't do that ever again. And then I went to Bed Bath & Beyond to buy him a new bath mat.

Although it seemed to me that Jon and I drank the same amount, I was the only one who blacked out, had horrendous hangovers, and felt remorse after getting out of control once again. But it always seemed like an accident, something that could happen to anyone, like a tax audit or fender bender.

The problem, Jon later determined, when we were past the point of being polite, but still very tolerant of each other's faults, wasn't that I had a "drinking issue"; it was that I didn't have an off switch, so I simply wasn't able to regulate my drinking. He offered to help. "When we're at a party, as opposed to a bar, you aren't counting your drinks and you lose track, especially if someone is refilling your glass. I can help monitor you in those situations and let you know when you're getting tipsy." It was pretty ingenious but it didn't work. Once I had a couple of drinks in me, I didn't want to stop, and I certainly didn't want him controlling me and telling me I seemed drunk when I was so clearly not drunk! "What are you, the wine police?" I'd say, *as a joke*! And then he'd get frustrated with me, and then I'd sneak and refill my glass again when I thought he wasn't looking—or maybe he purposely looked the other way.

But Jon loved me. He was kind, consistent, and made me laugh harder than anyone ever had, and although he wasn't exactly distant, he needed enough space to keep me moving toward him. My friends think this relationship changed my pattern because I'd worked on myself so much before meeting him, knew my own value, and was ready to finally accept love into my life or some bullshit like that. I think it thrived because he played so hard to get.

Although Jon asked me to move in after a couple of years together, he seemed in no rush to get married, so I started a full-court press to get him to propose. I asked him, I begged, I cried, I gave half-assed ultimatums—who was I kidding? I wasn't breaking up with him. I knew he was going to marry me at some point, but he moves at a glacial pace, so one night I drank too much white wine and repeatedly punched him in the arm, asking when he would ever marry me, until he pulled out some mugs he'd made at Color Me Mine for our third anniversary. One said, "Happy anniversary to my bitch" and the other one said, "Wanna get hitched?" I straight-up bullied him into a proposal he'd actually planned but hadn't quite gotten to yet. Aspirational stuff, I know. Look out for my next book about how to get a man to commit in just under four years.

A year later we were married at a restaurant with a view of the Santa Monica mountains in front of our immediate family and a few close friends. Even though it rained so hard we were forced to do the ceremony indoors, it was the happiest moment of my life to that point, so of course I drank way too much Veuve Clicquot and passed out in our Malibu hotel room without any married night action. Regardless, the following month I was pregnant. But it would be another five years before I quit drinking.

8. Do I Have to Quit or Can I Just Cut Down?

There are people for whom drinking is no big deal. I call these people the Take It or Leave Its. You've probably seen them at parties ignoring the crackers and Brie. These types are able to drink at a party or have a glass of wine with dinner and stop there. Then there are other people who drink more, but if it feels like an issue, they find a way to dial it back or moderate. And then there are those of us who find ourselves really struggling and unable to control our drinking.

If you're reading this book and thinking, *Wow, sucks for you. Luckily I can have a glass of wine and leave it at that*, well, cheers! Or maybe you're thinking, *Yeah, I might need to cut down a little, but that's easy for me.* Hey, that's fantastic! Maybe you're in the group feeling *Hey, thanks for helping me take a look at my drinking; I'd like to be more mindful!* Cool! You'll get zero judgment from me. I quit drinking because I couldn't moderate, not because I suddenly had a moral turnaround on drinking and would like to reinstate prohibition.

If I could moderate, I would never have quit. Nobody, seriously no one, not one single person who suspects they drink too much *wants* to quit drinking completely. Does a diabetic *want* to swear off dessert simply because their stupid defective pancreas can't produce enough insulin? Do *you* want to swear off all sweets because the last time you went to Outback Steakhouse with your coworkers you embarrassed yourself by demolishing the entire Salted Caramel Cookie Skillet since even though it was Charlotte's birthday, that bitch only ate the tiniest bite and then everyone else whined about how they were so full so it was just sitting there taunting you until you did everyone a favor and ate it all? No! You just hope it doesn't happen next time, right? For me it's the same with alcohol. *And* cookie skillets.

But maybe you're someone who is thinking, *I don't want to give up alcohol completely but I need to figure out how to control it better.* Valid! But I will say that moderating is a lot harder, nearly impossible for those of us with addictive personalities. If you find yourself attempting to moderate and failing over and over, just know that cutting it out completely is so much less of a hassle. But I commend anyone who is brave enough to even take a look at their drinking and try to make a determination if it's serving them in their life. If you've had a nagging voice in your head telling you your drinking isn't normal, you are not alone.

Before I quit drinking, the last thing I wanted to do was quit drinking. What I *wanted* to do was to control my drinking. But alcohol is as slippery as a baby in a bathtub, and just when I thought I had a grip on it, it would squirm out of my grasp and leave me leveled with a hangover on a Wednesday morning. It had to be proven to me over and over and over again that no matter how much I drink, I can never fully predict my behavior.

The number one question I get asked after people see me on a talk show or read something I've written is, "How do I know if I need to quit drinking or if I should just cut down?" That is a great question. It's also a question I can't answer for anyone else, since it took me years to answer it for myself. I'm not the kind of drinker who sets out to get drunk. The problem was, I never could figure out how to stay buzzed without accidentally overdoing it. I almost always went out telling myself, "I'm only going to have two drinks," and then I'd have one and my drinking would develop a mind of its own. *That margarita was so tasty*, my brain would say. *Let's have another!* My brain was like my hype man, always cheering me on to keep the party going.

Every single time I drank more than I meant to, rather than entertain the notion that I wasn't someone who was in control of my drinking, my hype man would go into self-preservation mode, supplying me with excuses: *You were drinking on an empty stomach! The bartender made the drinks too strong! You shouldn't have taken a hit off of that joint! You just lost track because it was an open bar!*

In my teens and twenties and even into my thirties, if I woke up with a terrible hangover or remorse over something that had happened the night before, I would promise myself to never drink again or at least limit myself to three drinks per outing, and I'd be very strict! At least the first time out, but eventually, after a few weeks or maybe a month, I'd let myself off the hook because the consequences were just not that dire.

So I got drunk on a first date and the guy never called again, oh well, he was probably an asshole anyway. So I was a little hungover when I had that job interview; I didn't really want the job anyway. If I started to suspect that I'd lost some control over my consumption, I tried to regain it. But my self-management style was pretty lenient.

I'd take a few nights off or at the very least one night off to show myself I could.

But maybe six months after I had my first baby and noticed that my occasional—okay, if we're being honest, semi-regular—weekend binge drinking when I was kidless had morphed into a steady two-to-three-glass-a-night habit, I decided that I wanted to make sure I could cut down a bit just to prove to myself I wasn't a wino. I just didn't like that wine started calling to me every single night and didn't let up until I opened that bottle. I wanted to *want* a glass of wine, not *need* a glass of wine. I wasn't going to be wine's bitch! So I made a few rules for my drinking, but nothing too stringent, because I didn't have a problem, per se; I just wanted to make sure the old liver wasn't working too hard. I'd make sure to take a day or two off per week, I wouldn't start drinking in earnest until after my daughter was put to bed (I certainly never wanted to chance slurring her a bedtime story), and I promised myself I'd never drive drunk. During that time, whenever I'd go a night without wine, I'd congratulate myself like I'd passed the California State bar exam. *Look at me not drinking*, I'd think. *I'm killing it over here!* But then I got drunk that Halloween and basically scared myself straight.

After I'd turned back to wine following the birth of my twins, I quickly realized my drinking was slowly climbing back up into *possibly* problematic territory. Nothing bad had happened. It was just that I was starting to drink a little too much every single night and I didn't want to entertain the idea that I'd ever need to completely stop, so I decided to try to control it a little better, make some more rules for myself to prove I was good.

Because I was a stay-at-home writer and my schedule was so loose, it was hard to decide what rules would work best; I needed to cut down but not remove the release valve I'd come to rely on. I started small: *I'm only going to drink on weekends—including Friday, because everyone knows Fridays are part of the weekend.* But by Tuesday afternoon, my resolve would start to slip and my hype man would clock in: *Girl! You didn't drink on Monday! That's awesome! But Jon is getting home early from work tonight. Don't you want to put the babies to bed and chill with him with a glass of wine? Come on! Plus, why are you going to say you're not drinking?* He might suspect that you're worried about your drinking if you're suddenly not drinking at all during the week.

So I'd make a more reasonable plan: *Okay, here's what I'm going to do: I'm going to only drink on week*days—*including Friday, because everyone knows Friday is a weekday. On Saturday and Sunday, I'll give my body a break—absolutely no drinking on Saturday or Sunday. No exceptions.* But then something would come up like dinner with some girlfriends and I'd crack open that wine bottle or have margaritas, and by the end of the night I'd be drunk and I'd wake up hungover, cursing my lack of willpower.

And then I'd have an even better idea: *I will drink every other day!* That seemed like a workable solution: *I can have wine tonight but tomorrow is Wednesday, so I'll take that day off and then I can drink Thursday.* But then it would be Friday and I'd be struck by the short-sightedness of my plan: *How can I not drink on Friday? It's the weekend.* And I'd be back to square one rationalizing my drinking.

Then the guilt would creep in. *I'm just being weak. Why can other people control it but I can't? Why doesn't Jon want to keep drinking when we've finished one bottle?* "Hey, let's open another bottle!" I'd say, as if I was just in a great mood and wanted to continue enjoying the night.

"I'm good with this," he'd say, gesturing to his still half-full glass.

"I'm pretty tired." When my husband turned down my offer to open a second bottle of wine it would infuriate me. *He's tired?* I'd think. *How much energy does it take to drink wine? One bottle between two people is like eating one cookie. What's the point? I want to drink until I'm satisfied, until I'm floating, until I'm not thinking anymore, until I feel the relief, until I'm done.* But I never felt done. More was always better. Many times I would open that second bottle anyway and pour myself a much-needed fourth glass. Often that would lead to a hangover the following morning, which would lead to more promises to keep a tighter rein.

But by that night my hype man would step in once again: *We're just in our living room, it's not like we're out somewhere where I can embarrass myself. I'm not hurting anyone! What's the harm of one glass?*

So I'd make a new plan: *I'm only going to drink beer. First off, beer is more filling, so after a few beers I probably won't even want any more.*

And then another new plan: *I'm only going to drink wine, because it's lower in calories.*

And another: *I'm only going to drink cocktails, because the sugar in wine is giving me hangovers.*

And another: *I'm not going to buy wine except for what I plan to drink that night, and I won't go out for more.*

The more I'd try to control my drinking, the more it would threaten to escape my grasp. My drinking was like a new puppy you try to contain in the kitchen by using baby gates. The puppy whimpers and cries to get out, and eventually you can't handle the whining anymore, so you take pity on the little guy and let it out, just for a few minutes, just while you run out to the store, but when you come home, it's shit on your rug, peed on the couch, and eaten your brand-new Birkenstock sandals.

I needed another new plan: I would try keeping track of my drinks in a journal, which I would call my "Alcohol Agenda." With my older daughter in preschool and having time to kill, I decided to take the twins out to the mall, where I paid six dollars to rent one of those double strollers that look like a fire truck so we could go to Papyrus, the high-end stationery store known for adorable tote bags and eight-dollar greeting cards. My thinking was if I bought myself a fancy journal in which to log my drinks, I would take it more seriously than if I just jotted it down in a notebook from the Dollar Tree. An expensive journal felt like it meant business and wasn't something I could just toss if I felt frustrated with my progress. I settled on a light blue faux leather–bound book embossed with the words "You Are Worthy of New Beginnings." This was not something I would normally pick out, seeing as I wasn't big on inspirational sayings, but I was turning over a new leaf! This was going to be a brand-new me! My drinking was going to be totally manageable now that I was putting it into writing. That was what was missing before: accountability!

I literally couldn't wait to start drinking just so I could feel the sweet satisfaction of entering my glasses of wine into the ledger like some kind of alcohol accountant. If this worked, maybe I would start a business helping people keep track of their drinks! I could make my own line of notebooks with cutesy sayings! This was a million-dollar idea!

That night my husband had to work late as usual—but it was fine, I was in a great mood. I rushed the twins through bath time, got everyone into their jammies, read the twins a story—skipping every other page because they were only one-year-olds, so they didn't know the difference—cuddled with my older daughter, and read her

Skippyjon Jones: Lost in Spice, and finally tiptoed out of her room so I could settle on the couch and turn on the TV. Finally it was my time: wine o'clock.

I grabbed my corkscrew and expertly opened a bottle of Ecco Domani chardonnay, eager to start my experiment. But I had a thought: *I really can't just pour a small glass, because I can only have two, so I better make them both count.* So instead of my usual small juice glass, I went into the kitchen cabinet under the counter and pulled out an actual crystal wineglass, usually reserved for company— except we never had company. This accomplished two things: It accommodated a much more generous pour and it made the ritual less ordinary and more like a special occasion. It was all about being more aware of how much I was drinking. Fifteen minutes later I was ready for my second glass. This time I really needed to fill the wineglass to the top or I'd be completely done with my wine allowance for the night by eight thirty p.m.

By eight thirty-five p.m., it became clear that this plan was going to be too strict. I tried to think about it more like a diet: You need to allow for "treats"; otherwise it's too hard to stick to and you'll end up bingeing, which is obviously counterproductive. So I decided that just for tonight I'd allow for three glasses because I was still getting used to the new plan. Plus, the important part was being aware of how much I was drinking. The real issue was more with unconscious drinking! This was basically practicing mindfulness! It was kind of spiritual, if you think about it. If I kept this up, next thing you know, I'd be teaching yoga at a meditation retreat!

When Jon got home from work at ten thirty, he found me asleep on the couch, having taken a Xanax, the now-empty wine bottle on the floor next to me.

Moderating my drinking was proving difficult, but I figured this was probably just due to stress; I had a lot on my plate. My smaller twin had remained extremely small despite everyone's best efforts. With the help of a nutritionist, we spiked her formula with high-calorie supplements, gave her straight Ensure, offered her every calorically dense food we could think of: pasta with Alfredo sauce, full-fat Greek yogurt, and quiche. But she remained severely underweight, and when she turned one, her pediatric gastroenterologist decided that she needed to have a tube surgically inserted in her belly to get her sustenance. The doctors call it "failure to thrive." Before we knew it, there were boxes of medical supplies piling up by our front door from the frequent deliveries; there was an IV pole in her room, and I had to attach a bag of special formula to it at night so that she would gain weight while she slept. If the tube got accidentally pulled out because she rolled over or puked, an alarm would go off. And it went off several times every single night, like a shrill reminder that I was failing my sweet baby girl. Wasn't that one of my main jobs as a mother? To feed my child?

The problem, I decided, was in trying so hard to control my drinking. All of these rules I kept putting in place were just making me want to rebel against myself. I didn't know how it had gotten this bad. I thought back to when drinking was fun, when it was social, and just a nice way to unwind; I thought back to when I had more control. I knew there was a time I could go into an evening without making sure there was wine in the fridge but I couldn't recall how long ago that had been. I knew people who were actual alcoholics, and I wasn't that. I didn't even drink that much. But I didn't like the feeling I got when I tried to cut down. It felt like I wouldn't survive without a glass of wine, like I couldn't parent, sit still, relax, access my emotions, cry, write, sleep with my husband; like I couldn't fucking breathe.

I made a decision: *I am not going to go against my nature. I am going to embrace who I am, and who I am is someone who enjoys a daily cocktail.*

I thought about Jon's family of WASPs. If we lived in Connecticut, it would be completely normal to enjoy dirty martinis or gin and tonics every night before dinner. We would pour them from a Waterford crystal decanter, monogrammed with our initials and received as a wedding gift from a second cousin probably named Greer or Haisley. Forget the fact that I hate gin. The point was, this would be expected and normalized. I'd never have to worry that I was drinking too much, only that I was drinking too little!

So even though I wasn't a WASP and no one I knew lived like that, I decided the best way to tackle the nagging feeling that I drank too much was to either drink less or raise the amount I considered acceptable. Since drinking less hadn't been working out, I decided to just embrace my love of daily drinking. I would own this part of my personality. After all, I was far from alone: It was me, the entire East Coast, and every mommy blogger on the Internet.

I was going to go ahead and just let myself drink every single night! I would try to limit it to a couple, but if I had more than that, so be it. I wasn't hurting anyone. I closed my eyes, took a deep breath in, and let it out through my nose—the full-body relief I felt was palpable. I went through a mental checklist in my head to be sure this was a responsible idea: I was a caring mom. I didn't get drunk in front of my kids. I did all my drinking out in the open like a normal person—it wasn't as if I had a bottle of Captain Jack hidden in my dresser drawer so I could run upstairs and sneak sips while the kids played outside, like my friend Jody. I didn't drink in the morning. Yeah, I was good to go. But I made one final line in the sand: I would not drink and drive.

This plan worked beautifully for a few months until I not only crossed my line in the sand, I hurdled over it like an Olympic pole-vaulter.

9. How I Almost Became a Lifetime Movie

I wake up on my couch fully dressed: I'm still in jeans, a tank top, and unbuckled sandals. Clothes plus couch can only mean one thing: I've had a fight with Jon. My memory of the night before looms over me like a tidal wave moments before it hits the beach. But I can't even process it quite yet because—no surprise—I'm sick. Like, so sick. This is a hangover for the ages. And if I have a hangover this severe, it must mean that I was quite drunk last night. And if I was drunk last night, then it would follow that I drove home. With my kids in the car. The tidal wave crashes violently, soaking me in shame.

I run to the bathroom and puke repeatedly, my stomach convulsing until the only thing coming out is bitter yellow bile. I raise my head, but my brain feels like there is a knife going straight through it. Hangover migraine. My favorite. This is bad.

My memories start coming through in flashes like a movie trailer: I'm at Stacy's house, drinking an apricot martini she's poured for me from a fancy glass pitcher. "This is so good," I tell her. And it is. I'm normally just a wine girl, but this hang-out/playdate/whatever you want to call it is next level. I feel relieved to be somewhere with other fun adults, having adult beverages. I deserve a fun night with all I've been dealing with and, damn it, I want a second drink. Stacy is only too happy to oblige; she's a great host.

My friend Diana had invited me to hang out at Stacy's house. Stacy was part of a big group of friends who got together every Friday night, some with kids, some without, and, for lack of a more mature word, partied. Now, Diana wasn't a big "partier"; in fact, she barely drank. I'd met Diana at a neighborhood progressive dinner party back when I only had one baby and was pregnant with the twins. Since I'd moved to the San Fernando Valley when I was pregnant, I'd tried to be open to suburban-mom activities. A progressive dinner party is one of those things where a type A neighbor organizes a dinner and enlists various other neighbors to offer their houses to host different courses. At the "main course" house, Diana and I became fast friends over a shared love of Trader Joe's Green Goddess salad dressing and the discovery we both had young daughters exactly a year apart.

Later, when my twins were little, I would often walk to her house, sit on her couch, and try to convince her to day drink with me. I would always make it sound super casual, like it was something that had literally just occurred to me because it was a hot day and "a beer sounds nice, do you happen to have one?"

Diana's sister, I found out, had a very serious problem with alcohol, which had resulted in Diana's family attempting several interventions, all of which failed. It was a painful subject, so I always tried to be sensitive to that fact and I never wanted to seem like drinking was all that important. But I really liked that beer.

Diana's house was a refuge for me. As the twins got a little older and started walking, I'd stick them in the double stroller, walk the six blocks to Diana's, and we'd sit them at a little toddler table in her kitchen and feed them pancakes—the kind you microwave; we weren't actually cooking pancakes, have you met me? With three kids aged four and under, one with medical issues, I'd say my stress level was pretty much always at least DEFCON 3, but watching my little twin struggle to take in calories could easily raise it to DEFCON 2. Diana and I would watch and cheer for every bite together. Sometimes we'd manage to get her to eat half a string cheese, and I'd practically throw a parade.

Diana thought I would have a great time with Stacy and her group of friends, and I was desperately in need of a great time, so I left Jon home with one of the twins, bringing my oldest and the other twin to the party with me.

I'm standing in Stacy's kitchen. A Black Eyed Peas song plays in the background. Fergie tells me she's gotta feeling that tonight's gonna be a good night. A man who looks to be in his early-to-mid-thirties—one of Stacy's friends, I presume—seems to be flirting with me. "Wait, those are your kids? No way do you look like you have a baby!" he says. "You look great." The way he pauses after the word "look" and then makes direct eye contact when he says "great" is 100 percent flirty. With the couple of cocktails I have on board, this feels extra intoxicating. It's not that I'm attracted to him at all—he sports a scraggly beard, and I'm fairly sure he works part-time as an extra on movie sets; it has nothing to do with him. It's me. I'm forty-two, sleep-deprived, and swimming in toddlers, formula, diapers, medical supplies, and Target runs. I thought I'd disappeared.

For the past few years and most especially the past year and a half, I've felt like I'm walking around with a sign over my head that says, "Just a mom." The last time I'd been in for a haircut I'd told my stylist, "Please make my hair look 'fuck off.' I'll take heroin chic over mommy," and yet I still came out looking less Courtney Love and more Connie Chung, if Connie Chung was just returning from maternity leave.

But this man is focusing on me. Am I looking cute? Is that even possible? I'm wearing my favorite low-rise jeans that I finally fit back into if I suck in my stomach nonstop, and I've attempted to camouflage my muffin top with a hot-pink tank I got at T.J. Maxx for nine dollars because I refuse to spend real money on clothes until I'm at least close to my pre-babies body, which I'm starting to doubt will ever happen. But I'm feeling good. And, yeah, this guy is definitely hitting on me, I think. Maybe he's just being nice, but whatever! I'm loving the attention!

Fergie shout-sings that tonight's the night and I gotta live it up.

My four-year-old and my eighteen-month-old twin along with a few other kids are being entertained by Stacy's nanny in her backyard while the adults chill in her beautiful home and I feel free, un-weighted, untethered. I haven't felt this way in . . . I don't know how long. God, I'm so happy Diana invited me here! I really needed this!

I attempt to leave my bathroom to go back to the couch, but I can't stop throwing up. Where are the kids? I definitely don't remember putting them to bed last night, probably because I didn't. I'm crying now. I feel shaky. The inside of my mouth feels like when you go to the dentist and they vacuum out all the moisture—I can barely swallow. I may need to go to the ER. I can't believe this is happening.

Jon is calling me. I see his number come up on my BlackBerry, trying to check in, but I don't answer. I instantly feel irritated. I never get to have fun like this. What could he need from me? I have two of the kids in tow. It shouldn't be so difficult for him to watch just one. I'd give my left ovary to just be in charge of one toddler for the evening! It sounds like a goddamned Hawaiian vacation to spend a few hours with only one kid. Think of the possibilities! A person responsible for one toddler can do whatever they want! Like go to the park—a trip to the park with three kids is a nightmare: One kid climbs up the slide the wrong way while the other one dumps sand in their hair and the third makes their way to the top of the structure and you have to climb up after them or they might step off and break a leg. With just one kid, a person could go to a restaurant! I bet people with one kid practically live at restaurants! Why wouldn't they? And fancy restaurants, too! They don't have to narrow their dining options to kid-friendly chains that offer menus you can color. Or a one-kid-haver can just hang out in the house, WHICH IS WHAT JON IS CURRENTLY DOING SO WHY IS HE CALLING ME? I'm here with two-thirds of our children. Dude, relax.

Fergie sings to me that we'll have a ball if we get down and go out and just lose it all. Stacy pours me a third martini. I'm definitely only going to sip this one slowly, because eventually I do have to drive. But that won't be for a while.

I sneak a look at the living room clock. Six thirty a.m. My head hurts so badly that I can't think. Can you die of a hangover? Jon has to be asleep in bed. God, he must be so angry. I wonder if he wants a divorce.

Diana walks up to me, sipping an Evian. "I gotta go. I have an early flight in the morning." She shoots a concerned look at the empty martini glass I had planned to sip slowly. "Are you okay to drive?"

"Yes! Of course!" And I do feel fine to drive. I am fine to drive.

"I've only had two drinks," I lie, "And I'm not leaving anytime soon."

"Huh. Okay. If you're sure." She gives me a look like she's definitely not sure, even if I think I am. "I'll talk to you when I get back. Love you." She gives me a hug.

"Love you too! Have a great trip!"

Diana means well, but she's seriously uptight. She won't allow her-self even one little drink just because she's leaving town in the morning? Is having a single drink going to impact her ability to pack? Jesus, live a little!

Stacy sees my empty glass and refills it once again. I start to protest, but this is a special occasion and I'm having so much fun and the apricot martini tastes so good. Did I mention Stacy is a great host? Why don't I ever entertain? I used to love having people over, back before I had kids. I should start having people over to my house on Friday nights for drinks! I can whip up some apps easily—maybe chips and salsa and spinach dip. I'll definitely need Stacy's martini recipe!

I'm finally puked out for the moment, so I lie back down on the couch, stinky, sweaty, vibrating. I try to lie perfectly still, breathing slowly in and out while attempting to put the final pieces of the drunken jigsaw puzzle together in my pounding head.

My BlackBerry is ringing. It's Diana, so I answer. "Jon called me looking for you. He says you aren't answering your phone. Can you please call him back? He's really worried." I look and see I have several missed calls from him. I guess I can't even enjoy one night out, can I?

I'm strapping the kids into their car seats, one in her Britax with the five-point harness—which I'd paid forty bucks to have professionally installed by Rick at Baby Town just to be sure it was completely safe and secure—and the older one in her highly rated Graco three-in-one booster seat—only the best for my precious cargo.

I drive home, occasionally covering one eye.

Jon stands barefoot in our driveway. He wears jeans, a blue T-shirt, and a furious expression. He rubs each of his wrists in turn, a poker tell that he is incensed. It takes a lot to get Jon to go from irritated past his tipping point to full-on angry—Lord knows I've pushed him often enough.

Jon is the kind of husband I'd refer to as "my rock" if I spoke in Hallmark greeting cards, which I don't. Normally he's incredibly patient and consistent, but right now, he's accusatory right out of the gate.

"You're drunk! What the actual fuck?" He doesn't give me even a second to explain. "I've been worried sick and it's fucking worse than I thought."

This is ridiculous. What is he, my dad? I feel fine. And I'm home, so there was nothing to worry about, was there? Now I'm actually mad too! I'm not a child. I am a grown woman! I can be trusted to know how much I've had to drink!

"I only had two drinks," I say, trying very hard to enunciate my words correctly, so as not to give him more ammunition. And then I stagger up the driveway, leaving Jon to unstrap the kids and bring them into the house, because I am very mad!

"Yeah, two drinks. That's why you can barely walk!" Jon calls to my back as I open the front door. "What the hell is wrong with you?"

And that's all I remember until I wake up on the couch. Now, lying here, barely able to move my head even slightly due to the unremitting throbbing still radiating from my brain, I'm struck as if by lightning by a truth:

I *was* drunk last night.

There it is, almost as if it were written on a page and underscored with yellow highlighter. I was drunk last night and I drove my car. I was drunk and I drove my sweet babies home. I got behind the wheel, drunk, and drove them. There was no rearranging of the words that would make this untrue; I wasn't an eighteen-year-old teenager making a stupid mistake; I was a forty-two-year-old mother of three with *everything* to lose. What the hell *was* wrong with me? I was stunned by my own arrogance.

The rationalization begins to creep in, attempting to protect me: *The thing is, I really hadn't thought I was drunk at all or I wouldn't have done it.* But the excuse feels like it's attached to my brain with used Scotch tape; no sooner is it stuck up there than it falls right off. I press the tape down harder, hoping to secure it: *The alcohol hit me harder because I haven't been eating enough. I'm on Zoloft. I lost track of my drinks. Stacy made them extra strong. This would never have happened with wine or beer. I was tired. I'm not used to drinking that much. My tolerance must be lower. Stress caused me to feel drunker—is that a thing? I bet it is. It sounds right.* But the Scotch tape is overused and coated with fuzz and the excuses won't stick.

There was that asshole truth again: This is what happens when I drink—not every time—sometimes I can manage to have one glass or two, but that's usually because there isn't any more or I'm trying to prove to myself that I can, but eventually I let my guard down and I accidentally lose control.

I'm at a crossroads: I can go into the bedroom where my husband is sleeping alone and beg his forgiveness, tell him how sorry I am, and I can promise him that I'll *never* let something like this happen again. I can swear to him. And I'll mean it, too. I can explain that we were having martinis and *you know I'm not good with hard liquor, you know I do better with wine or beer—the hard liquor just hits me different*—the same excuses I tell myself. And he will believe me. He trusts me. He knows I'm a good mom who loves our kids. This same mom who did this very bad thing is also the one who cuddles in bed with the twins every night, reading *Goodnight Moon* or *Pat the Bunny*, holding their little hands over the pages, helping them play peek-a-boo with Paul and scratching the flowers so they can sniff them.

But I know that I can't promise him that. Because even though he trusts me, I don't trust myself. I know that if I drink, at some point, I will drink and drive again. Not in a week, not in a month, maybe even not in a year—but at some point, I will get drunk again without meaning to and possibly make a very bad decision, because that's what happens to me when I drink. It sounds victimy even in my own head, as if once I uncork that chardonnay, big bad alcohol wafts out of the bottle like some demented genie, tackles me to the ground, and forces me against my will to do bad things—but how else could I explain myself? Sober me knows you don't drive when you've had more than one drink even if you feel fine. Haven't I been inundated with D.A.R.E. and Mothers Against Drunk Driving lessons since high school? For God's sake, a drunk driver killed my friend Amy, and I'd thought I'd never get over it.

But tipsy me never registers any of that. I'm always the last to know I'm drunk, and the next day I always feel surprised, as if I hadn't been the one doing the drinking.

I don't know if I'm an alcoholic; I don't think I am. I desperately hope I'm not. I just know that I never want to feel this *how the fuck did this happen* feeling again. I want to wake up without the sneaking suspicion that I picked a fight with Jon the night before, but since I don't remember what it was about I'm forced to pretend I'm still mad because it would be too embarrassing to admit I don't even remember going to bed. All I know is that I don't want to drink anymore but I don't know how to stop.

Still nauseous but unable to sit with the feeling that Jon may never speak to me again, I tiptoe into the bedroom and sit down next to his sleeping form. He's lying with just the top half of his body covered by our gray-and-white striped comforter, like he's had a sleepless night. Obviously this is my fault. I feel a stab of love, remorse, lust, and sadness at the sight of his bare legs, legs with just the right amount of muscle and hair, sexy but also regular. My guy. I've slept next to those legs for a lot of years now. I think about my kids sleeping on the other side of the house and the man sleeping right here. I have so much to lose.

He doesn't stir, so I nudge him very gently. After a beat, his eyes open slowly, but when he realizes I'm sitting there, he just seems disappointed, like he got the wrong thing under the tree on Christmas morning.

"Jon," I say, quietly, because my own voice might cause me to hurl. "I'm so sorry. I know I was drunk. You were right. I am going to quit drinking. I know I've said that before, but I mean it. I'm going to get help. I think I might be an alcoholic." I hear loud crying, which I assume is coming from the twins' room, but I realize it's me. Jon's face is now more concerned. Just to be clear: I'm not someone who uses tears to manipulate. Holding back tears is kind of my superpower, so when the tears are flowing, I feel less in control rather than more. I'm not huge on vulnerability. I'd never make it as a *Bachelor* contestant.

"I don't think you're an alcoholic. I don't even see you drink that much. You just can't drive when you've been drinking."

I can't believe I'm going to have to convince my husband I have a drinking problem. This is not the way it goes in the movies. Well, except *When a Man Loves a Woman*, which is one of my all-time favorite movies about alcoholism. Meg Ryan (arguably delivering her best work) plays Alice, who seems like a woman who is enthusiastic and fun when she's drinking, especially when she's being drunkenly flirty with her husband, Andy Garcia. But one day she gets extremely drunk, slaps her kid, and falls through the glass door of her shower, passing out cold and scaring the shit out of her kids, who think she's dead. Even after that, Andy Garcia's character, Michael, makes a lot of excuses for his wife. Is he loyal or is he in denial? I would have always said loyal.

"But I did drink and drive. I know better and I still did it. Obviously I'm not safe when I drink. I have to get help." And now that I've said it out loud, I'm scared that I can't take it back.

10. Asking for Help

I walked into the meeting with my friend Karina by my side three days after I'd driven drunk. It was a Tuesday at three in the afternoon, which, in retrospect, probably wasn't ideal for my first "actually here for me and not pretending to simply be mildly curious about whether or not I have anything in common with people who have a real drinking problem" meeting. Three p.m. is a great time slot for people who are chronically underemployed, people who have no kids to pick up from school, or alcoholics who have turned semi-pro and attend meetings from morning until night. I wasn't at all sure this seemed like a great hour to find people whose lives had any similarity to mine beyond our shared desire to quit drinking.

That morning when I'd decided everything had to change, I could only think of one person to call: Karina. I hadn't spoken to her about my drinking even once since she and Chloe had cornered me in her condo for the informal intervention a few years before. I really had to commend her: She wasn't one to keep her thoughts to herself, yet she hadn't mentioned it again. She never asked a single probing question like, "Did you ever stop hoovering all that Xanax?" or, "Are you ready to admit you're a mess?" or, "How about you stop now? *Before* you ruin your life?" That's how I knew I could call her. She wouldn't judge me—well, she might, but she wouldn't tell me she was judging me, which was just as good.

To be honest, though, I didn't completely think Karina could relate to my situation. She wasn't a mom, and it didn't even seem like she drank that much. She swore she had drunk alcoholically and that's why she'd quit, but I'd never really seen her get messy, and we'd been friends for at least fifteen years. Was it possible that I was drunk when she was drunk, so I just didn't realize she was drunk? I sort of doubted it. She was single and claimed she often calmed her first-date jitters with a shot or four of tequila, but last I checked, that wasn't alcoholism—it was just good planning.

I was already crying when she answered the phone. "Hi. I need to quit drinking. This time for real. Can you help me?"

"Of course. I can take you to my Tuesday meeting. Pick you up at two thirty." I knew she would be there for me. Getting asked for help is like catnip to reformed drinkers. But I was still flooded with gratitude. I felt relieved to have a plan, and even more relieved that she hadn't asked any questions.

I made it through Saturday, Sunday, and Monday coasting on shame. There wasn't much to tempt me; my husband wasn't drinking out of solidarity, and there was no alcohol in the house anyway—not because I'd thrown it all out. I would have dramatically cleared my refrigerator of all wine—sweeping the bottles into lawn-and-leaf-sized green Hefty bags, ceremoniously tossing them into the outside trash bins—but there wasn't any leftover wine. I bought wine every day, as if it was a surprise that I needed it again. Looking down the barrel at another long evening with babies, I'd realize there was no wine in the house, because I'd drunk it all the night before, and casually do a Trader Joe's run. I'd of course make up some other reason

I had to go, a necessity like a bag of fusilli pasta or milk or hummus, and then I'd tell myself, *Hey, while I'm out I'll just pick up a couple of bottles of pinot!* As if the thought spontaneously popped into my head every single night for the past several years. As if I could get through a night without it.

These three days (almost four) were the longest I'd gone without drinking since I'd started back in after bringing home the twins.

I'm extremely lucky I didn't have physical withdrawal symptoms, and I don't recommend going cold turkey as a technique. I have friends who drank less than I did who needed to go through detox to quit safely. Drinking every single evening without a night off even if you have the flu can lead to physical dependence. I didn't have physical symptoms, but I was already having a few emotional ones. Although, it was tough to tell if my mood instability was due to alcohol withdrawal or simply that having no alcohol with which to numb myself was making me even more painfully aware of how close I'd come to blowing up my life.

Although I was proud that I'd gone a few days with nary a drop, I knew from experience my resolve would soon crumble. My resolutions were like sandcastles. Each time I'd build them farther up the beach, but they were no match for the advancing tide of my drinking. There was a time that the tide used to advance and then recede, but somewhere along the line it had just continued to advance.

I knew I couldn't do this without support.

When Karina and I entered the church hall, it was like Norm just burst through the doors of Cheers, except this wasn't a friendly neighborhood bar; it was quite the opposite. "Karina!" said at least five different people. I stood glued to her side as she introduced me to a few people who seemed way too happy to meet me. I got a lot of very hearty "welcomes" and "keep coming backs," but this time, I was too sad to be cynical.

We grabbed a couple of folding chairs in the middle of the room that didn't already have a business card or car keys holding the seat of someone outside smoking or chatting. I leaned over and whispered to Karina, "Are any of these women moms?" I was desperate to find other moms like me, women who understood the unique pressure I felt to be perfect and the unique humiliation I felt in my failure. I figured if this was her regular meeting, she would know some of their stories. Karina gestured to a sweet-looking blond woman standing by the coffee, possibly in her early thirties, but in LA it's hard to tell. She could have been fifty with access to Botox and Juvéderm or twenty-three but ravaged by drugs and alcohol.

"I think she has a baby. Or a toddler. I'm not sure." I made a mental note to try to talk to her afterward. Karina didn't know about anyone else, but even one was good enough for now. Eventually everyone filed in and the chairs filled with alcoholics. Was I one too? I knew I didn't want to drink. And that's about all I knew.

The leader started the meeting, and there was an awful lot of business they had to take care of first. I found it very hard to concentrate on clapping for the person who'd done the coffee setup and to mentally follow the instructions on where to stack the chairs at the end of the meeting (spread evenly between two racks against the far wall) when my life was ruined. It was like these people didn't get the gravity of their situation. Here they were, talking about nonsense like we were at a PTA meeting and not in a desperate bid to get our shit together.

Two seemingly opposite lines of thought raced through my brain: 1) I'm probably not as bad as most people in this room because there is just no way that my two or three or four glasses of wine a night habit truly qualifies me as an alcoholic, and 2) I'm much worse than everyone in this room because only a few short nights ago I drove drunk with my kids in the car. The second line of thought was still burning in my brain like a California wildfire.

When the leader started telling his story, Karina grabbed my hand and held it and then kept holding it, and I was actually grateful. I'm usually not up for that level of physical intimacy with a friend. I've never been someone who just randomly slings her arm around the shoulder of a girlfriend outside of summer camp. I will do it under duress, like at a funeral, but even when I do, I'm overly conscious of it and will spend an inordinate amount of energy trying to determine how long my arm has to stay there to indicate comfort but not overstay its welcome. But Karina must've sensed that I was a woman on the verge, and this was our *Sex and the City* moment. Thank God for girlfriends.

I cried quietly the entire ten minutes the leader spoke, and when it was time for people to share, my hand popped up against my will, like it was a jack-in-the-box and some force outside myself had turned the crank. The speaker pointed at me immediately and my confession tumbled out unbidden, yet unstoppable. I had to start by saying my name and identifying myself as an alcoholic—which seemed like a big ask—kind of like saying "I love you" on the first date: Maybe I'll come to believe it at some point, but why force it if I'm not sure I even mean it? I said it anyway because it was the price of admission to unburden myself.

I didn't make eye contact with anyone—not that I could've seen much, since my eyes had basically become water spigots. "I'm Stefanie and I'm an alcoholic. I mean, I don't know if I am or not, but

I've been drinking too much for a long time and I really want to stop. I drove drunk with my kids in the car. I can't believe I did that. I didn't mean to; I didn't think I was drunk. And nothing happened, you know? I didn't get a DUI or anything. I got home safe. But I'm so scared it could happen again if I don't stop. Every time I do something stupid when I drink, I swear I won't do it again, but there is always a next time, you know? I can't afford any more next times. I *have* to be done."

People clapped, which felt awkward. You don't normally expect applause after recounting a humiliating experience. "I smoked crack and sold my parents' Honda to get money to buy more crack!" Huzzah! "I lost my medical license for getting drunk and sexting my patients!" Standing ovation! Okay, I realize people clap because it's brave to share on such a personal level, and they want to show support, but it felt so out of place after what I'd said. Who would want to support me? I'd just admitted something gross and unforgivable; I felt stripped bare and disgraced, like I was now wearing a scarlet letter signifying I was the worst of the worst, the bottom of the alcoholic barrel, a drunk mom.

I sat there in my chair, my face hot with shame and grief, while people passed purse-sized tissue packets my way and gave me sad-clown looks. I'd said it out loud and I couldn't unsay it. I also couldn't take back what had happened: I could only move forward, but I had absolutely no idea how I would do that.

Another crier raised her hand and shared that she was currently in treatment at a nearby rehab. I knew the rehabs sometimes drove a little group of inmates over in a van to take in a meeting out in the real world. She had a face full of makeup and some really nice black suede boots that hugged her calves. I pictured her packing for her stay and taking the time to consider eye shadow and footwear. Imagine giving a shit about how you looked? If I went to rehab, I would pack Target lounge pants and socks. I'd refuse to wear bras on principle. I'm unclear on what principle that is, but I'd stand on it nonetheless.

The more I thought about this girl, the less I felt bad for her and the more I felt sorry for myself. She was safe; safe inside those rehab walls, safe from all the outside stressors, like toddler meltdowns, writing deadlines, dishes, cleaning the bathroom, changing diapers, and trying to make a skinny toddler gain weight. She was probably busy with horseback riding and nonstop therapy. How could a person in rehab NOT get better? The odds seemed stacked in their favor.

More people shared, but my mind was consumed with racing thoughts: *Will I have to be coming here in twenty years? Can I ever take another Vicodin? Will I never get to feel that perfect feeling you get when you take those first two pills on an empty stomach? Surely they make exceptions for that? What if I have surgery?* I really fucked up my life. I'd taken it too far and now I'd given myself a life sentence that would be carried out in church basements.

What *was* wrong with me? I looked so normal on the outside; I *was* normal. I was a writer, a mother; I had friends and a husband. How was it that I couldn't keep this one tiny aspect of my life under control? I had privilege; I knew that. Other people wished they had it as easy as I did. I'm sure they thought, *What does she have to drink about?* And nothing against the other people in the room—many of them also looked normal—but the big difference was they all seemed thrilled to be here, or if not thrilled at least fine with it; and I was not, I was devastated. Even Karina seemed like she came here because she wanted to, as if it were a book club. This would be the world's dullest book club, because instead of reading the latest Oprah Winfrey discovery, the only book up for discussion was a boring one about people in the 1930s who couldn't quit drinking.

The meeting closed, as they mostly do, with a prayer, which I found uncomfortable. Obviously, having been to twelve-step meetings way back with Landry and most recently right before I got pregnant with twins, I knew there was a lot of God talk involved; I'd just put it out of my mind in order to get through it.

Once the meeting ended, people bum-rushed me, the newbie who'd cried. I'd allowed myself to be known, and now people wanted to know me—funny how that works. Women took my hand and pressed folded scraps of paper into it where they'd scrawled their phone numbers and told me to "call anytime! Day or night!" Lots had words of encouragement: "I've been there too," or, "You're in the right place." The blond woman of unknown age who had a child introduced herself to me as Donna and whispered, "I drove drunk with my son in the car and got a DUI." *Shit*. She gave me her number too.

One older lady, whom I'd noticed knitting her way through the meeting, waited to speak to me, so Karina left us to talk. She looked like a sweet grandma type, and carried a tote bag for her yarn balls and knitting needles. I couldn't imagine her committing a crime worse than speaking above a whisper in a library, but her voice was deep and gravelly, like that of a lifelong smoker who'd seen stuff.

"Listen, honey, one day you'll be grateful you drove drunk with those babies of yours. You're gonna be able to use your experience to help others." I was appalled.

"There's no world in which I'll ever be grateful that I did that," I shot back. She didn't flinch.

"I always tell newcomers, 'I wish you the gift of desperation,' because desperate people tend to stick around." And then she asked me what my plan was. I must've looked confused, so she told me to meet her at a women's meeting that was happening in two days and gave me the address. So I agreed because I *was* desperate and I needed a plan.

11. The "A" Word

When I quit drinking, I felt done—very sad, but very done. But was I an "alcoholic"? My image of an alcoholic was someone who drank all day every day, a person who would get the shakes if they tried to quit. I saw alcoholics as people in movies—like Nicolas Cage in *Leaving Las Vegas* deciding life wouldn't be worth living without drinking so, fuck it, he might as well drink himself to death. But I saw myself as more of a social drinker who drank every day, with or without other people present, more of an "alcohol enthusiast," if you will.

I quit drinking years before the word "alcoholism" was tossed out of the accepted recovery vernacular and replaced by the less judgy terms "substance use disorder" or "alcohol use disorder" which cover mild, moderate, and severe addiction, making it more inclusive for people like me who couldn't wrap their heads around the "A" word. In actuality, the *Merriam-Webster* definition of "alcoholism" is: *continued excessive or compulsive use of alcoholic drinks*—really not all that accusatory sounding. But the word "alcoholic" has a certain finality to it, like being diagnosed with an autoimmune disease or finding out you're color-blind. Alcoholism doesn't seem like something that just goes away because you started a plant-based diet. And if you announce you're an alcoholic, you can't change your mind; otherwise you're a "sad alkie who's drinking again" instead of a "person who just wanted to get healthy and sort things out before getting back to enjoying a glass of wine once in a while."

I wished there was a diagnostic test to tell me if I was really an alcoholic. There were tests that could predict whether you had the risk factors for heart disease or Alzheimer's. Why couldn't there be a blood test so I could know for sure if I really needed to go through all of this? I didn't even drink that much! It seemed unfair that someone like me, whose life was still totally fine, would have to say sayonara to booze for good. What if I was depriving myself of the one thing that gave me relief at the end of the day, the thing that was guaranteed to soften my chronic irritability, the substance that helped me connect with my husband, the magic elixir that turned just sitting on the couch watching *Housewives* into a good time, the antidote to a screaming baby, the seasoning that could give almost any activity more flavor?

So I wrestled with the idea that I could actually be an alcoholic. But I also tried to remain open, because I knew that if I didn't take some sort of action, the tapes would start playing in my mind, like reverse self-help: *You weren't that bad! Why are you being so all-or-nothing? You can have just one! In fact, everyone knows having a glass of merlot every day is actually healthy for you. There are all of those studies that say red wine has antioxidants in it that prevent heart disease. I mean, are you trying to have a heart attack?*

Karina quit smoking a bunch of times: twice through hypnosis; a few times using Chantix, the drug that supposedly works on nicotine receptors; several by just white-knuckling it; and many more by chewing Nicorette gum. Sometimes she lasted a day, sometimes a week, and once she went for over ten years. She always told me,

"Quitting is the easy part, but staying quit is hard." So why after ten years would she possibly pick up a cigarette? It seemed insane to me. I couldn't fathom getting completely over smoking, to the point that you really don't think about it anymore, and then smoking again, knowing exactly what will happen.

She said her relapse started with one cigarette: a clove. It seemed harmless enough. The idea just got into her head one day when someone was smoking a clove near her. Usually, as a nonsmoker, she would be disgusted by the smell, but somehow, this time the smell triggered a good memory, and a little seed was planted, and before she knew it, that seed sprouted roots, and over the next few weeks those roots bloomed into a plan: *I'll just smoke one.* And the idea of smoking one made so much sense to her. If she just smoked one, she could stop thinking about smoking. *Just one,* she thought. *One tiny little cigarette to stop the incessant thoughts about smoking one cigarette. Maybe even just a half. Maybe just a puff will do the trick. What's the harm in that?*

So she stopped at the store, bought a pack of cloves, smoked one, and then she smoked the rest of the pack because, fuck it, she'd be quitting again tomorrow so might as well.

And then for the next three years she kept smoking while talking about quitting constantly before she got the strength to try again.

I knew if I wanted to stay quit I'd have to do it differently this time. I'd proven to myself I couldn't stay sober on willpower alone. And although I'd scared myself straight with my risky behavior, I knew from experience that eventually the soul sickness I felt after driving drunk wouldn't feel so close behind me. Eventually, the shame would begin to fade in the rearview mirror until it was a blip on the horizon and then poof, I'd no longer remember why I'd thought it was a good idea to quit. And so, much like Karina convinced herself one ciggy wasn't a big deal, I would inevitably convince myself that just one little drink would probably be okay. That scared me.

But still, sitting in those meetings in those very early days, I had a debate going on in my head constantly. The part of me that couldn't take the L would tell me, *You don't belong here. You are nowhere near as bad as these people. Bless their hearts, but you don't have the same issue. Just look at your life! Still intact! Nothing is different. You haven't lost anything.*

But there was another voice, a quieter voice that would bravely argue: *Yet. You haven't lost anything yet. But are you willing to take your chances? Because the odds don't seem to be in your favor. You're playing roulette and betting on double-zero. In the end, the house always wins.*

So yes, I had to do it differently, but how? In the past, even when I'd gone to a meeting, I hadn't actually done anything but sit and listen. I hadn't actually asked for help. I despise asking for help. I'm an "I got this" type of person, preferring to handle things on my own because if I don't put myself out there, then I don't risk feeling let down. But handling things on my own obviously hadn't worked when it came to my drinking. I'd tried so hard to get this under control; I'd literally exhausted myself with the effort. I knew that something that helped people was getting a sponsor, which basically meant asking another alcoholic to help take you through the twelve steps. The thought of a person helping me do this daunting thing sounded tempting, like maybe it would be nice to do things someone else's way. But if I gave someone power, would I lose some of my own? I didn't love people telling me what to do. That's an understatement: I've always had a problem with authority, from parents to teachers to bosses. There's a thing inside of me that worries I know better about what I should be doing. Asking someone to sponsor me seemed as though I was giving another person free rein to make demands on me. But again, I had to change.

So when a woman named Betsy, who had kids a few years older than mine and about ten years of sobriety, kept calling me to "check in," I took a risk and asked her to be my sponsor.

One of the first things she told me to do was to read the Big Book—a book written by two white dudes in the 1930s. It may as well have been written in hieroglyphics for all it had to do with my life. I'm not a huge fan of old-timey stuff anyway. I don't even love movies that take place before the advent of cell phones. But I dutifully worked my way through it, even highlighting passages that seemed like they were written in the current century.

Next she had me make a list of all the ways drinking had made my life unmanageable. I grabbed myself a spiral notebook and listed out my most embarrassing and painful admissions like I was in a trance.

1. I drove drunk with my kids in the car.
2. I've slept with people and not remembered it.
3. I get hangovers so bad I have to go to the hospital.
4. I've left Jon to take care of the twins at night because I'm passed out.
5. If I was drunk at night alone, I wouldn't be able to drive my kids to the hospital if something went wrong.
6. I'm sure drinking is affecting my liver and not in a good way.

I ran out after those six and I wondered if I'd even proven my boozing bona fides. It seemed horrific to me to see it right there on paper, but if compared to other people's stories, would my stuff seem tame?

When it comes to hard-core drunk-a-logues, it can seem like a dick-measuring contest: *Oh, you got trashed and fell out of a third-story window? That's gnarly, dude, but I drank a gallon of Jim Beam and woke up three days later in jail because I burned down my house trying to bake Totino's pizza rolls in the oven.*

For a long time, I could only see the differences in my drinking compared to others' stories. I was obsessed with the Nevers: I never got a DUI; I never lost custody of a child; I never got arrested; I never broke a bone, went to rehab, got a divorce—the list went on. I teetered on the edge of believing my drinking could be defined as alcoholic, but couldn't quite get there.

When I was about six months sober, I listened to a guy with unruly white hair share at a meeting about being a "real alcoholic." He described his years of heroin addiction, sleeping in an abandoned van for months, and his twenty-seven stays in rehab. This was all fascinating—I was here for all the crazy stories! But then he said, "Unless you've been to rehab at least a dozen times, you probably aren't an alcoholic." The more he talked, the clearer it became that I was in the wrong place. My brain was on fire with the idea that if this guy was a real alcoholic, it was likely that I wasn't an alcoholic.

Maybe I was just a problem drinker. I wondered if there was a different set of meetings for people like me, people who just drank a little too much.

I called Betsy right when the meeting was over to share my good news: "I think I may have overreacted to my whole drinking-and-driving thing," I said. She didn't jump in right away, so I continued. "This guy said that if I haven't been to rehab a dozen times, I'm not

an alcoholic. Well, guess what! I've never been to rehab *one* time."
Personally, I felt this was a mic-drop moment but Betsy was still quiet.
Maybe she was realizing she also wasn't an alcoholic?

Finally she spoke. "Is your life better when you aren't drinking?"
Hmm. I had to think about that. There were times I really missed
drinking but, yeah, I was relieved to never worry I was too drunk to
drive; I liked waking up without a hangover; I felt proud that I was a
sober mom.

"Yes. My life is better," I said, truthfully.

"Then does it matter?" Point Betsy.

But despite this, for months I still obsessed on the idea that I
might not officially be an alcoholic.

I was stuck.

I got asked to lead a meeting when I was about nine months
sober, and I shared about how I just wasn't convinced I was an alcoholic but I knew I didn't want to drink. I figured I'd keep it real.
In retrospect, it might have been a little like going to a twelve-step
meeting for murderers and saying, *I know someone died, and I was
arrested with the knife in my hand, and yeah, my DNA was all over the
victim, but I'm not convinced I did it.* Kind of like OJ.

The women who raised their hands after I finished said things
like, "I'm so glad I *know* I'm an alcoholic," and, "I never wondered if I
had a drinking problem." This felt like a personal attack! I was highly
aggravated and called Betsy right afterward to tell her how awful people were to me. She just said, "Nobody is thinking about you. They
are thinking about themselves. Let it go."

So I did. And I kept going to meetings and kept doing the things
Betsy asked me to do.

I knew I wanted to stay sober slightly more than I wanted to drink.

But I often still felt sorry for myself that I had committed myself to sitting through these meetings, looking at my past behaviors and dealing with all of these uncomfortable feelings. Then one day I heard someone say this quote: "The defeated do not get to dictate the terms of their surrender." I was stunned, and it jarred me out of myself.

No one had done this to me. No one was telling me I *had* to do anything. But I'd tried to solve this thing in a million different ways, a million times, and here was the truth: I'd fought alcohol, and alcohol had won.

And that was when I started to really understand the idea of surrender. I know a lot of people have trouble with the concept. Some people think that if you "surrender," you are giving up your power. We all like to feel like we are in charge of our choices. I thought that for so long, but where did it get me? It got me doing a drunken walk of shame up my driveway after having made one of the dumbest decisions of my life, to drive my car after drinking. It got me checking out every night instead of enjoying my kids. It trapped me in an endless cycle of drinking, making excuses for my drinking, swearing off drinking, and then drinking again. But here was a radical thought: I could give up the fight. Drop my weapons. Raise a white flag. Wasn't that actually freeing? I've seen war movies (against my will, but my husband loves them), and there's that look in a soldier's eyes when they've been fighting a battle they know they'll never win, taking shrapnel, shivering in foxholes, feeling scared, and then they're captured—that look is relief. It's over. They'll soon be out of the line of fire, hopefully draped in a blanket, drinking soup out of a tin cup. Maybe it won't be comfortable, but it would be better than being bombed and shot at; anything would be better than that.

So yeah, the defeated don't get to dictate the terms of their surrender.

It wasn't necessarily going to be easy, and I'd be asked to do some things I didn't feel like doing, but I got to go somewhere safe, where I was surrounded by my fellow captured soldiers. I've Googled this quote trying to figure out who wrote it, but nothing ever comes up. So if you were the one who said it and you're reading this book, *thank you.* You really helped me that day.

But I *still* wasn't done obsessing about the idea of whether or not I was an alcoholic. I would Google "alcoholism," and, "Am I an alcoholic," and, "What's the difference between people who drink a lot and alcoholics." But due to confirmation bias, I found a lot of articles that seemed to prove to me that I was fine. In fact, one quote from a guy named Dr. Robert Brewer, who was the leader of the CDC's alcohol program, said, "A lot of people mistakenly assume that people who drink too much are alcoholics. The surprising finding was that nine out of ten people who drink too much do not meet the diagnostic criteria for alcoholism." Boom. Case closed. Look around! I'm certainly not the one in ten!

It was so confusing. I knew I couldn't drink safely anymore. But I didn't *want* to quit; I *wanted* to have the ability to control my drinking. And it was painfully obvious I couldn't. Or I would have. I'd backed myself into this church basement. Drinking might not have always led to dangerous or embarrassing behavior, but when I did something dangerous or embarrassing, hadn't alcohol always been involved?

Right about the time I was almost one year sober, I went to another meeting and heard a man speak. This guy was probably only in his fifties, but he had the craggy face of someone much older. He looked like he might've been a drummer for a metal band for the past thirty years. He spoke about having almost died from alcohol poisoning several times, having to have his stomach pumped in the ER. But even though it seemed pretty obvious to me and I'm sure everyone in the room that this guy's drinking habits were pretty bad, he shocked me by saying he'd also had the debate going on in his head for years. He said, "I wasted so much time obsessing over whether or not I was actually an alcoholic, but one day I thought, 'What if I died and went to heaven and met God or whatever, and I asked God, "Hey, dude, was I actually an alcoholic though?" and what if God said, "Ha ha, no man, you're weren't. You were just a guy who likes to drink a lot." Would I be sorry I quit drinking?' And the answer is, 'Fuck no.' Because without alcohol and drugs, I live my life with integrity. I'm proud of the man I am when I don't drink. That word doesn't fucking matter anymore."

Something in me changed right in that moment. This prophet in a Metallica T-shirt had finally helped me realize that it didn't matter what I called myself: an alcoholic, a person with substance use disorder, or just a woman who isn't living with integrity when I drink. I didn't want to drink anymore. And that was enough of a reason to do what it took to make sure I didn't.

12. What's God Got to Do with It?

A lot of things turned me off of the idea of traditional recovery meetings. For one, all the slogans: *One Day at a Time, First Things First, Easy Does It*. I don't like corny sayings. I've never been in HomeGoods and felt the need to pick up a pillow embroidered with *Home Is Where the Heart Is* or *Grateful, Thankful, Blessed*. Especially the "Blessed" one, because that's another thing that turned me off about meetings: the whole God thing.

In the beginning, I had serious concerns that recovery meetings were a religious cult. As far as the cult part went, it *seemed* to have all the trappings of a cult, but I had trouble finding proof. There wasn't a "leader" per se, and it didn't cost any money besides the buck or two you drop in a basket if you have it to give, but something about those slogans and the idea of "surrender" made me suspicious. Could that be brainwashing? It sure seemed like brainwashing—all these people sitting in rooms, constantly clapping for each other? But if it was brainwashing, I had to admit it was for a pretty good cause: to help you stop doing a thing that's ruining your life. Couldn't addicts' brains use a little washing? At the very least a good rinse? Also, realistically, any cult worth its salt won't let you just *leave*. I have firsthand experience with that.

In 1986, I was aggressively recruited to attend a Buddhist cult meeting where people kneeled on someone's living room floor in a Hollywood apartment and chanted *nam myoho renge kyo* over and over in an effort to invite material goods like a Porsche 928 or Apple stock into their life. I was young, it was hot outside, and there was air-conditioning. I figured it couldn't hurt to have an open mind. After all, I had just arrived in Los Angeles, and my only possessions at that point were a Mazda GLC with over a hundred thousand miles on it and a few suitcases full of clothes, makeup, and dish towels. Somehow, I gave the recruiters the phone number of the place where I was staying *and* the address, and they called repeatedly and tried to stop by for weeks until I threatened to call the police.

After that experience, I made sure to steer clear of anything that even smelled a little cultish. In 2009, I got a few direct messages on Twitter from the actress Allison Mack inviting me to be part of a "women's empowerment group" which turned out to be NXIVM! I didn't respond, because even the term "women's empowerment group" felt icky, and in doing so I narrowly escaped joining a sex cult!

But the thing about twelve-step meetings is that as paranoid as I was that they were a cult, I kept getting proven wrong. I'd watch people come into a meeting, sit in the back, and just listen, purposely avoiding talking to anyone or even making eye contact, and no one bothered them. Sure, I knew from experience that if people found out you were new, a few go-getters would ask for your number and call to "see how you're doing." Suspicious, right? But if you didn't call back, they'd give up way too easily. Pretty early on I started thinking, *If this is a cult, it's a fairly lazy one.*

But even if it wasn't a cult, it still seemed religious. When people write to me and tell me, "I want to quit drinking but I don't want to go to a twelve-step meeting because of all the religious stuff," I get it. It's tough to argue with, since the word "God" is in five of the twelve steps and referenced in two more! It seems impossible to avoid the spiritual bent of that program, which can look a lot like hard-core Christianity. I wasn't into it either—in fact, it's one of the main reasons I didn't want to go, and I only went because rehab seemed like overkill and doing it on my own had failed. I felt backed into a corner without many other choices, but I didn't have to like it!

The first time everyone recited the Lord's Prayer in a meeting, I was more than a little put off. I'm just not a religious person. In fact, I have a long history of *non-religion*. When I was a little, despite being Jewish, our family celebrated Christmas. I use the term "celebrated" very loosely. We got presents on Christmas morning and hung a stocking on the mantel; Santa Claus was the one who delivered those gifts and filled those stockings with a foil-wrapped hollow milk chocolate Santa, a Pez dispenser shaped like a snowman with a few packs of refills, and hard candies with soft centers in red, gold, and green wrappers. But we weren't allowed to have a tree, even though I begged for one every year.

When I'd ask why, my mom would give the same answer: "Because we're Jewish," she'd say, like it was obvious. I guess somehow a Christmas tree was taking things too far, like some sort of majestic, brightly lit "eff off" to our people. We also never baked any Christmas cookies, although that could have been due to laziness more than principles. But besides not getting a tree and refusing to bake, we did nothing to honor our so-called Judaism: We didn't go to temple or acknowledge, let alone celebrate, a single Jewish holiday. When I asked why, my mother explained that we were "culturally Jewish," which meant that we appreciated good New York bagels and ate pastrami on rye with a dill pickle once a week, but that's about as far as we went.

When it came to the God topic, my mom said she was an atheist and didn't believe in God. Sometimes I would try to engage her in talking about it, but she wasn't interested.

"There's no such thing. It's made up by people who think they need something like that to feel better." She made it sound final. But although she seemed quite sure of herself, I wasn't totally convinced. It just didn't seem likely to me that there was *nothing out there*; just empty space, because how did we get here?

"Evolution," she explained, "First there were microorganisms, and they evolved over millions of years into humans."

"But how did the microorganisms get here?"

"They just did." Case closed.

But then when I was ten, seemingly out of nowhere, my mom decided we were into being Jewish after all and there would be no more Christmases. My favorite holiday was canceled and replaced by Hanukkah, which was celebrated *all out* with potato latkes—made from scratch, one present a night for eight nights (before you get too excited, sometimes a present was just socks) and a forced reading of the criminally boring "Story of Hanukkah" every night of Hanukkah, every single year until I moved out. My parents also joined a synagogue, and I was forced to attend Hebrew school and go to services on Yom Kippur (the highest holy day in the Jewish calendar) and some random Friday nights. Yet there was still zero talk of God or any force bigger than us. It felt like such a farce.

Once I was out on my own, I was on a mission to get back to celebrating Christmas. My first order of business was getting a tree and decorating the living shit out of it. My roommate (also a Jew—we put a deposit down on our first apartment with her bat mitzvah money) and I bought ornaments, twinkle lights, and tinsel; we strung popcorn garlands and topped it off with an angel made of aluminum and glass. We also baked cookies, went caroling, and in all ways yuletided it up.

But my love of Christmas had no ties to religion, and any talk of God, especially Jesus, put a bad taste in my mouth. I definitely didn't believe in organized religion; I felt strongly that religious morality left a lot of perfectly good people out of heaven. But I wasn't atheist like my mom; I came to see myself as agnostic, having a vague belief there was *probably* something bigger than all of us but having no clear concept on what that was.

When Jon and I got married, his parents were a little worried I'd insist on a Jewish wedding, which was hilarious to me. The truth was that even though Jon was raised Episcopalian, he joked that he was more Jewish than I was. He'd grown up around a lot of Jewish kids and had the leftover yarmulkes from the many bar mitzvahs he'd attended through the years to prove it. We decided to ask a family friend who was a Presbyterian minister to marry us and my only request was that she not bring Jesus into our nuptials. Suffice it to say, when I got to those meetings, I still wasn't sure where I stood when it came to spirituality, but I didn't want to be strong-armed into believing in God.

When I first dipped a toe into recovery after the trick-or-treating-drunk incident, I tried not to pay too much attention to the God stuff, but now that I was diving in headfirst, I wondered how easy it would be to ignore. Most people know that the twelve steps were founded on Christian principles. Let me nutshell it for you: Basically, a man named Bill W. and a surgeon named Dr. Bob met in the thirties through a Christian fellowship called the Oxford

Group. The Oxford Group was trying to help people live better lives through their six spiritual principles. Their theory was that most people's problems came down to fear and selfishness. Now, this wasn't necessarily for alcoholics, just a baby self-help group like EST or Lifespring.

Dr. Bob didn't have any luck getting sober that way, but when he met Bill and they started talking alcoholic shop, a connection was made, and it helped Dr. Bob get sober. So they sat down and took the Oxford Group's six steps and extended them into twelve, but the basic premise was just one alkie talking to another. There's no formal religion involved. But that didn't stop me from worrying it wasn't for me.

It turns out that Bill W. was actually an atheist when he formulated his crazy plan, but somewhere along the way, he had a spiritual experience, credited that with his sobriety, and, let's be real, probably became annoyingly preachy. But does that mean everyone has to be spiritual? Hell to the no. Because here's the thing: The group talks about "a God of your understanding." And here's what I found out: A God of your understanding can be literally anything—trees, dogs, love, SpaghettiOs, the group, or sure, God, if you're into that kind of thing. It's just the idea that there's something bigger than us, which I'd always suspected anyway.

Lots of people I met early on in meetings had zero problem with all the God talk; they either grew up Catholic and talking about holy spirits was just normal to them, or else they just had a relationship with God, so prayer wasn't unsavory to them like it was to me. I was always a little suspicious of those people. Didn't they have any healthy skepticism? How do you get told things as a child about Jesus being born to a virgin or how a cracker is the body of Christ and just go, *Yeah, okay, cool, that makes perfect sense, nope, no questions,* even as an adult? But on some level, I was jealous that there were smart, discerning people who had beliefs that comforted them while I had to attack and question everything.

But I also met lots of atheists, folks who steadfastly ignored any and all mentions of God, skipped the prayers, steered clear of the threat of any sneaky spiritual awakenings, and yet still managed to stay sober.

I sort of did a combo platter: At first I attempted to force myself to believe in God, even though it felt like trying to stick a magnet onto plastic. I would say prayers along with the group and pretend I felt something, but I secretly didn't. But as cynical as I was and still am, I gave believing in a higher power the old college try.

Sometimes, during a good meeting, I felt the presence of something bigger than myself in the collective spirit of a huge roomful of people all there helping each other achieve a common goal: sobriety. I also found something spiritual in the Me Too, those moments when someone shared something about the way they drank, or the way they thought that felt like they were sharing my own closely held secret. I'd feel such profound relief that it was almost like being given a gift. It felt divine. And in a moment like that I'd think, *There it is! That's God.* I kept it really simple for myself: God was in connecting.

When I was about three years sober, a thirty-something professional woman, dressed for success in serious business attire, face full of expensive makeup, with newscaster hair, looking unlike anyone I could possibly relate to, broke down in sobs. She cried through a share that it was her first meeting but she'd driven drunk with her kids in the car and she was terrified it could happen again. Here I was in my ripped sweats, hair like an unmade bed, no actual job to go to, but in that moment, I truly knew her. I felt God in that.

And I realized that three years earlier, in this very room, I'd shared the exact same secret, and that it was possible someone else had felt God in it.

Sometimes, when I was struggling to feel any sort of spirituality, I would listen to Christian rock. I'm obviously kidding. But I would play "The Rainbow Connection"—both the Kermit the Frog version and the Kenny Loggins version off his lullaby CD—because, as my kids tell me, I am extremely cringey.

The lyrics of that song kind of speak to our continuous search for meaning and how difficult it is to just go on faith when we can't possibly know exactly what's out there. For me, trying to believe in a higher power is like trying to have an orgasm: The more I concentrate on trying to make it happen, the farther it floats away. It's when I completely let go that I feel it, sometimes in an explosive way and sometimes in just a small, satisfying shift in my consciousness.

13. A Year of Firsts

The entire first year I wasn't drinking, I was like a newborn fawn wobbling around on shaky sober legs, trying to figure out how to have fun, how to still be myself without an adult beverage assist. Alcohol had held my hand tightly, like a mom leading me through stressful situations and helping me navigate uncomfortable feelings and anxiety. I'd come to depend on my trusted wine riding sidecar in my system while I did mundane tasks like cooking dinner but also hard things like writing books.

Could I even write another book if I couldn't drink away the goblins in my brain that whispered mean things to me while I sat in front of my laptop struggling to put words on the page? *You have no talent. You're not funny. Why would anyone pay you to write? You're going to have to give the advance back because you can't do it. Ha ha ha. Maybe you should've gone to college. Also you need to lose ten pounds.* The goblins always managed to get in a little weight jab while they were at it.

Toward the end of my drinking, I'd gotten so used to alcohol being available to me when I needed it, losing it felt like giving up my security blanket. I simply wasn't used to doing life sober, and I wasn't looking forward to it. But life went on life-ing, running ahead of me, paying no mind to my inability to keep pace.

Now that I was sober, I wondered not only how I would do the little things, like hanging at home watching TV or going out for "girls night," but how I would do big things, like going on vacation or to a wedding? I whined to my sponsor, "What if I go to Mexico? What would even be the point of Mexico if I can't have margaritas?"

"Are you going to Mexico today?"

She was right in assuming that I wasn't going on vacation that very day, but I like to get a jump on anxiety so I can figure out exactly how I'm going to feel and then formulate a plan to avoid feeling those feelings.

"No, but I'm scared of all the things I just won't be able to do sober or won't want to do sober." My sponsor kind of laughed, which was annoying at the time, but now I understand why: The first year kind of sucks while your body and mind acclimate to functioning without substances. That's why it's tough to stick to sobriety if you don't truly want to be sober.

My first big test was when, with only a month of sobriety under my belt, my husband was nominated for an Emmy. Before you get super excited, it was a daytime Emmy and the awards show wasn't televised, nor would it be attended by any big celebs. But there was a whole-ass cocktail hour with an open bar, fancy-schmancy catering, and lots of time standing around in heels making small talk with people who could be important. All of this seemed really awkward without being able to drink.

I worried it was too soon for me to try to go to an event like this and attempt to enjoy myself as if nothing had changed, as if I hadn't recently had my ability to have fun surgically amputated. Would I be able to laugh? Would I find anything funny? Would I be able to loosen up? I honestly wasn't sure if my outgoing personality was truly part of my genetic makeup or if there had always been a chemical component involved. I tried to think back to when I was a little kid and remember if I'd been an extrovert or if I was actually shy. I didn't know. I'd been drinking since the first time I went to a party that didn't involve party hats and piñatas, so it was difficult to gauge. But I was going to the Emmys, whether I felt comfortable or not. This was my husband's day—it was not about me.

This felt similar to when I had to go to an event a month after giving birth to my first child. Right after I'd had a baby, I felt like a different person, one who didn't fit into my clothes or the world in quite the same way—a puzzle piece that had strayed too far from the puzzle and now didn't belong. And just like with being a new mom, where all I wanted to do was talk to other parents about how hard parenting was, as a newly sober person, I felt more comfortable with other sober people talking about how difficult it was to quit drinking. What would I talk about with a bunch of weirdos who could still drink?

I armed myself with outs: I could sneak away to call or text a sober friend if I felt tempted to drink, I could step outside for a pretend cigarette, and as a last resort I could just tell Jon I wanted to leave early. My husband is actually an introvert: I mostly ignored this fact when I was drinking, because I always wanted to keep the good times going, but now it came in handy to be married to someone who's always ready to leave a party.

I'm not going to lie, this first foray into the world without the option of liquid relaxation started out a little awkward, but I chatted with the few people I knew, actually watched the ceremony, nursed my Diet Coke, ate as much of the delicious food as I wanted (the five oversized warm chocolate chip cookies at the dessert bar hadn't been in my original plan, but sometimes you have to use the tools at your disposal), mingled until my social battery was drained, and was home in bed by eleven p.m.

I know many people contemplating living alcohol-free, or even cutting way down may worry about going out if they're sober because they feel like they have to have an excuse in case people ask why they're not drinking. If you're concerned, you can always order sparkling water in a rocks glass and dress it up with a little swizzle straw and lime like your water's going trick-or-treating as a gin and tonic, or you can tell people you just started a new medication or that you're doing a thirty-day cleanse. I support doing all or any of these things if it makes you feel more comfortable. What I personally know from having been an avid drinker is that people who drink a lot probably don't care that you aren't drinking, and usually won't even notice because they're too busy drinking!

Now having been in the sober game a minute, I can tell you that most people don't even ask, but when they do, I tell the truth. Sometimes I say, "Oh, I've already had my share of drinks for an entire lifetime," or simply, "I quit drinking." That usually does the trick. But of course there are exceptions. If someone is being pushy, questioning you about why you aren't drinking, that is someone who needs to take a closer look at their own drinking. Feel free to point that out to them! It's a fantastic way to extricate oneself from an annoying conversation.

Before I quit, when I would meet someone who I knew was sober, I would look at them like an exotic animal, someone cool and mysterious, someone I wanted to know more about, and maybe see if I could pet them. People who quit drinking have stories! People who quit drinking because they drank way too much are far more interesting to me than, say, people who just never had a taste for alcohol.

So now I knew I could go to a professional event and refrain from drinking, but that seemed like beginners' level. A couple of months after I quit, Jon asked if I wanted to go see Wilco—just like that, as if it were no biggie—oh, just go to a concert, the ultimate drinking activity besides, I guess, going drinking at a bar. I didn't have the best track record with going to see live music with Jon pre-sobriety. In part, I blame the fact that we don't have the exact same taste in music so I've felt it necessary to drink my way through a few loud bands like the Hold Steady and Bob Mould to earn girlfriend points despite not knowing a single song. More than once I overshot the mark and fell asleep during shows, ending my evening with negative girlfriend points, if he was keeping score. But this was a band we both liked, so I looked at it as a chance to redeem myself. I was going to prove to Jon I could go out and have a great time sober! I was still a lot of fun! We were going to *party* (sans alcohol)! Fuck yeah!

The night of the concert, I started seriously doubting my ability to have fun without drinking, so I lowered my expectations of myself from being a "party animal" to being "awake." I hoped they served coffee.

In line for refreshments, I saw there was no coffee, but I was kind of buoyed to see they served soft pretzels. I'd never noticed that before. Was that new at music venues? I'd been so accustomed to splurging my mortgage on two or three eighteen-dollar Miller Lites, I'd never even considered there might be snacks. So I got an eight-dollar bottle of Fiji water and a pretzel while Jon got a plastic cup of beer, like a regular person who hadn't been condemned to live out his days as a glorified monk and could still enjoy an adult beverage.

I sat self-consciously in my seat, nervously tearing off bits of pretzel and stuffing them in my mouth, taking sips of my water, pretending to myself it was fine while waiting for the lights to dim and the music to start. But it wasn't fine. I knew I stood out, my Fiji water a blinking neon sign saying, "I can't handle alcohol." I tried not to feel sorry for myself, but I couldn't help it. Was this how every supposedly fun thing would feel: decidedly unfun, like chocolate cake with no frosting? But as I looked around, I noticed a weird thing: A lot of people were drinking water. At first I thought it was a fluke, so I meticulously scanned the theater to make sure. All around me people had plastic Fiji bottles in their hands instead of overpriced cocktails or beer. Finally I leaned over to Jon and gestured around at the thirty-something hipsters with furry hats and tattoos sipping water and asked, "Is Jeff Tweedy sober? Is this like a sober band or something?" My husband just shrugged.

"Not that I know of."

"Well, I don't get it. Why are all these people drinking water then?"

Jon gave me a confused look. "It's a Monday night. Maybe they have to work tomorrow."

Whoa. What? Mind blown. I couldn't imagine people who could drink if they felt like it choosing not to. I'd always operated under the assumption that unless a person had a valid reason they *couldn't* drink, like they were sober or they were recovering from open-heart surgery or they were currently piloting a plane, they would drink—especially at a concert! But as it turns out, the whole world isn't drinking all the time; it just feels like it.

So with my first concert out of the way, I was feeling slightly better, but by November, six months after I quit, I realized with dread that the holidays were approaching. First up: Thanksgiving.

To me, Thanksgiving has always been a great excuse to drink. There's beer while watching the football game (not that I ever watched the football game—I just drank beer in solidarity) and wine the rest of the day. For me, drinking goes with cooking, socializing, lounging, arguing, celebrating. The idea of being sober on Thanksgiving sucked the gratitude right out of me. But once again, I realized that I was the only one who felt drinking needed to be the star of the show. Thanksgiving for our family consisted of me, Jon, my three kids, my brother, and his wife. Turns out none of the other adults seemed to care much—they didn't even finish a six-pack of beer between the four of them. Instead of drinking, I got hammered on carbs, hoovering mashed potatoes like Tim Allen on a coke binge. I may have gone to bed bloated, but I woke up hangover-free and proud of myself for surviving another milestone.

But in December the firsts kept on first-ing. Christmas sans alcohol was looming like a massive storm cloud darkening the skies. I dreaded this holiday full of the pressure to make it special but now with no outlet for my stress. Everyone knows drinking is synonymous with Christmas, and although I've established I'm a Jew who loves Christmas, I have to admit that no one does Christmas quite like WASPs. When we'd go back East to visit Jon's parents, his mom and dad did it up: They wore Christmas sweaters, trimmed their tree tastefully with soft golden lights and personalized ornaments, and played classic Christmas music quietly on the stereo—my first Christmas there, the music was so low I had to strain to hear if we were listening to Bing Crosby's "I'll Be Home for Christmas" or LL Cool J's "Rock the Bells." But my favorite tradition was the rum-heavy eggnog that flowed as freely as I needed. No one questioned going back for thirds on rum-spiked eggnog! It just showed you were in the spirit. I loved the camaraderie of cocktails, because as someone who didn't come from the most stable family situation, the need to belong created a bit of internal tension, and alcohol was the most reliable way I knew to melt that feeling away.

For the most part, I did fit in with his family, who appreciated a heavy pour. Although, a few Christmases before I quit, I'd possibly gone back for fourths or fifths on eggnog and had subsequently fallen down the basement stairs leading to the guest room, tumbling head over feet and landing next to my daughter's pack 'n' play. Even though the stairs and floor were covered in beige shag carpet, which helped muffle the noise, my husband and sister-in-law heard the crash and came running in, only to find me sprawled out on the floor. There was nothing to say besides, "I'm fine." In true WASP fashion, no one ever brought it up again, but I was mortified and promised myself I would be much more careful with my drinking. But starting tomorrow, because right then, the pain in my ankle called for another round.

The Taylor family eggnog tradition had been carried back home to Los Angeles, and every Christmas the sweet, rummy concoction took the place of wine, putting me in a celebratory mood while wrapping presents, reading my kids *The Night Before Christmas*, watching *Frosty the Snowman*, *How the Grinch Stole Christmas*, and *The Year Without a Santa Claus*. The toasty warm feeling I got from hard liquor was difficult to rationalize the rest of the year, but somehow during the festive season all bets were off.

But now I was sober, and I couldn't drink eggnog even if I wanted to—well, I could; my husband even offered to pick up a carton of it at Ralphs, but what would be the point of drinking cream, sugar, and eggs without rum or bourbon? If you think about it, what was the point of drinking it before? It sounds disgusting.

The idea of Christmas just felt flat without the joy I got from drinking. Now that I had kids, I put high expectations on myself to find the right gifts and make the holidays special, happy, and memorable. To me, alcohol had always helped release that pressure valve, like letting a little air out of an overinflated balloon so it doesn't pop. Parenting was already difficult the rest of the year, and Christmas only raised the level of difficulty more. And now with two-year-old twins and a five-year-old, I wanted to be present, but I also desperately wanted to put the experience in soft focus.

On social media we see all the fun Christmas Eve videos, the Instagram pics of perfect families with kids in color-coordinated outfits sitting around beautiful tables set with DIY centerpieces—most likely made using mason jars and sprigs of some sort—eating a delicious home-cooked holiday meal. But we rarely see how it went down in my house, with toddlers refusing to get out their non-matching pajamas, multiple meltdowns at Michaels craft store—even if I promised to buy them a puzzle or overpriced coloring book—the nine return trips to the grocery store to grab cinnamon or buttermilk or turkey dogs or Scotch tape or ibuprofen because I kept forgetting the one thing I went there for. And yes, I know I could make a shopping list. Shut up.

So that first sober Christmas I decided to be easy on myself. I was sober, goddamn it, so I was limited. I bought as many presents online as I could, avoiding the stress of malls, and I didn't try to disguise my writing on the gifts from Santa. We made chocolate chip cookies to leave for him from a giant roll of cookie dough, and I may or may not have eaten half the dough before it made it onto the tray. I made a lot of calls to fellow sober moms who I knew were also struggling. Thank God my oldest daughter didn't discover the Elf on the Shelf until I'd had a few years of sobriety under my belt, because remembering to move that fucker around every night would surely have driven me back to the bottle. On December 25, we ordered Chinese food like all the other Christmas-celebrating Jews. But I'm not gonna lie, I was relieved to wake up on December 26 with my first sober Christmas behind me.

But probably the biggest test of my sobriety was my first sober New Year's Eve. Now New Year's Eve is a struggle even for people who have no issue with substances and can enjoy a toast along with everyone else without having to stop and buy some stupid Trader Joe's sparkling apple juice like a toddler with a wallet.

There are so many expectations we place on ourselves for having the Best Time Ever, and yet, it rarely turns out amazing. I actually have a shitty track record with New Year's Eves even when I could drink my face off if I felt like it, and believe me, I always felt like it.

My first NYE with Jon was the momentous millennial Y2K. 1999 was going to become the year 2000, and Jon and I had big plans: We'd bought silly plastic champagne flutes, horns, a glitter cardboard top hat for him, and a glitter paper tiara for me that said "Happy New Year 2000." We planned to have sex, drink champagne, and watch to see if our computers combusted under the strain of not being ready for a new century. But a few days prior, I came down with the flu (which I'd actually caught from him, but who's bitter?), so we welcomed 2000 in my apartment, me in bed nursing a 102° fever, Jon sipping champagne, watching Dick Clark.

Another New Year's Eve that should have been amazing was the one we spent in Paris. Jon and I went to Europe right after Christmas because the flights were cheaper. We figured we'd wing our New Year's Eve, just plan it on the fly, how very French. Big mistake. We couldn't go to the bar in our hotel because it was off-limits to *guests* unless we paid $150 a person for a split of champagne and the privilege of being able to order appetizers off of a hotel menu where a Nicoise salad and some baked Brie bites would probably cost more than my Prius. So instead we took a train to the Champs-Élysées, where we hoped to see fireworks near the Arc de Triomphe but instead were swallowed up by a massive crowd of rowdy locals yelling and screaming—I'm pretty sure someone threw a Molotov cocktail—and then we couldn't get back to our hotel because the trains were too packed. We walked the five miles only to be kept awake by club music until four thirty a.m., courtesy of the hotel party we couldn't afford to attend.

The first New Year's Eve we attempted to celebrate as parents was worse. Our baby was a little over one year old, so, figuring we were ready to get back to living, we went to the home of another couple with a baby the same age to sip blended drinks and champagne. We planned to crash there so we wouldn't have to drive home and we could all wake up and make scrambled eggs and sausage the next day. It seemed like the perfect plan, the best of both worlds. Despite having a baby, we could take part in a special night of overindulging completely sanctioned by society. Sure, we had to pack like we were going on a ten-day cruise in order to hang out seven miles from our house, but it would be so worth it.

The evening started off well: good company, fancy cocktails. Once the babies were fed and asleep, we started drinking in earnest, and by the time the ball dropped at midnight *West Coast time*, I had that warm, boozy, "all is right with the world" feeling. I thought, *Even though I have a baby I can still party—okay, not in public, only at someone's house, and I have to bring half the contents of my house with me, but still.*

At some point, Jon and I stumbled to the guest room only to be jolted awake a few hours later by loud crying coming from next to our bed. Although Jon and I were fine hanging out in a different house, our kid was not having it. I tried explaining to her that it was New Year's Eve, but she kept crying. I wasn't drunk anymore and I wasn't hungover yet—I was teetering in the space in between. We attempted to bring her into the bed with us, we offered her a bottle, we changed her, but she just wouldn't stop crying. At this rate, we knew she was going to wake up the whole house, so we had to make the most fun-killing decision ever—pack up all our shit and go home at four a.m.

Are you seeing a pattern here? My bar is already low for New Year's Eve.

Unfortunately, my first New Year's Eve sober was going to be a category killer: We were going to a hotel, attending a wedding, and ringing in the New Year all in the same night. First of all, who gets married on New Year's Eve? Having a hotel wedding is pricey enough without making it the most expensive night of the year! I suppose for the guests this would be a money-saver since, hey, free champagne and a place to go. But this was going to be my first major drinking holiday spent *not* drinking. I'd given up booze in May, so I'd missed St. Patrick's Day—not that I'm Irish or ever celebrated anyway, but in case you were thinking, *Stefanie, what about St. Patrick's Day?* I figured I'd let you know.

So, since I had a bad track record with New Year's Eve anyway, it would make sense to spend a major drinking holiday safe at home in my pajamas, asleep right after nine p.m., when the ball drops in New York. But now I was being forced to wear a dress, attend a wedding of someone I barely knew, and turn down expensive champagne all night. This was a nightmare scenario.

The wedding was held at one of the more glamorous hotels in Hollywood and began, as most weddings do, with cocktails and hors d'oeuvres. I was at the wedding with Jon; my brother, Michael; and my sister-in-law, Racquel. Racquel and I were the only two people not having cocktails as far as I could tell, but the reason Racquel was abstaining was because she was pregnant with her first baby. It didn't seem fair. If Racquel hadn't been pregnant, even though she barely drinks, she would have had at least one cocktail and could toast with real champagne.

I couldn't. Not because I was protecting a growing fetus in my belly, but because I had done the opposite and not protected my own children outside of my body. And now I'd sentenced myself to this shitty life where I couldn't ever fucking drink again. The more I thought about it, the more sorry for myself I felt.

Trays were passed around containing bacon-wrapped scallops, tiny crab cakes, stuffed mushrooms, and small ramekins of lobster mac and cheese. To make myself feel better, I ate two at a time from each tray. Despite having a napkin full of mushrooms, I waved my arms to flag down the waiter in his fitted black vest and bow tie so I could grab a few more of those scallops before he ran out. He gave me a funny look, but fuck it, who knew when the scallops might come around again? It was either stuff myself with scallops or I was going to start swilling champagne. Did he really want that on his conscience?

As I posed for a picture with Jon in front of a giant fountain, smile plastered to my face as if to tell the camera lens, *Of course I'm having fun, why wouldn't I be? I never needed to drink to enjoy myself,* I'd never felt so separate from the rest of the world, the normal people. Unlike the crowd at Wilco who were choosing not to drink because they had to work the next day or just didn't feel like it, I couldn't. I was deprived, and I was grieving my self-imposed deprivation.

But then I had another thought: I was *also* choosing not to. I was making a choice, the same as all the people making the choice to drink. I'd been chatting with people I didn't know, and sure, that was a little boring and uncomfortable without a drink in my hand, but what if I had been drinking? Would it have been that different? The truth is, it probably still would have been kind of boring, but I just would have been buzzed. And if I was buzzed, I couldn't stay buzzed for long. I'd either spring into super-drunk mode or get tired and want to go home; I was like a broken bike with only two gears and no brakes.

Once I accepted my sober state and stopped fighting it, I was able to enjoy the ceremony, which was beautiful. There were readings and sweet and funny vows and beaming faces and, well . . . I'm not going to bore you with too many details, because that couple is long since divorced. Maybe it was because they got married on New Year's Eve, maybe not. We'll probably never know. What I do know is that night I came home sober, paid the babysitter, and went to bed grateful that this New Year's Day I wouldn't wake up with a hangover. Plus, there was no need to make a New Year's resolution not to drink, because I'd already quit.

14. Where Everybody Knows Your (First) Name

There is a lot of help out there for substance use disorders, whether you are looking to quit entirely or just cut down. There are treatment centers, online self-help programs, medications, addiction specialists, virtual support groups, and in-person support groups, like twelve-step meetings. I know a guy who stopped drinking completely through something called SMART Recovery, where SMART stands for Self-Management and Recovery Training. It bills itself as an alternative or supplement to the twelve steps. Last time I spoke with him, he hadn't had a drink in ten years. There's another group called Women for Sobriety, which is a peer-support program tailored specifically for women overcoming substance use disorders. I also know of people who have read Allen Carr's book *Quit Drinking Without Willpower* and said it changed their lives and they never again needed to touch a drop. And those people can fuck right off. I'm kidding! Good for them. I'm glad solving their alcohol problem only cost them $13.46 plus shipping. Must be nice.

For me, a book wasn't going to cut it, and neither was taking up running or switching to an Ayurvedic diet to balance the energy in my body; I wasn't going to solve my issue by eating more legumes. A lot of things work for a lot of people. And here's where I talk about what worked *for me*. The twelve-step thing was accessible (there were meetings everywhere, all day long), it was free, and Karina was willing to take me. Talking about going to meetings is controversial, because, as you've heard, it's anonymous. What happens in twelve-step meetings stays in twelve-step meetings. There is a good reason for that—actually, many good reasons—but the main one is that if I publicly tell you that I went to meetings to help me stop drinking and then I start drinking again, you'll think, "See? It doesn't work!" Which is valid. But, on the other hand, anytime I've spoken about sobriety in a public forum like TV or online, I get emails from people struggling, asking me how I did it, and I have to tell them I went to meetings. It's simply what *I* tried, and it was one of the things I found very helpful.

It's not a miracle. It's not a treatment center where there are doctors and meds and therapists—although there are plenty of doctors and therapists there, but they are also trying to stop drinking—it's just other people struggling and helping each other, and those twelve steps you've heard about. There are no contracts to sign. No one can make you go. Well, I guess you can get court ordered to go—which I don't necessarily agree with—but no one can really make you listen. There are also no rules. That was good news to me, because have you met me? I don't like to be told what to do.

Whether you are doing the SMART Recovery, Women for Sobriety, or any other treatment option that involves meetings, being around other people who are also trying to stop drinking is huge, because you will see that you are not alone. When I was drinking every night, making bargains with myself, disappointing myself by promising myself I wouldn't drink that way again, and then drinking that way again, it was incredibly lonely. I was sure I was the only one.

My compulsive nature, be it my inability to eat one cookie or the weird urge I feel to pick at my skin or scalp, felt like a deep dark secret. My lack of control around alcohol, and the fact that it led to me endangering my babies, made me feel ugly and freakish—like a person with an enormous moral failing. But when I went to meetings, I could breathe a sigh of relief, because we all have secrets. Hearing other people share their secrets made me feel safe, because people there got me.

I can remember taking my older daughter to the hospital when she was around fourteen months old. My husband was out of town and I was home alone taking care of her while she threw up over and over and ran a high fever. She wouldn't drink or eat anything, shaking her head violently from side to side when I tried to give her a bottle. I held her sweaty little body in my arms and spooned small teaspoons of water into her mouth, but she'd spit them out. She was so weak and I was terrified, so I paged the pediatrician for the third time that day. The doctor feared dehydration and instructed me to get her to the hospital.

Before I left, I made sure I had my medicine with me. I kept an old prescription bottle for migraine meds with its outdated label and child-safe cap in my purse. It contained a few Xanax, Motrin, a couple of Vicodin, and some Imitrex (the actual migraine med) in case shit went sideways, and shit was definitely going sideways.

My daughter ended up admitted to the pediatric intensive care unit for the night because they couldn't find a vein to get her re-hydrated, despite many tries and much screaming—both hers and my own. With my husband stuck in Virginia due to a snowstorm, I was alone and scared. But I had my pills. I swallowed them one after another without water while my daughter lay on my chest, her tears spilling down her face, soaking the shirt I'd been wearing for two days. There was little I could do to comfort her besides keeping her close, so I did what I needed to do to comfort myself even though I felt ashamed. I was definitely not taking these pills as directed. But how did people get through times like these without something to take the edge off? Why didn't they have a bar right there in the hospital? That seemed like a real missed opportunity. People in meetings understood this type of thinking. For the first time, I felt like if these people could stop drinking, maybe I could do it too.

Another thing meetings did for me was create accountability. The second time I showed up at what accidentally became my regular Saturday meeting, I was asked to take a commitment. Commitments are little jobs that people need to do to help the meetings run. I didn't especially want to, but I wasn't in a position to say no because, again, I really wanted to quit drinking. My first commitment was called "coffee cleanup." At the end of the meeting, my new friend Shayna and I would have to grab the giant metal coffee urns, bring them into the church kitchen, empty the grounds into the trash, rinse everything out, dry it with paper towels, and put it all away. You might be wondering why. I wondered that all the time. I'd stand in the kitchen away from everyone else thinking, *What does this have to do with not drinking?* The answer is everything and nothing. The act of cleaning out the coffeepot in and of itself didn't keep me from drinking, but it did help get the coffee ready for the next meeting and, more importantly, it kept me coming back to the meeting. It kept me accountable.

Before I quit drinking, I wouldn't have used the word "accountable" to describe myself. But there was something about having a job at the meeting that made me feel like I had to show up. I don't love responsibility, but I despise disappointing anyone, so I'd show up, week after week, sitting through meetings, some good, many annoying. Sometimes during a particularly irritating meeting I'd go home and think, *What am I doing? I don't have anything in common with these people, this is a waste of my time, I can do this on my own. Maybe I'll just read that Allen Carr book!* But then Saturday would come and I'd think, *Shit, I have to do that coffee cleanup and it's too late to ask someone to cover for me. I'll just go one more time and let everyone know they can find another sucker to slave away in the kitchen washing dishes, because I'm fine and this whole thing was a big mistake and clearly overkill. I'm not that bad, certainly not as bad as most of these people!* So I'd go to the meeting. Those recovery people are tricky motherfuckers; they know what they're doing.

It certainly wasn't always easy. But meeting after meeting, week after week, I wasn't drinking, and my thinking was changing. It was happening almost in spite of myself, because many times, inside my head, I was kicking and screaming like an angry toddler who didn't want to take a nap!

Meetings served as a daily reminder that I didn't drink. It was so easy to forget. Sometimes I'd be in Trader Joe's, just innocently doing my shopping—not for the week, because I'm not much of a planner—and I'd absentmindedly find myself going down the wine aisle and thinking, *I'll just grab a bottle of white for the chicken piccata I'm microwaving for dinner tonight,* before remembering that, *Oh, god-damn it, I'm sober.* But in those moments, the fact that I didn't drink anymore almost came as a surprise to me. Like, *What? Me? I don't drink? That's so strange. And unfamiliar.* Alcohol had become such a part of my life, my identity. Drinking felt instinctive, like the way water runs down a rock the same way for so many years that it makes a groove. Trying to make the water run a different way doesn't hap-pen overnight; the water will naturally try to get back to that groove, the easiest way for it to flow. It was going to take time and effort to wear a different, new, sober groove into the rock.

Some days I was on a natural high, in total alignment with the universe, certain of the presence of God, wondering why I hadn't gotten sober years ago. *Where has this peppermint tea been all my life?* I'd scream in my head. *It's fucking delicious!* And then the next day I wanted to murder a senior citizen for not using their blinker.

Sometimes I would sit in my car in my driveway, listening to music, tears streaming down my face because I was so desperately sad, literally grieving wine, pining for it like an ex-lover, wishing things had been different—that it hadn't come to this: saying goodbye forever. I was scared to death I'd never feel like myself again. But, really, who was "myself"? Did I want to feel like that person? I'd always used something: food, pot, Vicodin, Xanax, or wine to blot out fear—fear that I was too much, too needy, too loud, too dumb. Unlovable. But ironically, wine often made me too much, too needy, teary and loud and dumb. Maybe what I wanted was at best to be a better version of myself and at worst to get some quiet in my brain.

It was key to keep myself surrounded by other sober people. Just as I'd been living in a bubble of people who liked to drink the way I did, meetings helped me feel like I was in a different bubble, surrounded by people who were trying to live full lives, lives with lots of laughing and fun, but lives without alcohol. I found women to socialize with outside of meetings: Many of these women became close friends—I attended their baby showers and birthday parties; we supported each other's business ventures and attended plays. We knew each other in a deeper way, a way other people couldn't know us. Because of this, we could keep each other honest. Honesty is key. The more I shared my story with my friends and with people in meetings, the less easy it was to play it down and tell myself it was just one night, just an accident, nothing I'd done before or would ever do again. People knew the truth about me, and I knew the truth about them.

One day I was walking through Ralphs comparing the price of the Lean Cuisine five-cheese rigatoni to the Smart Ones three-cheese ziti marinara when my friend Meredith called. I picked up immediately because she was one of my recovery friends and that's what we do for each other. We made a moment of small talk and then she got right to the point, "Hey, I've been thinking that I may not be an alcoholic."

"Oh, okay." I had to laugh a little, but only because I related.

"It suddenly occurred to me that I might've gone a bit overboard in thinking I can't drink ever. I wasn't really that bad." Except I knew that she was.

"Well, remember when you told me that you took your son to that eight-year-old kid's birthday party at Dave and Buster's and you got so drunk another mom had to drive you both home? And it was eleven a.m.?"

"Yeah. That's true."

"And then you had to avoid making eye contact with her for the next six months because you were so embarrassed."

"Shit. You're so right. I forgot about that. Never mind."

"Of course. See you Saturday."

15. Not Without My Xanax

"Why do you want to stop the Xanax completely? I thought it was helping you." Dr. Steinberg just stared at me. I couldn't read his expression, but that's usually how it was with psychiatrists.

"Oh, it's not that it doesn't help; it helps. Actually, 'help' is a giant understatement." Dr. Steinberg continued to say nothing. That's how they get you; they don't say anything, and you're forced to keep talking or risk both of you just sitting there in awkward silence until you pass out from panic.

"I don't *want* to stop taking Xanax completely." I overemphasized *want* so he'd see that I wasn't a crazy masochist, and then I dropped my bomb. "I actually quit drinking thirty-one days ago. And . . . well . . . I've weaned myself off the morning Xanax, but I still take a milligram at night because I'm scared of the withdrawal." Now I thought I could read his expression: surprise. He merely raised his eyebrows slightly, but I saw it. I studied his face. Was there also a slight hint of annoyance? If so, I deserved it. I was a liar.

"So do you feel you were abusing alcohol?"

Fair question. After all, Dr. Steinberg was an "addiction specialist," but I hadn't realized that when I came to him for Xanax. Here's what happened: A few years before this, I'd finally been diagnosed with postpartum anxiety, because it turns out that lying on my un-made bed next to my eleven-day-old infant counting her breaths and panicking because a website I found told me she should be taking forty to sixty breaths per minute *and it seemed like maybe she was breathing too fast and might die* wasn't normal baby blues. I hadn't known that the oppressive feeling that I had to be constantly scan-ning every situation for potential threats, counting breaths, reading the entire Internet about vaccines—becoming convinced they cause SIDS—or thinking my husband's female boss was hitting on him was called hypervigilance and it's part of anxiety; all I knew was that wine made it slightly better.

I was given a prescription for Zoloft and another prescription for Xanax. I was told I could take a milligram in the morning and one in the evening to help me sleep. Now heretofore, as far as benzos go, I'd only ever tried that tiny dose given to me by Karina and it hadn't done much. I've always operated under the premise that more is better—which is how I came to be writing this book.

The first time I took a whole milligram of Xanax, something mag-ical happened: I felt . . . relief. I didn't feel tired, particularly, which I hear is the common complaint for lightweights and nonaddicts. I didn't need a nap. I felt completely normal except that the worries that were usually on a level nine were now hovering around a three on the scale of zero to *my house is on fire!* Was this how non-anxious people experienced the world? It was almost like cheating. Some peo-ple had to do an hour of cardio or, worse yet, practice mindfulness, to achieve what I found in pill form. The .25-milligram Klonopin hadn't been helpful—sort of like trying to knock down a cement wall with a baseball bat when what I needed was a bulldozer—and a whole-ass milligram of Xanax was that bulldozer. So I took it "as needed," but I seemed to need it quite often. And of course I combined it with wine. It seemed to work even better with wine.

Sure maybe I was a little overly reliant on a pill, a drink, a *something* outside of myself to help me feel more like myself, but I honestly hadn't seen anything wrong with taking benzos, until I'd accidentally stopped taking benzos. I'd gone through a brief period of taking them every single day since my twins had come home from the NICU, because it was *stressful*, and then I ran out of my last prescription. I hadn't seen that psychiatrist in a while so I just figured I'd be fine without it. No biggie.

A couple days later I found myself in the fetal position in my bed in the middle of the afternoon. I had a feeling I can only describe as "the walls closing in." Seemingly out of nowhere I was shaking with nerves, as if I'd just been told I had to give a TED Talk on the tensions in the Middle East while naked from the waist down. I had absolutely no clue why I was feeling this way, but it was getting worse every minute. Making a call on my phone seemed like a bridge too far—I tried to imagine myself picking up the phone and pressing the numbers, but once someone answered, what would I say? I couldn't even put into words what was wrong with me. I'd heard the term "cold sweat" before, but it always seemed like something you said if you were being overly dramatic; but now I could put a feeling to those words. Cold. Sweat. I was sweating, my heart rate wouldn't slow down, but I was so cold.

Since Jon and I brought the second twin home from the NICU, things hadn't been great for me mentally. I had a new OB for my second pregnancy and I'd told her about my bout with postpartum anxiety with my first baby and that I was on Zoloft. She let me know, in no uncertain terms, that if I went off it during my pregnancy (which she didn't advise but which I did anyway), I would need to be back on it before I left the hospital. She was motherly, super smart, and no-nonsense, embodying all the qualities I look for in a therapist, teacher, doctor, lawyer, or judge. I never want to feel like I'm smarter than a person who has authority over me once I'm in a position where I've mentally accepted that I need to listen to an authority figure. I want to trust them implicitly so I can blindly follow their advice. There's nothing I hate more than the feeling that I need to do my own research. I didn't go to med school, so I don't want to have to read a bunch of literature to make sure you know what you're doing!

Sure enough, once I delivered the babies, Dr. Smartypants didn't forget. She ordered my Zoloft and made sure the nurses had given me a few doses before she'd sign my exit papers. And I'd felt okay for a week or two, but it turned out fifty milligrams of Zoloft was no match for a hurricane of plummeting hormones, colicky babies, my natural predisposition to anxiety, and a double dose of sleep deprivation—so I'd sprinted back to self-medicating with chardonnay and regular doses of the Xanax while waiting for the storm to recede.

When Jon came home and found me paralyzed with unexplained dread and unable to tell him what was wrong, he told me to page Dr. Smartypants and tell her my symptoms. I managed to make the call only because he sat next to me on the bed holding my hand and stroking my hair gently, like he was soothing a senior dog with arthritis.

When Dr. Smartypants called me back, she immediately asked about the medications I was taking. I reminded her about the Zoloft and told her I had also been taking Xanax but had recently run out. "When did you run out?" she asked.

"I don't know. Maybe a couple of days ago. Two or three. Is that really important?" Thinking hurt my brain. It could have been two days or five years. Time felt meaningless. Whatever was happening to me was a medical emergency; a heart attack maybe, and I didn't think it seemed all that pertinent to ask about how often I was taking a little Xanax! Get it together, Dr. Smartypants! Let's remember who has the degree.

"You're in classic withdrawal, my dear." What? I didn't even know how that could be. I wasn't addicted! "I'll call in a prescription for a few pills to get you feeling better, but then you need to find a psychiatrist if you need more."

And that's how I'd found myself in the office of Dr. Steinberg. I'd gone through my insurance to find a psychiatrist who took Blue Shield, was in my neighborhood, and was taking new patients. Dr. Steinberg checked all the boxes. His office was in a big newer medical building on Ventura Boulevard less than a mile from my house. Unfortunately, street parking was impossible at that time of day, so I was forced to park in their underground lot, which would cost a dollar every fifteen minutes, and there was no way Dr. Steinberg's office validated parking. Whatever. It would all be worth it for the security of regular Xanax prescriptions.

But as I stood in the modern lobby, next to a giant fern, looking up at the big directory to find the suite number, there next to the name Dr. Steinberg were the words "addiction specialist." Wait, what? How had I not noticed that before I made the appointment? No, no, no. The last thing I wanted to deal with was an addiction specialist who might mistakenly think I was an addict! I didn't want to start my search over, because finding a psychiatrist who takes insurance and new clients is like finding a helpful clerk at the DMV. I was going to have to do my least favorite thing: act.

During our first visit, I told him my whole story, minus any mention of my nightly wine habit, my off-and-on—depending on when I could get them—love of painkillers, or the true nature of my dependence on Xanax.

"Xanax works much better than Klonopin or Ativan for me," I said *super casually*, as if I were just letting him know Motrin seemed to work better on my headaches than Tylenol—every person's body chemistry is a little different, *amirite?*

Dr. Steinberg had a New York accent, wire-rimmed glasses, and a "doesn't suffer fools" demeanor, so I wasn't sure how this was going to go, but luckily, he quickly agreed to prescribe me my Zoloft and, more importantly, my two milligrams of Xanax a day—one in the morning and one at night.

I wasn't taking Xanax to get high. I was taking it because it made me feel sane and calm, like I had a little blue pill barrier protecting me, keeping me safe from the rougher elements of reality. I also knew that if I had to stop abruptly, I'd risk withdrawal. I understood I was technically addicted, but I was terrified of stopping.

The thing about benzodiazepines is that although they don't cause a typical euphoria like drugs with the potential for abuse, if you've been taking them for a while, your body can quickly become physically dependent, which causes withdrawal.

Now, less than a year later, I was back in his office because I had quit drinking and needed to figure out how to completely quit the Xanax. I'd already managed to wean myself down to just the one pill

I took at night before I went to bed, but now I was newly sober, trying to do it right, and I wanted to be off of all of it. And now he was asking me if I'd been "abusing alcohol." I felt like a piece of shit. Had I been "abusing alcohol"? Yes, I had been. But would I have considered myself to be "abusing alcohol" when I was asking him for Xanax? Okay, also yes. I guess on some level I knew that taking Xanax and mixing it with alcohol wasn't a winning combination. I'd seen Anna Nicole Smith's reality show; I knew how it could get out of control, but at the time, I also felt fairly sure that being medicated was the only way I was going to survive this period in my life.

Postpartum, I didn't feel like I could endure the days without some sort of medical intervention. And since I wasn't drinking all day because I wasn't an *alcoholic*, I needed a Xanax in the morning and then some wine in the evening, like a *normal person*, and a Xanax to get to sleep, which wasn't weird, because lots of normal non-problem-having people had trouble falling asleep. And sure, my husband often (always) had to get up with the babies in the middle of the night because I was sleeping (passed out); there was an understanding that I needed to sleep because the sleep deprivation was harder on my mental health than it was on his. This was all on the up-and-up.

But, another truth bomb: I knew that this hadn't been moving in a good direction before I'd sat in Dr. Steinberg's office for the first time. I was aware that I was keeping my drinking from the doctor for fear he'd tell me to stop.

I wasn't a complete stranger to misrepresenting myself to doctors: I'd also convinced quite a few doctors over the years to prescribe me Vicodin for migraines and other maladies. I just liked anything that could alter how I felt. My love of painkillers began innocently enough: I was given one for a migraine when I was around ten.

Migraines are the worst kind of headaches for me: They laugh in the face of common analgesics like aspirin or ibuprofen, and back then, a migraine could make me feel like I wanted to die for upward of eight hours. I'd been getting them fairly regularly since about the age of six, possibly due to stress, but possibly due to genetics, since my father had them his whole life as well.

This particular day, I'd walked the mile or so home from school with an excruciating headache, every step radiating pain. When I reached my duplex, I climbed the stairs, let myself in with the key I kept on a piece of orange yarn around my neck, and took to my bed, waiting for someone, anyone, to come home and help me. A few hours later, my mother arrived and found me crying inconsolably.

Typically my headaches frustrated my mother, and if a baby aspirin and a cold washcloth on my head didn't do the trick, I was out of luck. But maybe because it was an extra bad one, or she was in a good mood, or she simply didn't want to listen to me cry anymore—whatever her motives—she offered me a narcotic like codeine, possibly left over from some of her past dental work.

I can remember the pleasurable pressure in my face, and the slightly numb feeling. And it's not that the pill took my headache away but that it somehow made me not care about the pain as much. It also magically eased my fifth-grade angst for about an hour, or at least until I fell asleep and woke up in the morning, finally, gloriously, headache-free.

When I was old enough to have my own dental work and get my very own prescription for painkillers, I abused them immediately, starting with getting my wisdom teeth out at eighteen. I can't remember a time I ever took pain pills "as directed"; I was always fudging the timelines and running out long before a refill was due, *if* a refill was due. As I got older, before modern, nonaddictive drugs like Imitrex were invented, I started getting prescriptions for Vicodin to deal with migraine pain. The problem was, once I got a prescription, I couldn't save them for an actual migraine. I took them every day, multiple times a day, until the prescription ran out. I loved the security of a new prescription. I'd get a giddy feeling standing in line at the pharmacy and breathe a sigh of relief when I was handed my stapled brown paper bag securing my new bottles of twenty, fifty, or even a hundred pills. I'd take them on an empty stomach to get the best possible high, and I'd be so sad when it started to wear off so I'd pop another one an hour later, hoping to keep the same feeling going longer. A bottle of Vicodin was like a can of Pringles to someone else: I couldn't eat just one, and I couldn't stop taking them or thinking about them until they were gone.

If my regular doc wasn't loose enough with the prescription pad, it wouldn't be long until I'd be in search of a new GP who would be more understanding about my migraines. I liked the feeling I got from a couple of Vicodin more than wine: Vicodin made me feel warm and fuzzy and laid-back. It made me want to go through my contacts and check in with friends I hadn't talked to in a while. I would think about people I didn't like and wonder if maybe I'd been too hard on them. No one seemed that bad on a Vicodin high.

I loved to mix a pain pill or three, or however many I could get, with a beer. For years I played poker with a group of comedians, and one in particular was prone to having dental work or knee surgery or some sort of malady that involved him having pain pills at his disposal. I'd always ask shamelessly if he could spare a few, then I'd wash them down with my Miller Lite and inevitably go all in with a pair of twos. Later, when I got sober, one of my longtime sober poker buddies, Stanley, told me he'd worried about me like crazy on those nights and had even followed me home one night in his car, going five miles out of his way just to make sure I was okay.

About six months before I quit drinking, I had my last Vicodin hurrah: I'd gotten my doctor to call in a script for breakthrough migraine pain and, apparently having way too much trust in me, he gave me a bottle of a hundred pills, which was supposed to last a year. I went through them in a week. For me, it doesn't matter if we're talking pills, wine, or Pepperidge Farm mint Milano cookies: I can't stop until they're gone. I was actually relieved.

I never got addicted to pain pills, but it wasn't from lack of interest; it was only due to not being a go-getter. The thing was, as much as I loved having pain pills at my disposal, I lacked the ambition to keep the prescription train moving forward. There were no easy options: I could doctor shop, which would entail going to multiple medical providers at the same time and pretending I didn't already have a prescription. It was one thing to try and tell my doctor I'd accidentally misplaced my pills and could he please refill it early but quite another to make an appointment, go to a new physician, and lie my ass off. Even if I did have the acting chops, which I don't, it would also entail going to multiple pharmacies, which seemed illegal. Another possibility was to attempt to order the pills from Canada—I'd heard of pharmacies that weren't super strict about prescriptions—but it would be very expensive and how would I explain to Jon all the plain brown packages I would be receiving from our neighbors to the north? The whole thing seemed exhausting—it was seriously so much easier, and legal, to just go to Trader Joe's and buy wine.

After Dr. Steinberg recovered from his disappointment that I'd been hiding my excess drinking, he encouraged me to wean myself off of the Xanax very slowly so as to not experience withdrawal, which might make me want to drink to help take the edge off said withdrawal, thus throwing me into a vicious cycle. He didn't need to tell me twice, because I was in no rush to feel like crap. I made my follow-up appointment and felt proud that this was the first time I had gone to see him for a reason other than needing a refill.

When I got home, I counted out the number of Xanax I'd need for my tapering plan and then put the rest into a little baggie and gave it to Jon to hide in case of a mental apocalypse. That night I started my plan: I broke my one-milligram pill into two and took only one of those before bed. I did it every night for a week; then I broke the half pill into two for a couple of weeks and then took that tiny piece and somehow broke that into a tiny piece and so on until I was clinging to a crumb of Xanax. Finally the day came when I was basically just dipping my finger into a bit of blue dust in the bottle before throwing it out, and I was done.

For a brief while it was all good. I felt fine. Better than fine, actually. I started to get a little cocky: *Is this all? I should have dropped the Xanax and quit drinking years ago; this is smooth sailing!* But one morning, out of nowhere, I woke up and that old familiar panic had set in. Nothing extra stressful was happening beyond the normal insanity of my life, so I hoped it was just a blip and it would fade throughout the morning like the remnants of a bad dream, but it persisted. I tried to muscle through my day, but by the next morning it was worse. The feeling was awful, like being on those spinning carnival rides where the floor drops out from under you and you're stuck to the wall, unable to get off or make it stop. I wondered how anyone could just sit with crazy thoughts coming a mile a minute, heart beating like a hamster, and not drink or take a pill to fix it?

I tried going to a meeting, but it didn't make me feel better. Afterward, I scanned the faces in the room, checking to see if anyone seemed to be suffering like I was. But people were just sipping their coffee, munching glazed donuts, and laughing; basically acting like this was a fucking breeze while I felt like my nerves were hooked up to a car battery. What if this was my new normal state of being? Was I destined to feel this way every day for the rest of my life?

I tapped my friend John on the shoulder and asked if he had a minute to talk to me. John was in his early sixties, a comedy writer with a dry sense of humor who always whispered funny things to me when we sat next to each other in meetings, but when it came to recovery, he was dead serious.

"John, I'm having horrible anxiety. This can't be normal." John's gray-blue eyes fixed on me.

"It's *completely* normal. Everyone I know feels anxious in the beginning of sobriety. All the guys I work with go through it. Don't believe anyone who says they feel fantastic all the time; either they're not doing it right or they're full of shit." I immediately felt a lot better . . . for about ninety minutes, and then I was anxious again.

I tried everything I could think of to take the edge off: I wrote about it, I ate some Trader Joe's–brand chocolate sandwich cookies (not my favorite, but they were all I had in the house), I read a few pages of Augusten Burroughs's book *Dry*, which usually soothed me, but nothing worked.

A few hours later, I was feeling decidedly worse, and I had a sad realization: If I were going to get through this, I would need to take a Xanax. I'd just have to explain to Jon I needed just one little Xanax and I'd make sure I saw where he hid them—Jon's idea of a good hiding place was basically the top drawer of his dresser, maybe behind his gym socks and cuff links. Due to this, I was the one who was in charge of hiding the Christmas presents and the sex toys.

I decided to call my sponsor in the program and make my case. She'd understand. She'd have to. And if she didn't answer, I'd take matters into my own hands. Naturally, she answered the phone right away—so annoying—so I got straight to the point. I told her how awful I felt and all about how I had been "diagnosed" with anxiety, so I really needed a Xanax to feel better—I was a special case. She said, "I understand. But that's between you and your doctor. You should make an appointment. Let them know you're sober and see what they tell you to do."

She didn't understand at all. Set up an appointment? I didn't need a Xanax *next Tuesday*, I needed one *yesterday*! Maybe I needed a sponsor with more experience. She'd only been sober eleven years.

And then I started sobbing.

"I really don't think I can do this," I told her.

She was quiet for a bit and then she said, "I know you want a Xanax. You want one because it's a surefire way to make you feel better. But if you take one now, then tomorrow when you feel anxious you'll have to take another one, because you'll think you can't feel better without it, and the next day same thing. Then you're right back in the addiction cycle." Ugh, she was right. I knew that was the way it would go. It felt so grossly unfair. How had it come to this? I felt so desperate, like a child who needed a mom with a lap to curl into. Every goddamned single coping mechanism, even my failsafe, I couldn't use. It was like I was on the *Titanic*, finding out the last available lifeboat had just sprung a leak.

"How am I going to get through right now?" I was still crying.

"Just like this," she said, her voice patient and kind, like that of the mom I needed. "This is the guts of it. Getting through these moments, the times when it's hard, when every muscle in your body is tense and you're forced to go on faith when I say that it will get easier. Can you trust me?"

"Yes." I wasn't sure I did trust her, but I didn't have a choice. I couldn't afford to go backward.

That night I messaged my friend Rachael Brownell, a writer in Seattle who'd written *Mommy Doesn't Drink Here Anymore*. She had been sober at least sixteen months and she'd contacted me when she'd heard I quit drinking, telling me to reach out anytime. "Hey," I typed. "I'm anxious and I really want Xanax. I'm not going to take one but I feel like I'm dying." Her message back popped up immediately with those two little words that are like a fix to an addict:

"I understand." And then a second one: "Can you get through the next hour?"

"No."

"How about thirty minutes?"

"I don't think so."

"Five minutes?"

"I can do five."

"Okay, I'll be right here. Message me again in five minutes and don't take a fucking Xanax." And so it went for almost an hour until at some point I realized I'd stopped thinking about Xanax and I went and made my kids some macaroni and cheese.

Ever so slowly, too slowly for my instant gratification–loving ass, my anxiety receded. For a few months I felt it lingering like a toxic ex trying to sneak back in until it finally lost interest and disappeared into the background. Has it gone away completely? I'm sorry to say no. I still experience waves of anxiety to this day, such as when I travel or when I'm forced to be a passenger in someone else's car. I don't know why, but it drives me to the brink of insanity, and I constantly hit an imaginary brake pedal and let out little scared noises, which don't endear me to the driver, especially when it's my husband. Here's the part where I tell you how to deal with anxiety without using drugs or alcohol right? Ha ha. I wish I had a magic bullet. You can try magnesium or biofeedback or listening to classical music or going to a petting zoo, but at some point, if you're like me, you will want to pop a Xanax. And the bad news is that you can't. But the good news is that it will get better. If you find yourself in the throes of terrible anxiety where you feel like you can't possibly get through even the next five minutes, I promise you that you can. You'll just have to trust me.

16. Sober Wife, Happy Life?

I was sitting at a café with my friend Shayna after my Saturday meeting, eating French fries and nursing a lime Perrier, when the topic turned to sex—specifically, sex with our husbands; more specifically, the sex we weren't having since we'd stopped drinking a few months before. I had broached the topic first, because even as I happily dipped a fry into a side of ranch, it was weighing on my mind. I'd been comparing my sober life to my friends' sober lives and felt nervous that I was doing sobriety wrong somehow, because I wasn't having all the sex—or any of the sex. I was dying to see if this was a me problem or if maybe, possibly, someone else felt like I did.

I trusted Shayna to be honest. She was gorgeous—an actress, tall, with long straight brunette hair—and married, with three kids similar in age to mine. She had been sober a few months longer than I had, so I sort of looked to her to lead the way.

"Jason and I had insane sex. I was crazy—dildos, role-playing, some light BDSM. But I was fucked up all the time! I was always at least two wine bottles in. I don't know who that person was, but I can't even imagine doing that shit stone-cold sober! I don't even want to masturbate. I have literally no sex drive at all. The whole idea of sex just seems awkward."

Oh, thank fucking God. I understood exactly what Shayna meant. I found it challenging to simply chill on the couch watching *Jersey Shore* with Jon without a little wine to help me relax. I'd sit there, jaw clenched, fidgeting like a kid with ADHD in algebra class, acutely aware of the fact that I was just *sitting here attempting to enjoy television*. And that didn't even involve seeing a penis. If watching TV with my husband felt like writing a term paper, what would actual sex be like? How could I do it?

I felt like quitting drinking should improve my marriage. My wine addiction was something that separated me from my husband, created distance between us. And despite the fact that Jon loved me, constantly, consistently, always, and I loved him back equally, I had picked fights when I was drinking to create even more distance. So it should follow that quitting drinking should foster closeness, right? I was removing a major barrier to intimacy. But therein lay the problem: I needed a barrier to intimacy because I was afraid, terrified even, and I had used alcohol to numb and to give myself a safe distance especially when it came to sex. Sex without the alcohol assist I was used to seemed impossible.

I shared with Shayna that I'd been feeling the exact same way, and then I quietly started obsessing on cheesecake.

"I have an idea," Shayna said. "Maybe we just need to rip the Band-Aid off. Let's make a pact that we will fuck our husbands tonight. If we make a commitment to each other, it will help keep us accountable." Although her idea struck fear in my heart, I knew it was a good one.

"What if we give ourselves a week and start with a blow job? You know, baby steps," I said.

"Even better." We clinked our glasses of sparkling water. Solidarity!

"Should we get a piece of cheesecake to celebrate?" I asked.

"Obviously." Shayna was so smart. Taking commitments at meetings helped me to keep attending them even when I didn't feel like it, so maybe committing to a sex act would help me attend to my marriage.

I considered myself happily married, and I really wanted to want to have sex. For my husband's part, Jon had been giving me space and following my lead as to what I needed—which was good. But he also wasn't treating me like a delicate flower, implying that everyone should tiptoe around me because I could no longer handle life—and I also appreciated that. Although, if I'm being honest here, I could've used a little more acknowledgment of the huge thing I'd done, the enormous sacrifice I'd made: Quitting drinking had made my whole life spin off its axis. I'd *voluntarily* stripped myself of my main coping mechanism for my family, and even though I knew it was my own fault that it had come to this, it was still incredibly difficult, and I'd been hoping for a little more fanfare. I hadn't expected a parade, but I would have appreciated a few whispered sweet nothings like, "Let me do the dishes tonight because you're probably exhausted from all that drinking you're not doing."

Between going to meetings, crying, talking on the phone to other sober people, and grieving my old life, sobriety felt like a full-time job, and my responsibilities as a mother continued unabated: kid care, grocery shopping, stories and bedtime, microwaving dinner, going to the park. Jon helped when he could, but he was working full-time and I had the more flexible schedule.

Jon was also very supportive of my recovery, but I knew it was hard for him because he didn't totally understand. He hadn't seen me as an *alcoholic*; therefore, he was admittedly worried about things changing that he never thought needed to change. I'm sure that's the case with many men married to women who drink too much.

But the truth is that he didn't know everything.

He didn't know I would be half a bottle of wine in by the time he got home but that I'd shove that open wine to the back of the fridge and uncork a new bottle so he didn't know exactly how much I'd had. He wasn't aware when I'd had a few glasses of white wine at Susan's house or a margarita at a restaurant at lunch after taking a kid for vaccinations. He didn't know that I often loved to make spaghetti with sauce for dinner not just because it was simple but because my special recipe called for copious amounts of white wine. Fancying myself a regular Gordon Ramsay, I'd pour one glass for myself and then pour a liberal amount into the sauce straight from the bottle, then another for me and a bit more in the sauce until I was drunk and the pasta was gummy. Of course, I'd open a new bottle to split with Jon with our dinner. He didn't know that I always gave myself a more generous pour because I knew he didn't need it as much as I did. He didn't know that when we finished the bottle, panic would set in if we didn't have another bottle chilling. And if we *did* have another bottle, Jon didn't know that even that wouldn't feel like enough, because there wouldn't ever be enough until I felt completely out of it. And when I was passed out by nine thirty p.m. from too much wine and Xanax, Jon didn't know it was because my casual love of alcohol had become a dependency; he just assumed I drank this way because I was stressed and tired.

So now that I wasn't drinking, it made sense that it wouldn't make such a big difference to him. My drinking wasn't affecting his life too much as far as he could tell, so he wasn't excited for me to suddenly have to attend meetings several times a week—meetings that he suspected might or might not be a Jim Jones–level cult. It wasn't obvious to him that I needed to change everything. The signs weren't there: I hadn't been physically addicted, I didn't have yellow eyes or sallow skin or broken capillaries or wine bloat. And once I quit, there were no big changes on the outside to indicate the work that was going on inside. I think Jon honestly felt that I was being too hard on myself. And my being hard on myself made it a little harder for him.

I went to a meeting every Saturday morning and left him with our four-year-old and the twins, who weren't yet two. I knew it was stressful for him, because the second the meeting was over, he'd blow up my phone with texts: "Are you almost home?"

"What's your ETA?"

"Should I feed them?"

"What should I feed them?"

"WHERE DO WE KEEP THE STRING CHEESE?"

I would start getting these texts before the meeting was even over. The vibration of my phone would instinctively cause my hands to sweat. *He's waiting. He's getting upset. This is my fault. I'm the one who's a fuckup, who needed to quit drinking, who can't do it without these meetings and this support, but I'm making his life harder. What's wrong with me?*

In the beginning, I felt like I shouldn't go out after meetings with people I'd met. Even though I needed the support, it felt indulgent somehow, leaving him to do all the heavy lifting. It made it especially difficult knowing that when I'd been drinking, I'd left him to deal with so much on his own, mostly things in the middle of the night like the feedings. Even when the twins were up at the same time at midnight and he had to feed them in tandem, he did it without complaint. Even if he'd worked all day, he'd load up on Rockstar energy drinks and motor through so he could let me sleep. I kind of owed him my presence at this point.

I told myself at the time that it was because he was better with the sleep deprivation than I was—and that was sort of true. He was used to pulling all-nighters from writing term papers in college when he'd put them off until the night before and, much later, writing scripts for jobs where his bosses had no boundaries. He had a way of pinning his ears back and pushing himself through without complaint.

We'd always handled stress differently. When a wave of stress rolled in, I thrashed about, complaining loudly, wanting others to join me in my pain—finding solace in solidarity. Jon reacted by ducking under the water, gritting his teeth, and waiting for the wave to pass over him. These two different approaches have led to some of our biggest fights: When we'd been together about nine months, we went on vacation to Mexico. On the last night of our trip, I thought it would be fun to take a sunset cruise on a pirate ship that was billed as having a mariachi band, a filet mignon dinner, and free-flowing cocktails. It sounded like the perfect ending to a beautiful trip but Jon was hesitant. "It's going to be like a booze cruise," he warned. I didn't have much experience with this, but "booze" and "cruise" were terms I could get behind, so I voted yes and Jon rolled his eyes but obliged me.

I realized our mistake about ten minutes in, but that was ten minutes too late, since we'd already left the shore. The club music started thumping immediately, at a volume so loud it was impossible to hear each other talk, and right away the guests were corralled like cattle and harassed into participating in sad party games involving attempts to say dirty phrases with a mouthful of ice cubes, wearing blindfolds, and feeling people up. It was like forced attendance at an X-rated baby shower. I tried to drink, but it was only making me angrier.

About an hour in, we were marched downstairs into the belly of the boat and given some dry, stringy meat of some sort and a single glass of cheap burgundy, then pushed single file back upstairs and straight into the wall of sound. The music was relentless and ear-splitting. It wasn't like anyone was dancing. We were just standing, all seventy-five of us, squished together on one side of this hell boat. And then the final blow, the coup de grâce, a *cockfight!* *A fucking cockfight.* On what was supposed to be a pleasant sunset cruise! Were these people kidding? Was this some sort of payback to America for swiping California? "Please respect our culture," the Mexican cruise director pleaded as four wasted sorority girls started sobbing. I was furious and would have loved to speak to a manager, but they were all busy doing tequila shots.

Through it all, while I ranted and seethed, Jon ignored me, silently videotaping on our camcorder. His non-reaction to what I felt was an insanely stressful situation made me even more upset. "This is unbearable! I need off this boat! How can you just stand there videotaping? Can we swim to shore?" I yelled this because I was so mad, but also because it was the only way to be heard over the music and boat engine.

"There's nothing we can do about it but wait until we get back to shore," he yelled back. And with that, his eye went back behind the viewfinder and he was done interacting. So I drank and bitched while Jon, who had taken a mental escape to a completely different vacation, stoically recorded our pain. By the time we disembarked, we weren't speaking. As we rode in a cab silently back to our Puerto Vallarta motel room, I'm sure Jon was enjoying the quiet, but I felt abandoned, positive this spelled the end of our relationship. We were completely incompatible.

Later, when we had both calmed down enough to talk about it, we came to the realization that we were both doing what we needed to do to endure a terrible situation. It wasn't that he couldn't empathize with me; it was that he didn't want us both going down with the ship.

And much later, Jon would tell me that when we had twins, he knew it would be like the pirate ship and that the only way he would get through it would be to duck under that wave. But once again, even though I knew intellectually what was happening and that this was his way to get through it, while I struggled and tried to swim against the tide, I felt all alone. So I leaned harder on my survival tool: wine.

Despite Jon's initial reaction that I didn't need to quit drinking, that I was overreacting, being too hard on myself, that I was a great wife and mom, one who cared desperately about the well-being of the kids, not some derelict swilling Mad Dog by night and sleeping all day, once he realized that I was serious about needing to quit, he was on board.

For the first three weeks I was sober, Jon was sober too. He didn't bring any alcohol into the house and he didn't drink outside of the house either. It was nice of him and felt good at first, but then it started to irritate me. "I haven't had a single sip of alcohol in almost three weeks," he pointed out to me one day. He hadn't actually made a concerted effort not to drink, but since he hadn't brought it into the house, he didn't think about it. I'm sorry, but that's not an accomplishment. It gives "skinny people who forget to eat" vibes and it made me feel worse.

When we first met, he told me he drank way too much in high school and college. I got inexplicably excited that it seemed like he might have even had a problem there for a while. It made him more complicated, possibly troubled. But sometime after college, a close friend of his got into a drunk-driving accident, scaring the hell out of him, and he'd cut way down after that, never really drinking compulsively again.

It's not like I wanted Jon to have an issue with alcohol—one of the many things I loved about him was his consistency. He never got drunk or out of control. In fact, I could only think of one or two times I'd ever seen him extremely tipsy, where I was on the verge of being worried about him, but he never crossed over to drunk. Both times we were on vacation without anywhere to drive or anyplace to be in the morning. In the seven years we'd been together, I'd been the one passing out, throwing up, losing track of my drinks, and making the decision to drive when I shouldn't. Somehow, at the time, I assumed Jon was drunk too, but only because I was too drunk to realize he wasn't. It was just a little embarrassing that all this time I had been the one with the issue and he had mostly drunk to keep me company. And now he'd only been *refraining* from drinking to keep me company.

When Jon was ready to get off the wagon, he was sweet about it. "Would it be triggering for you if I bought some beer? I don't want to bring anything in the house that would tempt you." I wasn't excited to have alcohol in the house but, on the other hand, I didn't want him to feel like his whole life needed to change. I felt guilty and worried that I wasn't going to be as fun, and since I already wasn't having sex with the guy, how much of a killjoy did I want to be? I told him it was fine to keep beer in the house but that I wasn't cool with wine and I didn't want to buy alcohol for him.

Shayna and I checked in with each other via text the day after our pact.

"Did you do it?" she wrote.

"Yup," I texted back. "I almost didn't recognize it. Lol."

"Lol," she texted back. Like we were fourteen. "Now we have to go all the way."

Getting intimate with Jon post-sobriety did make me feel like a teenager. I was scared and self-conscious. My husband felt like someone I didn't know and someone I knew all too well at the exact same time. I'd always armed myself with at least a few glasses of wine if I knew we were going to get busy, even well into marriage. I thought it made me looser, more relaxed, and sexier because it lowered my inhibitions. I had always been embarrassed that I needed this, like I was defective somehow. But it was the only way I knew how to let someone get close to me in that way. Trying to be intimate without a drop of wine or even one tiny little benzo made me feel way too exposed—naked under floodlights on the field of Giants Stadium–level exposed. It wasn't a sexy feeling, unless that's what you're into, and hey, I'm not kink shaming here. But, sure enough, as Shayna predicted, it was like ripping off a Band-Aid.

I'm not going to sit here and say it was fun. It was genuinely scary for me and awkward, but I wanted to stay married, so I put on my big-girl panties—or rather, took off my big-girl panties—and got the job done. I will assure you it got easier with practice. Drunk sex can feel fun and uninhibited, but physically it's more challenging to orgasm, because you're anesthetized. Sex is way more satisfying when you can actually feel things below the waist.

I know a lot of single women who quit drinking and then wonder how they will ever date sober—I agree, it sounds mortifying. But if you are single and quit drinking, you don't have to go on a date until you're ready. You can literally shut your vagina down for business like a ski resort in July. *Sorry, no action is happening at this time. Try fishing instead.* Eventually you'll need to reopen, but there's nothing wrong with taking your time and getting used to operating at a higher level of awareness. Many potential relationships will end after one date because sober people tend to ask more questions and have a more difficult time ignoring the inevitable red flags that come with the answers. But hey, at least you won't be three months in before you realize you're dating a Holocaust denier or someone who writes *Twilight* fan fiction.

Once Jon and I got sex out of the way, it was time to move on to something even more intimate: date night. I wondered how it would be to go out to dinner and just sit and talk. Had we ever really done that sober? Surely at some point we'd had an evening out that didn't include drinking. Yes! When I was pregnant! But I'd been high on hormones then, so I wasn't sure it counted. Anyway, it had been a while.

Seated at the sushi bar with Jon, I immediately felt weird. I've loved sushi since the first time I tried it after moving to Los Angeles. I'd started with a California roll. Eventually, over the years, I worked my way up to uni, the slimy yellow edible part of a sea urchin, which Jon always said tasted like "licking the bottom of a boat." I savored ikura, those little translucent salmon eggs that burst salty water in your mouth when you eat them like a piece of Freshen-Up gum. But tonight everything felt wrong. Sushi without sake and large quantities of Sapporo seemed depressing. Sushi was my favorite food—I could eat it every day for the rest of my life—and quitting drinking was going to ruin it for me.

I didn't want my decision to quit drinking to affect Jon's enjoyment, so I told him to go ahead and get some sake if that's what he really wanted to do. I meant it, sort of, but I figured he wouldn't take me up on it. Unfortunately, he didn't pick up on my passive-aggressive vibes and he ordered himself a large Dassai. When our server put the sake down between us and tried to hand each of us our little cup, I quickly handed mine back. I didn't need it sitting in front of me like a bright orange traffic cone, forcing me to drive around it: *Danger, don't look here, or prepare to be reminded of your sake-less life, devoid of any pleasure.* I tried to remind myself that sake tastes like drinking lighter fluid; you really don't get used to it until halfway through the second bottle. But I still felt bitter as I sipped my stupid hot green tea.

Jon sat looking at me expectantly. Then he shifted his gaze to the sake bottle and back to me like he was a golden retriever trying to indicate that his water bowl was empty.

"What's up?" I asked. If he was hinting at something, I wasn't picking up on it. He looked down at the sake bottle again, and that's when it dawned on me that this bitch actually wanted me to pour his sake into his cup like we always used to do for each other, as if this wasn't hard enough for me—as if I wasn't already questioning my sobriety and all I was sacrificing because I'd made one fucking mistake and misjudged how many martinis I'd had that one night.

I'd thought Jon understood how difficult this was, but the fact that he expected me to pour his sake into his glass as a newly sober person was beyond. I imagined myself knocking over the sake bottle, standing up from the bar, and storming out of the restaurant. But if I went and got the car from the valet and drove home, how would he get home? Would I have to come back and get him once I'd calmed down?

I opted for the simpler, honest approach.

"I'm not doing that," I said.

"Why not?" He was genuinely confused. "I'm not suggesting you have any, but you can't still pour it for me? It's our tradition."

"No. I'm sorry." He had the nerve to be hurt.

As kind and supportive as Jon tried to be, we fought a lot that first year. It reminded me of the first year of our relationship and the year after we had a baby. When we first started dating, I was quick to anger, not trusting Jon's intentions, constantly scanning for red flags. But I was able to soothe myself with alcohol, calm myself down even though I didn't know that was what I was doing. And it's not as if it worked. Many an argument escalated due to my drinking leading to dramatic storm-offs on my part, hoping Jon would come after me, proving to me he could tolerate my emotional instability. But I would have told you it wasn't the alcohol. I would have told you he was being an asshole. And later, after I'd calmed down, I would be sorry, and I would get scared he would break up with me or that he would have changed his mind, and I would swear to myself that I wouldn't get drunk again. And then I would.

I was a raw nerve in that first sober year, often taking simple disagreements and blowing them up into huge fights. One time, before my Saturday meeting, I'd left the house so furious I could barely focus on anything else, because inwardly I was stewing and plotting my divorce. I missed half the meeting because while a fellow alcoholic was earnestly recounting the gory details of their various arrests and 5150s, my brain was singing Gloria Gaynor's "I Will Survive" and ironing out the logistics of my separation: Would I move out? Would I make him move out? Would he sleep on the couch while looking for an apartment? *Being single again will be difficult but I'll be fine!* By the time I met up with Shayna afterward, I'd worked myself into a ball of seething resentment ready to file paperwork at the courthouse that afternoon.

"Okay, here's what I want you to do," Shayna said, once I told her how upset I was. "Get out your phone. You're going to send him a text right now."

The hell I am! I thought.

"Tell him you're sorry and that you love him." Had she gone back to drinking?

"But I need to tell you what he did!"

"First text him, then you can tell me." Shayna knew Jon wasn't an actual shitty spouse, that he was trying his best, that we were having normal disagreements, and that the problem was most likely with me. She knew because she was going through the same thing.

"Hey asshole, I'm sorry. I love you," I texted.

Within a minute I got a response: "I love you too, dumbass."

And with that, all my anger dissipated. But then a minute later another text came in: "Should I feed the twins or wait for you? Are we out of string cheese?" And I was mad all over again.

I would have told you at the time that those early days of sobriety put a strain on my marriage. But by learning how to show up clear-headed for the good, bad, and tedious, I became a better, more consistent wife and mother. The truth is that my marriage was stressed by a million other things, and at no point would drinking have made any of it easier, but it definitely would have made things worse.

17. The Moms on the Other Side of the Fence

When I came out on my blog that I was quitting drinking, one woman commented, "On this side of the fence, you'll find moms who don't drink; Girl Scout moms who chaperone camping trips, moms who volunteer at your kids' school, moms who still get together and laugh and have fun, moms who are present and can be depended on. You're so welcome here." When I first read that comment, I didn't know what to make of it. It seemed impossible that I would become a mom like that: a mom on the other side of the fence. I'd grown quite comfortable on my side, thank you very much.

Up until this point, I had surrounded myself with a lot of moms who drank like I did. It may sound crazy, but it simply hadn't occurred to me that I could relate to any mom who *wouldn't* find it necessary to drink.

Prior to quitting, the only actual sober mom I'd known had gone sprinting back to drinking again only a few months after having a baby—which I found completely understandable. Lucy called me one day just to say hello and then slipped into the conversation that she really didn't think she was an alcoholic anymore. Our husbands had worked together and we'd hung out socially a handful of times. I knew she'd been sober a few years and that she took it very seriously.

She even traveled with her own six-pack of LaCroix in case of a nonalcoholic-beverage emergency.

We'd been pregnant at the same time and had our babies two weeks apart, but I thought she'd been adjusting way better than I was. Anytime I asked her how it was going she'd say, "Perfect," which annoyed me to no end, since I was a complete mess. I just assumed she was one of those Stepford wives who enjoyed watching her baby's eyelashes grow, while I would have given my kidney for a nap. But then I got that call. "I just started thinking about it, and now that I'm a mom, I'm realizing my drinking was never all that bad. I'm nothing like the stories you hear where people swap their babies for crack. I just drank too much in college. I'm a responsible person. I just want to have a beer. It's really not a big deal at all; I just thought I'd mention it so in case you see me drinking, you'll know why."

"Good for you! Sounds like a rational decision." She got no argument from me! In fact, it was the witching hour, and right at that moment, an IPA sounded insanely good.

But now that I'd swapped places with her, I wondered exactly how I'd fit in with the drinking moms. As it turned out, not all my drinking mom friends were doing so hot.

I was at a preschool pickup around Thanksgiving of the year I quit, and a mom named Jody approached and asked if we could talk. We sat on a bench outside of the pre-K classroom where our four-year-olds were finishing their handprint drawings of a turkey. "So, um, how did you do it? How did you quit?"

I was momentarily shocked, but I shouldn't have been. Jody and I had become fast, easy friends because our daughters were friends, and while our kids played at her house, we would drink chardonnay and commiserate about how much chardonnay we drank. We admitted to each other that our drinking had ratcheted up post-baby—that we rarely took a night off of drinking—*but*, we reasoned, if we felt this way, everyone must feel this way! It was nice to re-assure each other that we were okay, just trying to keep our heads above water in this vast sea of anxiety.

We made each other feel normal.

But now I had broken ranks, and although I hadn't explicitly told her, I knew she knew, and now it had seemed like she was possibly avoiding me, although I could have been being paranoid.

I'd done a few TV appearances at this point, including an in-terview with Elizabeth Vargas, and although the director of our preschool congratulated me and told me I was "brave" (what else was she supposed to say: "We had no idea you were a degenerate drunk and we're seriously rethinking you being room mom"?), it was the possible judgment from other moms that had me the most concerned.

I worried that some might think that because I'd publicly admit-ted to having a drinking problem I must be a shitty mom, and I also worried that others would judge me for not holding up my end of the secret agreement that we all had to drink to deal with the stress of parenting. Would I be kicked out of my social circle? Would my casual mom friends worry that now that I was sober I was judging their drinking? Would they think I'd done an about-face and decided they were all alcoholics?

The truth was I was mostly bummed that I couldn't make it work with alcohol and jealous that they still could. Walking away from drinking felt like getting a divorce, and I worried my friends would feel they had to pick sides and their allegiance would be with alcohol. "Sorry, Stefanie, you're so great and we loved having you around, but we've just known chardonnay longer. Plus, chardonnay's a lot more fun these days."

So maybe my quitting had made Jody uncomfortable by shining a spotlight on her own drinking habits, or maybe she'd been struggling this whole time and finally had enough, like me—like more and more of us, it seemed.

It didn't matter. I was just happy she felt like she could come to me.

"Well, I asked a friend of mine who's sober for help, and she took me to a meeting," I said. "Are you thinking about quitting too?"

I couldn't see her eyes, because she was wearing Jackie Kennedy Onassis–sized sunglasses that covered most of her face, and she was staring straight ahead. But then I caught a tear sliding out from under her shades and landing on her lip. "It's gotten really bad. I think I need help."

My heart went out to her. Here I'd been jealous of Jody because she could still drink. I'd thought we drank the same way, yet her life was staying on track while mine had veered off the road. But the truth was that the grass wasn't greener on the drinking side of that fence.

I slowly got used to being the sober mom among the drinking moms. The thing that really helped was meeting other sober moms. In my recovery meetings, I sought out the moms like the fruit at the bottom of a yogurt; that's where the real joy was for me. Moms clumped together during meetings and socialized after meetings at Fatburger or Starbucks or the mall. I loved sober moms because I could count on them to be just the right amount of pissed off at having to be sober at the exact time of our lives when we could all really use a drink. Some had gotten into the parenting game when they were already sober, which sucked for them but was helpful to hear about.

I met my friend Jess when I'd been sober only a few months. She'd been sober about fourteen months but she had a baby boy who was only a few months old. So if you do the math, she'd quit drinking and then gotten knocked up a few months later, which didn't give her a lot of non-pregnant sobriety experience. I've discussed the idea that some women don't have trouble staying sober when they're pregnant because those hormones are like God's sedatives and somehow make abstaining from alcohol seem like a totally reasonable idea. Anyway, once she had her son, she was hit with the wave of depression and anxiety a lot of us experience—but now the only bottle she could reach for was full of Enfamil.

I saw Jess at a weekly meeting I attended in a church, which shared space with a preschool. During that hour, children napped just down the hall. I always wondered if the parents of those babies took issue with a bunch of drunks talking about God knows what crazy bad decisions they'd made just a few doors away from their sleeping little angels. I also wondered if the parents of those preschoolers ever passed the door where our meeting was held on their way to pick up their kids and, knowing what went on inside, thought about coming in. I was grateful I was securely on the meeting side of the door and not untethered on the outside.

Jess always seemed downright unruffled, even when she was lugging seventeen pounds of baby around in her infant carrier and sporadically rocking him as he slept in front of her chair. Every time I saw her she had a smile on her face, which made me inexplicably angry—although to be fair, everything made me angry in those early days. It's actually not inexplicable; it just doesn't make me look empathetic. She was one of those people who made sobriety look too easy. In fact, she made it all look easy: sobriety, motherhood, hair care, all of it. She reeked of mindfulness and serenity, while I was afraid my anger, fear, and insecurity leaked from my pores, creating a stench that would repel people like her.

But one day, it was her time to share and as I inwardly rolled my eyes, bracing against her good mood, preparing myself for some "life is beautiful" platitudes, she surprised me by bursting into tears. "This parenting shit is so hard and I feel like I'm failing every single day." I snapped to attention, all ears. "I'm not cut out for this. I guess I thought it would be different; I thought it would be better, but now I'm wishing the days away and I feel so guilty about that." And then she just sat and cried quietly. I know the meeting must've gone on, but I couldn't take my eyes off of her. In the three minutes she'd held the floor, she'd transformed into the Most Interesting Person in the Room with her stunning confession. Her veneer might have shattered, but all I saw was a golden opportunity to help sweep up the pieces.

Right after the meeting ended, I made a beeline to talk to her, but an older grandma type with like a billion years of sobriety beat me to it and was attempting to give her what I'm sure she believed was helpful advice. "Honey, appreciate your sweet baby. They grow up fast and you're missing it!"

I was just in time to put a stop to this insanity. "She's not missing anything," I said gently, putting my hand on Jess's shoulder in what I hoped was a protective gesture. "That's the problem: She's present for every second of it and she needs a break." Then I introduced myself and told her she was coming over for some herbal tea. Jess may have been farther along in her sobriety but I was farther along in parenting. I was thrilled to be in a position to offer help. Sometimes you just need someone to see you, really see you.

Jess was a great addition to my sober-mom posse, which slowly grew into a little community. Luckily, I also had a small core group of moms who barely drank—a couple who preferred cookies to alcohol and one who'd grown up with an alcoholic mom. But then my older daughter started kindergarten, and outside of my bubble, being sober in the land of drinking moms felt like wearing Forever 21 in a sea of Fendi.

The kindergarten moms took their drinking very seriously. It was a small, tight-knit community, at once welcoming and intimidating, but early on I felt my nondrinking status made me an outsider. When I was invited to bring my daughter over to play with a few other kids at our mom friend Lena's house, there was always wine. I'd self-consciously sip my water and make conversation, all the while eyeing the way they drank, wishing I'd been able to keep it to one glass like these women seemed to do.

I tried to convince myself I was being ridiculous, that no one cared. Why would they give a shit if I did or didn't drink wine with them? It was stupid to imagine the other moms would think I wasn't "fun" or "cool" because I didn't drink. I mean, come on! We weren't in a sorority; we were moms in our thirties and forties.

But one afternoon Lena called. "Hey, are you going to Jen's on Thursday for margaritas?"

"I don't think so. I didn't know about it." Silence.

"Oh shit. I'm sorry. I thought for sure all the kinder moms were invited." Maybe it was an oversight, I thought. These bitches wouldn't exclude me because I didn't drink, right? That would be crazy!

Lena must've turned around and called Jen, because thirty minutes later my phone lit up. "Hey, I'm really sorry. I just wanted to explain. We were mainly getting together to drink margaritas, and since I know you don't drink, I didn't want you to feel uncomfortable." I didn't know what to say. I knew this wasn't exactly the truth: She wasn't worried about me feeling uncomfortable; she was worried about *me* making *everyone else* feel uncomfortable.

"It's fine," I lied. "Don't even worry about it."

So that was it. It was worse than I thought: I wasn't just boring; I was a literal buzzkill. This is exactly what I'd been worried about. When I drank, I thought moms who didn't drink weren't fun, and now moms who *did* drink thought *I* wasn't fun. I guess I had it coming.

When I first quit drinking and told my small group of mom friends, they were all surprised. "But I've never even seen you drunk," my friend Lara said. Lara knew I liked my wine; she just didn't know how much I liked my wine. Lara was the mom I attempted to strong-arm into ordering a margarita with me when we went to lunch when our girls were six months old. Once I knew she wasn't into it, I didn't drink much around her. She wasn't a "fun mom friend." If you'd asked me then, I would've said she was over-responsible, always worried about being out of control, about taking her eyes off the prize even for an instant, whereas I was desperate to focus on anything besides the prize. I felt overwhelmed by the enormity of our responsibility, so I longed to check out. I imagined that she only felt calm when she was 100 percent checked-in. Because of this, I never considered her fun to party with. But now that I was sober, I realized Lara was someone I could count on, someone completely trustworthy and consistent. And also fun.

When Jen had called me to tell me why I wasn't invited, I was angry. I wanted to tell her off. Who did she think she was imagining me as a threat to her good time? She wouldn't know a good time if it bit her on the tit! I used to do stand-up! I'm a great fucking time! But the more I thought about it, the more I realized it really didn't matter. I was a middle-aged mom with three young kids who lived in yoga pants and ate at IHOP; not getting invited to margarita night was the least of my worries.

Lena called sometime later and told me the get-together had been dull and that I hadn't missed much—just a bunch of moms standing around drinking and discussing ideas for fundraisers. I was secretly pleased.

On my blog, a few weeks after I quit, I posted a picture of my kids with the caption "They're worth it." The truth was, I quit drinking for my kids. It's not the popular thing to say. You'll hear over and over, *You can't quit drinking for someone else; you have to do it for yourself.* Well, screw that. I say, whatever motivates you. The desire to be the best mom I could be was the most powerful motivator. If I had been single with no kids, I might never have had my moment of desperation. Am I going to discount it because some randos think you can't get sober for someone else? Absolutely not. That's stupid.

I think what may be true is that you can't *stay* sober for someone else, but if you *get* sober for someone else, down the line you may end up having the realization that you actually were a big huge lushy-lush who really did need to quit drinking. At least that's what happened to me.

In case you're wondering, Lucy, the mom who started drinking a few months after she had a baby, seems to be doing fine, according to what I sleuthed on Facebook. Jody, that mom from preschool, ended up needing to go to treatment after a few attempts to quit on her own, which weren't successful. I tried to follow up with her many times—no pressure—but I stopped hearing back from her. I hope she's doing okay. But remember Lena? The mom who felt bad I wasn't invited to the party? Well, she just celebrated a year sober, and I was the first one she called.

About ten years into sobriety, I was at a New Year's Eve get-together at Lara's house with our small mom group while our fifteen-year-old kids were at another party about twenty minutes away. The moms at the party wanted to drink champagne, but they knew our kids would need a pickup shortly after midnight. Of course I offered to do the late-night drive. As I drove everyone home, stone-cold sober and responsible for a car full of my friends' kids as well as my own, that comment on my blog came back to me. *"On this side of the fence, you'll find moms who don't drink; Girl Scout moms who chaperone camping trips, moms who volunteer at your kids' school, moms who still get together and laugh and have fun, moms who are present and can be depended on. You're so welcome here."* I teared up. I was so proud to be on this side of the fence.

18. Outed

I published my first book, *Sippy Cups Are Not for Chardonnay*, in 2006, but even afterward, I'd continued to write about my life on my blog. One of my major themes, as well as my go-to method for bonding through humor, was talking about drinking wine. But now I'd made the decision to stop drinking and I wondered how I could write another entry without telling on myself? I thrived on this special type of connection to moms—most of whom I only knew virtually but many of whom had become friends in real life. It would be fraudulent to complain about some trivial parenting thing when my life had undergone a seismic shift. I didn't dare say I'd driven drunk; it was one thing to tell alcoholics about my drinking—hell, I figured the way I drank was probably aspirational to the "swilling mouthwash in the shower" set—but it was another thing entirely to tell moms, *probably* judgy moms who drank a ton themselves, that I'd lost control. What would they think of me? Would they be disgusted? Would I lose the support of the community I'd come to rely on? I also worried that they would hear my confession as an indictment of their own nightly habits. I needed to really keep this about me, and the decision *I* made. But I had to do it. So, a few days after that twelve-step meeting, I sat down at my computer and, heart thumping, crying harder than a preteen girl seeing *The Notebook* for the first time, I spilled the news that I quit and braced for impact.

But the comments that rolled in were loving and supportive, many of them from moms questioning their own drinking habits. Once again, my blog had helped me feel less alone.

Then, ten days after I'd hit "publish," my BlackBerry started vibrating with calls. The first voice mail was from a producer at *Dr. Phil* asking if I would come on the show to talk about quitting drinking. *What?* How the hell did the *Dr. Phil* show know I'd quit drinking? There were other messages too, from other television shows and from a few magazines.

I was mortified. What could I possibly have to say about quitting drinking, when I'd literally done it less than two weeks before? I racked my brain to figure out how my so-not-newsworthy news had traveled so goddamned fast. Were there cameras in my house? *How did all of these people know?* That's when I decided to Google myself, and within one click of my mouse, I found out a woman named Lisa Belkin, who wrote a parenting blog for the *New York Times* called *Motherlode*, had dedicated a post to me and my admission. She called it "A Mother Gives Up the (Wine) Bottle." How clever.

First, she'd listed off my books, which up until that point all had alcohol in the title and she said, "You are beginning to see a pattern here? Wilder-Taylor likes to drink. She likes it too much." And then she excerpted my confessional blog post almost in its entirety, which was a little lazy, if you ask me. But now, simply due to her reach, a few million *New York Times* readers knew that I'd quit drinking, as, it seemed, did a dozen TV producers. Mystery solved. Here's what she excerpted:

I found myself drinking more than I had before I became a parent and I drank with other moms to bond and unwind (yes, I'm the cocktail playdate mom and I stand by it being a healthy thing to do in moderation, in walking distance, if you're not me). Before I got pregnant with the twins I had pretty much stopped drinking because I felt it was becoming a habit so when I was pregnant, it was extremely easy not to drink. But when the twins were born and I was home and my milk was dried up and postpartum was setting in, the simplest thing to do seemed to be to have a glass of wine.

It was only too darn easy to fall back into the pattern (especially once the babies started having a regular bedtime) of having my wine every night. For some people I'm sure this is a nice thing, a tribunal thing (a drink at the end of the day with their spouse or friends). For others it might be a once in a while treat to go out and have a couple of cocktails. For me, it's become a nightly compulsion and I'm outing myself to you; all of you: I have a problem.

Of course I read the comments on Lisa's post. These were strangers, and most of them were not kind. One wondered about my marriage. Another said I was addicted to validation and needed to find real friends and not just *NYT* readers. One said I had a warped attitude toward parenting and kids and I needed to find a job and a therapist, oh, and I wasn't cut out to be a stay-at-home mom. I felt sick to my stomach, completely exposed. I hadn't submitted my story to the *New York Times*; I'd simply made a confession to my small circle of readers. I wasn't looking for attention; I was looking for connection. But now here was my dark secret being paraded out on the world's stage.

My first reaction was to think, *What a bitch*. I was pissed—Lisa Belkin had outed me. True, she did it after I had outed myself, but that seemed beside the point. It felt cruel. She didn't ask my permission or give me a heads-up or even offer me the opportunity to give a comment. Where was her journalistic integrity?

I'd actually met Lisa Belkin years before at a book signing during a women's blogging conference in San Francisco. I'd been flown there and put up in a nice hotel to promote *Sippy Cups are Not for Chardonnay*. The night before the signing was the first night of the conference, and there were a lot of parties. As I have established, I don't do well with endless drink opportunities, especially when I'm out of town and unaccountable. Everyone who drinks too much understands out-of-town rules: Basically, out-of-town rules are that there are no rules—sort of like, "What happens in Vegas stays in Vegas," but for *everywhere* you don't live.

By the time I'd gone to bed that night, the room was spinning so hard it's a wonder the centrifugal force didn't cause me to wake up on the floor. The second my eyes popped open and saw the hotel's digital clock displaying "06:00," I knew I was in bad shape. For a second I wasn't sure where I was; all I knew was that I was parched and sick. I ran to the bathroom and puked up the cheap buffet food from dinner the night before. There are only so many ways I can describe a migraine in this book, so trust me when I tell you that this one was so bad I knew I would have to go to the ER if there was any chance I'd make it to my eleven a.m. event.

Somehow I staggered down to the hotel lobby, doing my best to shield my eyes from any direct light coming in from the lobby windows, and cried at the concierge desk while they called me a cab and directed me to San Francisco General. I had to ask the cabbie to pull over twice so I could puke in an alley.

Once in triage, I was given IV fluids but the stingy nurses didn't offer me a single narcotic. I tried to hint to the nurse nonchalantly, but I didn't want to seem like I was a drug seeker. "Excuse me, hi, so is there any chance you could give me a few Vicodin? Sometimes it's the only thing that works on my migraines. I have a prescription for it at home but I forgot to bring it with me." It was worth a try.

"Sorry, the doctor just ordered fluids and magnesium for the nausea." Magnesium? What the fuck? That's like a glorified vitamin. What do they prescribe for a broken leg? A kale salad? What kind of a shitty fucking hospital was this? Didn't these amateurs understand I needed some hard drugs to get me through this?

As upset as I was, the irony wasn't lost on me that I was at a conference promoting a book that makes light of moms and drinking and now I was in danger of being too hungover to show up at my own signing. I promised myself I would never drink again. Well, for sure if I had to get up early the next day.

Miraculously, the magnesium and fluids did help and I made it back to the hotel with enough time to change my clothes and grab a coffee and an English muffin before sliding into my place at the book-signing table, where I'd been positioned next to Lisa Belkin. She looked annoyingly well rested, and she'd gotten there early, like a professional. What a show-off. We sat side by side for the next two hours, signing our respective books and chatting up attendees and each other. We exchanged business cards and said we'd keep in touch.

And now, many years later, she was outing me in her column. Did she not remember me? Lisa, I thought we were friends!

I ignored most of the media requests, but the *Dr. Phil* show kept calling until I finally picked up. "Look, I literally quit drinking ten days ago," I told the producer, after he made the request I knew was coming.

"That's okay! We won't put you in the hot seat. You'll be our expert. It could be so helpful to moms going through the same thing."

"No. I'm so sorry. I don't have anything to say about this topic. I quit drinking because I had a problem, but I haven't changed my stance on moms and drinking."

It's true I hadn't changed my stance, but my quitting drinking certainly complicated things. Although my book *Sippy Cups Are Not for Chardonnay* had alcohol in the title and it was packed with jokes about the power of alcohol to soothe the stress of new motherhood, I wasn't trying to encourage moms to drink; I didn't include cocktail recipes. Trust me, moms were already drinking. But by rebelling against the idea that I had to have a parenting philosophy or breastfeed for seven years or teach my baby Mandarin in utero, I tapped into the "Fuck it, let's have a glass of wine and do less" bad-mommy zeitgeist. What sealed the deal was that shortly after my book started getting a lot of attention, I was asked to do a segment on the *Today* show about "cocktail playdates," where I defended the right of moms everywhere to bond over a glass or two of wine while watching their kids together.

I had no idea that any of it would be controversial. It wasn't as if I was suggesting chugging beers or slamming tequila shots while innocent toddlers wander around un-gated pools! I certainly didn't think I was promoting alcoholism—I was just giving voice on mainstream media to what was already happening in the blogosphere. In my mind, there was nothing scandalous about having a glass of wine while in the company of children. After all, *I* certainly didn't drink too much. I was modeling moderation!

Back then, because I'd done that *Today* show segment, I was asked to do other shows and give quotes to tons of magazines and online articles discussing this mommy-drinking trend. I was usually up for giving my defense of moms and drinking—after all, it was the feminist thing to do. No one was judging dads for knocking back a few brewskis while watching the game, right?

But my private drinking wasn't the same as what I was promoting so it was incredibly embarrassing to have been all rah-rah drinking and then only a few short years later to come back on my blog, tail tucked between my legs, and admit that my public-facing persona had been a farce and that I had a problem, even if I hadn't known it then.

But four months after my Belkin outing, a writer for the *New York Times* named Jan Hoffman reached out and asked if she could do an interview with me. I hadn't responded to any of the previous media requests, but with slightly more sober time under my belt, I figured, *Why not?* I hadn't even meant to be public about quitting drinking. It's just that I have no filter. What you call dredging your soul for deep dark secrets I call dinner conversation—I will tell the stranger I'm seated next to at Benihana that I have a raging UTI while enjoying the onion volcano—so my thoughts on sobriety weren't something I was going to be able to keep to myself for too long. I decided I may as well lean into it. I figured, hell, my honesty about parenting helped women feel less alone; my talking honestly about quitting drinking might do the same for women struggling with alcohol.

The article, titled "A Heroine of Cocktail Moms Sobers Up," appeared on the front page of the Sunday Style section. I hadn't expected that. Again, the comments online were *not* kind. After I read a few that suggested CPS come take my kids away and others of a similar vibe, I had to have Jon screen them and only read me the few nice ones. Now I was *really* out there, and there would be no turning this car around.

Next I went on *The Dr. Oz Show*—this was right when he got his own spin-off show after being Oprah's darling and we all loved him—way before he was crowned the king of pseudoscience. I opened up to him about the way I drank as a new mom, my postpartum anxiety, and my decision to quit. Still no mention of the drinking and driving. After this episode aired, I braced for negativity, but instead I started getting emails and Facebook messages, dozens a day, from women who related.

"Saw you on Dr. Oz. Last night I got drunk and passed out in bed with my five-year-old while reading him a story. I'm scared I might have a problem. What do I do?"

"Hi Stefanie, I never used to drink much before I had a baby but now I go through a box of wine every couple of days. Do I have a problem?"

I couldn't believe it. Here I'd thought when I was drinking, raising my virtual glass of chardonnay in the blogosphere every night, that the world drank with me and that when I had to quit, I'd failed somehow, like I just couldn't hang with the big kids, and I thought I was alone.

I responded to each and every message with words of support, but I let them know I couldn't tell them if they had a problem or not, considering I'd only recently figured out that I had one. But now I felt encouraged that my story was helping people.

Less than a year after I quit drinking, I was asked to do a segment for ABC's *20/20*. It would be with Elizabeth Vargas. "She's very interested in hearing about mothers and drinking," the producer, Shana, told me. "We're going to have a woman who is currently struggling with alcoholism and some New York City moms who do regular cocktail playdates, but they feel it's a fun, positive thing and have no issues with it."

Well, that sounded familiar. Except now I would be on the other side, like some sort of cautionary tale: *Look! Here's what happens when your "cocktail playdate" is just an excuse for chugging wine because you suck at parenting! Check out this chick: She couldn't keep it to just a glass like these classy normal moms smiling with their Bugaboo strollers, Lululemons, and fresh blowouts. Of course they have time to do their hair! Because motherhood isn't that hard!*

I wasn't sure I was up for being presented as an example of wine drinking gone wrong.

"We would love to do a sit-down interview with you and get your whole story. Plus, we also have the author Mary Karr." Wow, Mary Karr was going to do it? She'd written *The Liar's Club*, which was a great book. The interview was to be filmed in Manhattan, so I'd get to go on a trip, and stay in a hotel, without my twin two-year-olds or my five-year-old. That was worth the price of possible embarrassment alone!

The drink cravings started shortly after takeoff. I was nine months sober and thought I was getting used to my booze-free existence, but life with three young kids was relentless—and I was on a plane, which is sort of like being on a cruise in international waters where you can gamble and commit murder or at the very least be intoxicated in public—there are no laws! Does drinking on a plane even count? When the flight attendant started wheeling the bar cart down the aisle, I thought about how easy it would be to order a glass of wine or, better yet, a Seagram's 7 & 7—my favorite plane cocktail. I was completely anonymous. Who would know?

I would know.

And I was on my way to go on national television to talk about sobriety.

I landed at JFK sober and headed to the hotel. Hotels are like drinking booby traps. Everywhere you look there are alcohol ops: restaurants, bars, minibars, room service, and so much privacy, sweet privacy. In the past when I'd stayed in hotels in New York while promoting my books, my ritual was to order a few glasses of red wine from the restaurant and take them to my room to drink by myself. I wasn't partying; I told myself it was just a nice way to unwind and enjoy child-free time before getting up at the crack of dawn. Plus, after my take-out wine I could drink one more from the minibar and it wouldn't seem like any big deal. So being back in a hotel, by myself, was a little triggering.

Because the restaurant had already closed due to the late hour, and I hadn't eaten, I decided the best approach was to go to the bar and order some food in the company of other hotel patrons rather than hang in my room with the minibar. I thought about what people say in my twelve-step meetings: "If you don't want a haircut, stay out of the barber shop," but in this case, the barber shop seemed a safer option than just leaving myself alone in a room with a pair of scissors.

The lounge was dark and inviting, a great place to have an affair or a relapse; I was definitely tempting fate.

I sat at the bar and ordered a Diet Coke with a slice of lemon because I'm sophisticated. As the bartender scooped chunks of ice into my glass and sprayed soda from the gun, he introduced himself as John and started chatting with me until he was called away by other customers. The next time he came over, he placed a shot of something in front of me. "On the house," he said. "Welcome to New York." I stared at it for a second—a total movie moment. *Oh no! Will she drink the shot and ruin everything? Don't do it, Stefanie! You've worked so hard!*

"Thank you so much but . . . actually, I don't drink. I'm sober." I choked the unfamiliar words out, hating the way they sounded, the way they separated me. It felt like an overshare that would make a stranger uncomfortable, like announcing I had irritable bowel syndrome.

"Oh, that's great! Good for you!" John said, removing the shot glass in a lightning-fast swipe, like Tom Cruise in *Cocktail*. And then John told me that he had been thinking he needed to cut down because he'd been drinking too much. I'd apparently flipped a switch, because he spent the next hour telling me about how he worried about his mom too because she was an alcoholic and how alcoholism ran in his family and could be traced back many generations. We laughed and talked and he told me he was so glad he'd talked to me and I'd given him a lot to think about. By the time I left the bar to head back to my room, I almost laughed that I'd even contemplated drinking in the first place.

Elizabeth Vargas and I sat on tall chairs facing each other surrounded by lights and cameras in a hotel room set up just for these interviews. She listened to my story very intently, asking questions like she *really* wanted to hear the answers. I told her my bottom had been when I woke up on my couch fully dressed with a hangover so bad I had to go to the ER.

"Whoa, the ER?" Elizabeth asked, taken aback but clearly intrigued.

"Yeah, it was a really bad hangover."

I was open about everything *but* driving drunk. I told myself that I was leaving out the drunk-driving part in these interviews because it might cloud the issue; people wouldn't be able to relate. If I admitted to driving drunk with my kids on television, other women who had been struggling with their drinking might think, *Well, I'd never do that, so I must not have a problem.* Plus, it was highly personal! I shouldn't have to share everything! Anyway, my story was already embarrassing enough without me completely decimating my own character. So I shared freely about my feelings of loneliness and despair and how it had become obvious I just couldn't stop drinking, but I carefully steered around the darkest part and hoped no one would suspect something was missing.

Sitting there with Elizabeth, I actually felt loose and comfortable because she asked questions and soaked in the answers as if we were just two friends meeting at Starbucks for nonfat lattes and I happened to be telling her a particularly juicy story. At the time, I just figured she was extremely good at her job but I later found out that, yes, she *is* good at her job, she's an Emmy Award–winning journalist, but she was also a mother struggling with alcohol addiction. I'm not pulling a Belkin, by the way, and outing her. A couple of years after my interview, she publicly checked herself into rehab, discussed it on a very special episode of *20/20*, and then wrote a beautiful book about it called *Between Breaths: A Memoir of Panic and Addiction.*

After that show aired, the messages poured in from women admitting to struggling with their drinking. Any doubts I'd had about putting myself out there were quelled simply by knowing that women (and men) needed to see themselves in someone else in order to realize they might have an issue.

Around the time I admitted to having a problem, more and more of my contemporaries were having their own reckonings with alcohol, many coming out on their blogs or being quoted in online articles. Some of these were writers with "alcohol" playfully in the title of their sites and others were bloggers who earnestly talked about crafting or cooking and hadn't even mentioned drinking before they announced they were quitting. It was like a chain reaction. Just as we "bad mommy" bloggers and authors lined up like dominoes on bookshelves and the Internet, one by one we were beginning to topple. Articles were published challenging the culture of moms drinking, questioning the use of alcohol to combat the stress of motherhood, and suggesting that moms could use more support in finding balance.

On the other hand, moms continued to fight for their right to party while wearing their "Rosé All Day" T-shirts, and the industry continued to market products to them such as wine brands with names like MommyJuice or Mommy's Time Out.

When I was about four years sober, I was asked to appear on Katie Couric's new eponymous talk show, *Katie*, to discuss this very issue. At this time I was hosting my own talk show called *Parental Discretion with Stefanie Wilder-Taylor*, a PG-13 comedy show aimed at moms. The show aired late nights on Nick Jr. much to the chagrin of parents whose preschoolers fell asleep to cartoons and woke up to me using the word "vagina."

I hadn't done many appearances to discuss drinking since *20/20* because I was afraid of being pigeonholed as the "alcoholic mom." On the other hand, since I had an even bigger platform now with my TV show, it seemed like it might be the right thing to do to continue to share the message that regular moms could also struggle with their drinking. The network execs at Nickelodeon were fine with it, so I said yes.

About a week before I was going to tape the show, I had a long call with a producer who pre-interviewed me about my story: how I decided to quit drinking, what I thought of the whole mommy drinking culture . . . all the greatest hits. I was told I would be on with a woman who ran a Facebook page called Moms Who Need Wine, which I believe they thought would make strange bedfellows, possibly sparking a debate, but I was looking forward to telling my story while also defending her right to enjoy wine.

The night before I was to fly to New York, I got another call from the producer. "Hi, Stefanie. So someone from our team found a video of you reading a story on YouTube where you talked about driving drunk with your children."

Fuuuck.

About two years after I quit drinking, I'd written a piece for a live show called *Listen to Your Mother*. It was in front of a small audience and it wasn't being recorded as far as I knew; I certainly hadn't thought it would end up on YouTube! "Anyway, Katie would really like to ask you about it." I suddenly felt like I was in an X-ray machine and this producer could see straight through my opaque relatable story veneer to the broken shameful underbelly.

"I'd really rather not bring that up," I said. "It's not a part of the story I'm comfortable sharing."

"Oh, uh-huh, uh-huh, I toootally get that, but Katie is reeeeally interested." *I don't give a fuck if Katie is interested. How is that my problem?* I thought.

"Well, I'm really sorry. I'm just not prepared to discuss that part of my story on national television. Also, I host a show for moms—on a children's network—so it's not appropriate. I hope Katie can understand that."

"Can you think about it? I know Katie thinks it will be helpful to moms for you to share your *whole* story." So I thought about it for one second and came to the same conclusion, which was *fuck no*.

"I'm sorry, I know you're taping tomorrow but I don't want to do the show if that's going to be brought up." There was quiet on the line for a second and then she agreed that we didn't need to talk about it and Katie wouldn't ask.

I flew to New York the next day as planned.

I don't remember a lot of the taping itself. Except that when I was seated in a comfy chair on Katie's lovely set, relaxed and ready to give my personal commentary on the mommy-drinking trend, she set her steely eyes on me and said, "So. I know you drove drunk with your children in the car. Why would you do that?" I would have been less shocked if she'd slapped me. Now, I don't have a copy of this segment, and I've really tried to block it out, so I can't promise that's word-for-word the exchange but it's got to be close.

I really didn't know what to do, so I did the thing I was trained to do in recovery: I told the truth. It was the first time I'd told that part of the story on television. It felt a lot like being pushed off of a high dive when you aren't prepared. But the thing about unexpectedly falling is that once you hit the water, you have to swim, so I simply told her what had happened, how accidentally driving drunk was the turning point for me, the moment the light went on and I knew I could never drink again, and that I hadn't.

Now, do I think that Katie Couric blindsided me with this question because she was trying to help mothers everywhere like her producer said? Hell no. I think the way she seemed to cross-examine me and put me on the defensive was clearly meant to knock me off-balance and get a great TV moment. But here's the thing: Katie did me a favor; she ripped the Band-Aid off and exposed my wound to the air so it could finally heal.

19. Whac-A-Mole

I love sweets. I'd spent the last few decades being "on" or "off" sugar since I'd more or less recovered from my eating disorder in my early twenties, but when I could no longer rely on alcohol for relief, sugar was most definitely *on*. My reasoning was simple: You can't get pulled over for driving under the influence of chocolate, so if I had to do something to take the edge off, sugar was the lesser evil. My thought process seemed to be reinforced by the fact that twelve-step meetings serve donuts and cake; millions of addicts can't be wrong. So I allowed myself dessert every night as a treat and just considered it #selfcare.

Daily dessert slowly evolved into just allowing myself sugar throughout the day—a frozen yogurt with my kids in the afternoon, a mint from the bowl leaving a restaurant, some cupcake batter when helping with my daughter's school bake sale. And even when I found myself sitting in my car devouring a large box of Lemonheads like an eight-year-old, I rationalized; I gave myself a break; I tried not to worry about it.

This may come as a surprise, but I recommend this approach, because if you are really trying to quit drinking, the truth is that early sobriety can be brutal, and in the beginning, you have one job and it's to not drink. You have to do whatever it takes, and if that means eating Ho Hos every day for a while, do you. But if you're like me and food or sugar is one of your issues, eventually it will catch up with you.

Most true addicts aren't just addicted to one thing—we just happen to like one thing way more than others—so when we quit one addiction, often another one pops up in its place. In recovery, we refer to this as Whac-A-Mole syndrome, named for the arcade game where you hit a mole over the head with a mallet only to have three more pop up until pretty soon you're overwhelmed with moles and just need a drink to calm down! I was actually caught by surprise by a few new addictions that popped up for me to replace alcohol.

One night when I was a month or so sober, I discovered *Brick Breaker* on my BlackBerry. *Brick Breaker* is a game where you repetitively, hypnotically, smash bricks. Think of it as a precursor to *Candy Crush*. If you've ever lost an hour to playing *Candy Crush* nonstop, you kind of understand; if you've ever lost an entire weekend, we may have something in common.

I found the game by accident while lying on the floor in front of my daughter's crib, desperately scrolling around while she cried and refused to sleep.

I didn't know *Brick Breaker* would make my brain's reward center light up like a dog losing its mind over peanut butter, but I was also vulnerable. Without my usual pain relief like Xanax, wine, or Vicodin, listening to my daughter cry made me feel like I literally had no skin. But once I found *Brick Breaker*, magic happened. Not the same magic as drugs or alcohol—let's not get too excited—but it took the edge off slightly.

Unfortunately, when you light up the reward center in an addict's brain, you can't simply switch it off. I started having a Pavlovian response to late-night baby stress where I would immediately reach for my BlackBerry and lie in a tense trance, holding onto my sanity with each broken brick. And that would have been fine if *Brick Breaker* was just something I did, albeit compulsively, late at night when I desperately needed something to calm my brain instead of drinking. But that wasn't the case. Much like wine, *Brick Breaker* was habit-forming. First I would play it while waiting for an appointment or standing in a line, but eventually I was sitting staring at my BlackBerry, slack-jawed, breathing slowed, mind somewhere else for hours. This went on until my husband pushed me kicking and screaming into getting an iPhone. I didn't want to make the change, because I was scared to lose *Brick Breaker*. But the more I thought about it, I realized this might be a blessing in disguise—like *Brick Breaker* rehab.

When I got the iPhone, I avoided downloading any games, because now that I didn't have a BlackBerry, I was experiencing freedom, and I didn't want to sink back into a *Brick Breaker* hole again. Unfortunately, *Brick Breaker* was a gateway drug to games like *Bejeweled* or *Threes*. *Bejeweled* is basically *Candy Crush*'s third cousin—same basic idea, equally addictive. I would watch Jon play it sometimes when we were supposed to be watching a Netflix documentary together. I'd just sit there with no phone feeling judgy. "Can you put that down and pay attention to the show?" I'd ask him in a bitchy tone—because we've been married awhile—and he would put it down. Because he's not an addict.

But then one day I thought, *Let me just try this. I'm sure I'll be fine. It's been so long since I played* Brick Breaker, *I'm sure I can handle a game on my phone now. I'll just play it socially, like when Jon's playing his,* and then I let Jon teach me how to play it and I was immediately hooked.

I literally could not put it down, no matter how hard I tried. I played anytime I was lying in bed, I played to put myself to sleep, I played while watching TV, and I played while talking on the phone. Jon started getting irritated and he'd make comments. "You really play that constantly." "You have a problem." "Can you put your phone down for a little while at least?" I was pissed. That was rich! He was the one who turned me on to it. This was as if a heroin dealer got someone addicted to smack and when they want to do more being like, "You're doing too much heroin! It's annoying. Can you just not?"

But deep down it bothered me too. I tried to moderate, tried to cut down, but I couldn't. It felt beyond my control. Sometimes I would try to quit cold turkey by deleting the app from my phone completely. I would get a sudden burst of resolve and hold down the app icon for a few seconds until it started to blink, offering me the X, which I would will myself to press and boom, it would disappear. I would last for a day or sometimes a few days—once I lasted a few weeks—but sooner or later I would miss the feeling the games gave me, the shot of serotonin when I got a high score or moved up a level. I needed that feeling like I used to need wine.

Smartphone addiction in itself is no joke: Checking email became and still is an obsession. I don't drink now, so I can't get pulled over for drunk driving, but I could get a ticket for trying to delete a Bath & Body Works sale alert while I'm driving. I have tried to put the phone in the backseat, where I can't easily reach it, but I usually last only a minute or two until I reach around and grab for it, rationalizing that I need to plug it into the charger or pull up a murder podcast, and then I quickly scan for a new email or text. Why can't it wait until I get to the grocery store, which is five minutes away? What will change if I don't see a message *right this second*? If you're a psychiatrist and you're reading this and can help explain it to me, email me! I promise I'll get back to you immediately!

I hit a bottom with *Threes* not that long ago when I found myself playing it at a stoplight. I realized that was just as dangerous as drinking and also illegal, so I deleted the app from my phone once more. I'm sure it will be back.

The sugar thing is much harder. After letting myself eat all that sugar in the first few months, things got dark. The first Halloween after I'd gotten sober was when I hit my lowest point. That holiday was always challenging for me once I had kids. There was a sweet spot between the time I was too old to go trick-or-treating and when I bought a house and moved to the Valley. During those years, Halloween didn't affect me directly; I was aware it was happening because the grocery store aisles were littered with massive bags of candy and spooky decor, but since I lived in an apartment I never needed to buy anything. But once I had a house in the burbs, things took a turn.

Our neighborhood, in particular, is a popular one for trick-or-treaters, and I wanted to be a house with good candy—not full-sized candy bars, we aren't the Kardashians—but also not Dum-Dums or Smarties. I wanted to be the Hershey's family with the mini Reese's, Almond Joys, and Kit Kats. I'd always buy way too much because I didn't want to run out and have to face a little vampire or Sponge-Bob empty-handed or, worse, have to turn out our porch light like a Halloween Scrooge.

When I wasn't in an "off-again" period with sugar, I'd always let myself have what I wanted on Halloween as a way to make up for feeling so ashamed as a kid that I was insatiable when it came to candy consumption.

But now that I was sober and candy was one of the few vices I had left, the slippery slope landed me right at the very bottom. It started slowly enough: I ate a few of the mini candy bars we'd set out in a novelty bowl featuring a giant hand that grabs at you when you reach in to take a piece. I was just getting in the spirit, I told myself. I cracked open my first mini Snickers the way I would pop open a bottle of wine at the end of the day, and then ate a few more while helping my almost-two-year-olds into their costumes. With my twins dressed—one in that old puffy bumblebee outfit, the other as Giants running back Tiki Barber, and my almost-five-year-old as Ariel for the third year running—we were ready to hit the road. I shoved two mini Krackles in my mouth, and as we walked out the front door I reached back for two more. It felt like scratching a chocolate itch. But I was really, really itchy, and the scratching only made it worse.

As we walked from house to house, I kept dipping into the twins' stash despite their protestations of "No, Mommy! That's mine!" It was dark but I wasn't picky, so I ate whatever I fished out. Those Sixlet chocolate balls were so tiny that I needed to combine them with something more substantial. And what the hell was up with those little boxes of Milk Duds? How are three Milk Duds supposed to do the job? I'm not saying we need to hand out movie theater–sized Milk Duds but there has to be a middle ground between the big box and one the size of my thumb.

My kids were young and had small legs and lacked stamina, so after going around one large block, they were tired and ready to come home. But I wasn't. I forced them to go to "just a few more houses!" I mean, come on, free candy! I was already feeling that irritable, speedy, slightly nauseous feeling that comes from bingeing sugar, but I couldn't stop, I was on a bender.

For the next few days I just kept eating the candy because it was in the house and there was so much of it, no one would notice if a lot of it were to go missing. A mini Snickers after breakfast, five frozen Milky Way bars for lunch. I tried to tell myself I was doing my children a favor: Too much sugar was obviously bad for them. It would be ridiculous to give barely two-year-olds any more candy than what they had eaten on Halloween. I *had* to eat it. It's called good parenting.

Two days later I found myself lying on the couch with a plastic treat bag sitting on my stomach, rifling through the dregs of the stash—all that was left were empty wrappers, mini boxes of Nerds, a few random vanilla-flavored Tootsie Rolls, and for some reason a few pennies covered in Sour Patch sugar. I was already bloated and sick to my stomach, but I was in a trance that couldn't be broken and I needed more.

I knew there was still some leftover candy in the cupboard from what we'd put out for the trick-or-treaters. Sure enough, there was chocolate. I could eat it. Or I could throw it away. *I* should *throw it away*, I thought. But if I threw it away, even in the outside trash bin, I could change my mind and go get it. It's not like the candy would cease to exist; it just would have changed locations. But it would still be protected by a wrapper. I didn't trust myself; I could and, let's face it, probably *would* go back and rescue it. If you're disgusted right now, I fully understand. If you're like, "Yeah, I get that," then hello, friend!

I knew if I didn't want to make myself any sicker I would have to destroy the rest of the candy—so I dumped it all in the sink and ran water over it until it was inedible, and then I took the soggy mess out to the trash. And then I called my sponsor.

"I don't feel sober," I told her. I was crying, feeling like a failure. I figured she would just tell me to go for a walk or read self-help books or some other bullshit advice that wouldn't be helpful to me, but she didn't. She listened and related.

"I get it. It's normal. Who can blame you? You don't have your coping mechanism anymore. Your brain is trying to protect you from feeling sadness, anger, or even boredom. You're simply looking for other ways to feel better." For some reason, this made me cry harder. I was just so sad. It felt like it was always going to be something. On the other hand, a good cry was a relief, and I didn't feel quite so desperate or alone.

I have to always be hypervigilant about compulsions. I wish I could be addicted to things with some value, like reading books or bathroom remodeling or running marathons.

By the way, there really are some healthy addictions out there, and running I hear is one of them. I've known lots of ex-addicts who traded an addiction to drinking or meth to an addiction to running actual marathons, which then led to an addiction to constantly talking about running marathons. Some people who are really into running claim that they get an actual runner's high. I'm not quite so sure about the runner's high thing, though. Either these people have never actually been high on drugs or I'm doing it wrong. I went through a short period years ago where I decided I'd jog for exercise because I couldn't afford the gym. I got up to three miles and at one point almost made it to four, and I never felt anything but an intense desire to stop jogging immediately.

But any kind of exercise can absolutely help reduce compulsive behavior. It makes sense because it's rooted in science. Exercise releases dopamine, stimulates neuroplasticity, and gives you a sense of well-being. Kind of like drugs!

So if you remove the alcohol and find that another *unhealthy* addiction crops up in its place, like cigarettes, cannabis, food, gambling, shopping, excessive phone use, porn, or Twizzlers, you're not alone.

Sugar is an ongoing battle for me. I have gone years in an "off" mode. I tell my kids I'm on a "sugar break," so it's clear it's about my addiction rather than an unhealthy obsession with my weight. But sometimes I lose my sweebriety and I'm off to the races for a while until things get bad enough for me to quit again.

My sobriety means no mind-altering substances, but I try to be gentle with myself with the rest. The point is, if the sugar makes my life unmanageable, I know there is help out there and I'm not afraid to reach out. But for now, I'm off to check my email. Who am I kidding? I already checked it four times while writing this paragraph.

20. Tools of the Trade

Most of us drink to have fun, to feel good, or to ease anxiety, but the truth is that alcohol is a depressant, so there's a rebound effect after we drink that causes us to feel irritable and low. When I would stop drinking for a while or cut down quite a bit, I would feel better. The problem is that although I was feeling better, it was easy to forget *why* I was feeling better. This seems pretty universal—our brains are not always in touch with our bodies unless we're super into yoga, meditation, and mindfulness. But even then, I imagine when we're not at a two-thousand-dollar retreat listening to our breathing all day, we may lose the connection between not drinking and feeling better, and then seemingly out of nowhere, we may be struck with the idea that this whole not-drinking thing is ridiculous, that drinking is in fact just the thing we need to get back to doing. This is normal and it happens to everyone. No one likes change. Our minds and bodies will fight hard for the status quo, even if the status quo is trying to kill us. When I quit drinking, my whole outlook had to change in order for it to stick—but how to change your outlook? Here are some things that worked for me:

Finding my part: I needed to understand why I drank and how I personally contributed to my need to drink. It was easy to look at factors outside myself: my childhood, my natural tendency to anxiety, and the stress of parenting small children. But I'd had plenty of therapy to talk about my childhood and still drank; I'd taken loads of Xanax and still drank; I'd had the means to hire help with my children and, yeah, I still drank. What I needed to do was confront how my own behavior and my sometimes-warped perceptions of situations exacerbated my need to drain a box of wine. In other words, I needed to see my part.

Note: Don't get me wrong about therapy. Therapy can be lifesaving when it comes to dealing with a lot of things that might be holding you back. Therapists have been invaluable in my life and my kids' lives. But let's face it, therapists can be very nurturing and on your side, and sometimes what I actually needed is someone to tell me the truth. In order to live a better, more honest life, I needed someone to cut through my bullshit and be real with me.

For instance: I did a lot of volunteering at my kids' elementary school. I chaperoned field trips to old-timey museums, chaired fund-raising committees, and took on the job of doing outreach to make sure that everyone in the community knew about our little school. And I'd complain about it a lot. I was overextended! I was tired! What was up with all the people who didn't help? One time I showed up to the campus to help with Teacher Appreciation Day. All the kids were asked to bring in a flower for their teachers and I was tasked with helping assemble the mass of flowers into individual vases. There were a lot of us volunteering that day, and one particularly controlling mom had extremely specific ideas of how the flowers should be arranged.

Now, I'm no florist, but I don't think making simple arrangements has the difficulty level of, say, separating conjoined twins, right? Well, apparently I did it wrong, because the controlling mom snapped at me when I cut the stem on a flower to match the others in the vase I was working on. "No, no, no! It's supposed to stick out above the rest!

Now this arrangement is ruined." Jesus, lady. Relax! How dare she freak out like that when I took time out of my busy day to be here, putting in hours to support our school! Why? Because I appreciated the fuck out of those teachers, that's why! Where was my appreciation for appreciating? I didn't say anything, but I quietly seethed the rest of the day, plotting her demise.

That night I vented to my sponsor about it, complaining about how much I do for the school. "Why do you volunteer so much?" she asked, point-blank. What a bizarre question. She was also a mom; I knew she had to understand where I was coming from. I had kind of thought I was preaching to the choir here.

"People need to show up to help out with this stuff or it won't get done."

"Yes, but why you specifically?"

"Um, because it's the right thing to do!" I wasn't sure what she was getting at.

"So you like to be seen as doing the right thing? Sounds like your ego is involved." This was patently false. Me? Have a big ego? Wrong! I was being selfless! I was an amazing, selfless, helpful person who had been mistreated!

"I don't think so."

"But when you weren't seen as doing the right thing, you got angry and felt judged. Why would it matter, if the goal is just the greater good of the school?"

Well, hell; she had a point. Who cared if that mom didn't think I arranged flowers correctly? The point was that all the teachers got arrangements and felt appreciated. Why did I need kudos for showing up and doing what needed to be done? And when I really thought about it, it's possible that mom also really cared about the teachers feeling appreciated and she just wasn't managing her own anxiety well. Maybe it wasn't about me.

It was kind of freeing to be able to just let it go; I wasn't used to that. I was used to carrying around resentments for days, building a case against offenders in my mind, telling eighty people about it, and then feeling surprised that I need so much chardonnay later to un-wind from all I had to endure.

This type of "checking in with my motives" has had to become a daily practice, because left to my own devices, I am quick to blame others. It's just easier.

Taking the focus off of me: Another thing that helps me not focus on me and how unfair people are to me—and, while we're at it, how unfair *life* is to me—is to try and focus on other people and what *they* need.

When I had kids, part of the shock was that I suddenly had other humans whose needs had to come before my own. But once I got used to the job of cooking, cleaning, feeding, driving, comforting, reading stories, and making holiday magic, I found that I could once again work self-obsession back into my schedule. In recovery, I found it was helpful to me to help others, even when I didn't feel like it. When a friend calls to vent, I welcome the opportunity to get out of my own head. When someone emails me to ask about quitting drinking, I relish the chance to write them three paragraphs about how getting sober changed my life and to ask how I can help. I'm not kidding. Message me on Facebook and test it out!

Some people are naturally good listeners, and I love those people, because I love to be listened to! Unfortunately, simply sitting quietly and listening to someone doesn't come as easily for me. I either want to jump in and share my own experience—which, in my defense, comes from wanting to relate but can come off as self-centered—or I want to jump in and give advice and suggestions for how they can live their lives better according to me. I have to work hard not to do this. Sometimes when I'm arguing with Jon he will literally say, "Let me talk!" I used to get so defensive, snapping back, "I am letting you talk! You're talking! So talk!" But somehow that didn't endear me to him the way you'd think.

I've gotten better at just shutting my mouth, trying not to look irritated, and letting him continue talking even if I'm sure he's completely wrong. Sometimes a magical thing happens where I'm actually able to empathize with his point of view and shock myself by realizing he's right.

Thinking through the drink: Even if you are getting out of your own head, seeking support, seeing your therapist, reading the entire self-help section at Barnes & Noble, being painfully honest with yourself, meditating, connecting with your spirituality, going on wellness retreats, and slathering yourself with essential oils, sometimes you're just going to want a drink. That's normal, and it doesn't mean you're doing anything wrong.

Even after many years of living an alcohol-free existence, sometimes I find myself wanting a drink seemingly out of nowhere. One night I was at a Buca di Beppo eating dinner with the family. As usual, the place was a cacophony of restaurant noise: babies crying, servers clapping out happy-birthday songs, and the clatter of busboys turning tables over for the next customers. I tried to stay present in spite of the overstimulating environment—and I honestly felt fine nursing a Diet Coke while my husband drank his Peroni beer—until a waiter walked by with a tray full of gorgeous drinks and stopped at the table next to us. I couldn't take my eyes off of that tray, and one sexy drink in particular: an espresso martini. It was as if the overhead lights dimmed and a spotlight showcased the glass like a prize on a game show. I could make out the layers of vodka, dark coffee liqueur, and espresso topped with three adorable little brown coffee beans. It looked like heaven.

And that's when the fantasizing started: What if that drink was for me? Wouldn't it make this dinner so much more enjoyable? I'd be less annoyed at the noise! What would it feel like to just have a tiny buzz after all this time? I could taste it, the sweetness of the liqueur, the bite of vodka that would leave a pleasant burning sensation as it went down. I was triggered, romanticizing drinking. My God, it had been so long since I'd had a drink; was it possible I could have just one?

That's when I employed a tool I learned in recovery called "Think Through the Drink." Using this tool, you follow what would happen if you had a drink, ate that donut, played that hand of blackjack, took that Xanax, through to its inevitable conclusion. For me, it probably wouldn't go the way you might imagine. If I had one espresso martini, I don't think I'd end up having five more, fighting with the waiter, and then commandeering the car keys from my husband, driving the whole lot of us home in a blackout. No, it wouldn't be that dramatic— at least not at first. Here's a more likely scenario: I'd order the drink and really love the feeling, especially after not having had one in so long. Immediately, I'd think about having another one. If one drink makes me feel more relaxed, makes the noise slightly less oppressive, two will feel that much better, right? But I'll stop at one just to prove I can. The next day I'll think, *Well, I managed to have one simple drink last night at dinner, so why not experiment with having one glass of wine at home? And since I'm just hanging out at home, not driving anywhere, why not have two?*

Soon I'd be back to having a couple of glasses of wine every night, and that would go on for a while until one weekend I'd go to sushi and order a large sake and a large Sapporo *all to myself*, because *that's how I roll*! Knowing me, I'd probably insist on going out for another drink or four after dinner, *because now that I'm drinking again, I might as well! We never go out! Let's live a little!* The next morning, I'd wake up with a crushing hangover, not remembering whether or not I paid the sitter or if I whispered good night to my children, who—before that espresso martini—had only known me as a sober, present mom, and I'd be full of regret. So I skipped the martini and tried my best to ignore the noise. By the next day, the craving had totally passed and I was grateful I hadn't caved.

Pausing: Years ago, a batshit mom of another child at my kids' elementary school had the audacity to yell at my fourth grader in front of a bunch of other children for the crime of not saying hello to her kid loud enough for her to hear. My daughter came home crying and told me what had happened and I promptly lost my shit. This was the final straw in a whole fucking bale that had been building since the kids were in kindergarten, and I was seriously done. Every year it was something with this lady—from getting eighty-sixed from field trips for stopping at 7-Eleven to buy herself a Big Gulp and gum while leaving all the kids in the car, to spying in the classroom and reporting all the kids' reading levels to the other moms, to calling other parents and making out-of-pocket comments accusing their kids of being mean. We didn't like each other and had exchanged words over the years, but this time, she'd crossed the line! You don't come for other people's kids! She was a mom bully and I'd had an ass-full of her antics.

So I sat down at my computer and hastily shot off an email missive exposing this woman's crimes that would rival Erin Brockovich exposing PG&E for contaminating groundwater. I sent it to the mom but to really make my point I cc'd the new principal of our school. I didn't bcc, I *cc'd*: I wanted that bitch to know that everyone would now be fully aware of what kind of person she was. And then I sat back in my chair reveling in the self-satisfaction of a job well done.

A while later, I hadn't heard anything back.

Yes, it was after hours, and obviously the principal might be, I don't know, having dinner with her family or something, but still. As the time ticked by with no response from either of them, I started to get a little worried. *What if the principal thinks I'm the crazy one?* Then I went back and reread my email. It sounded a little manic if you didn't know the backstory. Our principal had only been hired the month before, so she hadn't had a chance to experience that mom's insanity in order to compare it to my track record of being an involved mom who was a big-time volunteer! Now that I had a moment to think about it, maybe I didn't want my introduction to the new principal to be me sending an unhinged email complaining about a petty mom beef. What did I even expect her to do with this info? You can't exactly expel a mom, although that would be amazing. The more I stewed about it, the more I wished I hadn't been so hasty. I wished I'd paused, like I was trained to do in recovery, but I'm a slow learner.

By nature, I'm an emotionally reactive person who is always pretty sure I'm right—at least at first. But on those rare occasions I find out I *wasn't* right after all, I usually come to that conclusion after damage has been done.

Jumping in with my first thought never works out well for me. And the email to the head of my kids' elementary school was no exception. My husband and I were called into a meeting to get to the bottom of the issue, and although the principal was polite and took our concerns seriously, nothing happened to the other mom. In fact she probably felt empowered by getting away with her crimes, and she went on to torture me for another few years until we mercifully switched schools entirely.

By simply taking a beat and running stuff by a trusted friend, you can avoid a lot of situations like this!

Nowadays, I employ the pause as often as I can. I still write angry emails, but I leave them in drafts until a sane person has looked them over. If I am upset by a text, I don't text back immediately. Also, here's where I'm going to go against a lot of standard marriage/relationship advice: Sometimes I go to bed angry, and I think it's okay! Better than okay! Optimal! For me, if I can find a way to not say everything I need to say when I need to say it, it's a sign of growth. It takes strength to walk away mid-argument to pause and reconsider whether I am actually this fired up over my husband's ridiculous desire to paint a bright orange pop-wall in our bedroom or if something else is making me edgy. And no, I was *not* about to get my period. I have not been "about to get" my period in seven years.

Pausing is also helpful when it comes to eating cookies and purchasing everything in my Amazon cart. So if you've quit drinking or are thinking about cutting down, the pause is your new best friend.

Gratitude: I have a lot of privilege. Not only do I have a home to live in, work I love, healthy kids, a supportive husband, and the ability to buy a new pair of shoes should I choose, I also have a lack of obstacles that many other people face. Given this, you'd think it would be virtually impossible for me to bitch about my life. Oh, but have you met me? I'm always up for the challenge. No matter how many things I've watched or read to inspire gratitude—*It's a Wonderful Life*, *Oprah*, everything on the Hallmark Channel—feeling thankful isn't second nature. My default is to feel at least a little bit sorry for myself for whatever isn't working out in the moment, be it a crowded mall parking lot or having to spend two hours on hold with Blue Shield only to get disconnected *again*.

I don't think I'm alone in this, otherwise we wouldn't have to have Thanksgiving or even Teacher Appreciation Day. We all need to be reminded of the gifts we have in our lives. My kids don't sit around thinking about what a great mom I am 365 days a year. That's why we have Mother's Day. Obviously they should take a moment each and every day to really think about how good they have it compared to their friends whose moms do things like set boundaries and refuse to order takeout every night, but for whatever reason, they don't.

Taking time every day to list the things I am grateful for has been a real help for me to not get into the mindset that my life is so very hard and everything is a struggle and, fuck it, wouldn't it be better to just have a glass of wine? So although my lists aren't always earth-shattering, they do remind me that things are pretty much okay. For example, today my list reads:

The existence of coffee
I have food and shelter
My husband still makes me laugh
My sobriety
My dog Penelope's stupid cute face
I don't have a boss
I have health insurance
Living in California
Kenny Loggins
There are clean sheets on my bed

Now if your list looks anything like mine—especially the Kenny Loggins part—that would be so weird. Seriously, we need to be friends! Call me immediately! Obviously, when there isn't anything terrible going on in your life, gratitude is easier to come by. Sometimes we go through awful things: health issues, relapse, job loss, breakups, or losing loved ones. Sometimes we just feel like shit for no real reason. It's during those times that I try to lean even harder into what has been proven to help me, even if it doesn't feel like it's doing any good, even if it seems like it's making it worse. It's during times like that I just have to simply ask myself, "Would a drink actually make any of this better?" We both know it wouldn't.

21. Sorry About Your Bachelorette Party

If I wanted my sobriety to stick, I knew I would have to sort through my baggage, mining my past for mistakes I'd made and then attempt to make them right. For some people this might mean apologizing to an ex-business partner for sinking the company due to their cocaine addiction, or perhaps, even tougher, apologizing to their child for being drunk at their school play—embarrassing them by being a one-woman standing ovation for the entire show. I didn't think I had any real biggies like that, but there had been this one little incident that had been nagging at me, so I figured I would start with this low-stakes apology.

"Is this about my bachelorette party?" my friend Cynthia said pretty much right after she answered the phone. *Wow*. Seeing as how I'd only emailed with her sporadically over the past few years, I'd expected we would exchange a few pleasantries first, maybe a "How are you? How are the kids?" I was completely unprepared for an immediate callout. I mean, yes, it was in fact about her bachelorette party but I hadn't thought that would be the first thing she thought of—not even in her top ten! I was momentarily stunned into silence.

My friend Cynthia had quit drinking about six months after I did and had recently messaged me about it on Facebook. We'd been friends in our twenties, having met doing stand-up, but had pretty much lost touch. In contacting her I'd hoped to kill two birds with one stone, so to speak: catch up with an old friend and get practice making amends before going on a major apology tour—sort of a repentance dress rehearsal—so her response caught me off guard.

"Um, actually yeah. How did you know?" I asked, finally.

"I just figured you'd apologize eventually. I was very hurt for a long time." Okay, this actually stung. I hadn't even thought she remembered, let alone held a grudge about it. I mean, it had happened like eight or nine years ago and wasn't a huge deal. This was supposed to be an easy one! I'd figured since Cynthia was newly sober herself she'd cut me some slack, say something like, "What? I don't even remember that! Don't be crazy! You're too hard on yourself. We were all drinking too much in those days."

What happened didn't seem that bad: Cynthia was getting married, and since I was one of her close friends, I was asked to throw the bachelorette party along with her other close friend, Justine. I really wasn't much of a planner in those days—or these days—but in those days even less. In fact, I was irritated to be given so much responsibility when I had a lot going on in my life: I was carrying on a flirtation with a married man at my job, for one, and it had been taking up a lot of my mental space. Despite my well-documented fear of intimacy, and my attraction to unattainable men, I had never so much as considered dating a married guy, but Tom was love bombing me before loving bombing was an officially recognized way to fuck with someone's head. And, at thirty years old, I was petrified I would never be a person someone could love with the kind of intensity I heard in songs and saw in movies—so despite the fact that he had a bit of a pill problem and a bit of a wife problem, I decided not to let that cloud the love story that was unfolding. After all, he'd already told his wife it was over and he was moving out any minute.

So when Justine and I planned a Vegas getaway for Cynthia and Tom said he wanted to fly in and meet us, I figured, *Why not?* And even though I knew that Cynthia would hate it and I knew it was wrong, I didn't care. I preemptively blamed Cynthia for being self-ish. *Why does anyone need a bachelorette party anyway? You're getting married, you have someone! Why do you need to celebrate your last days being single? I'm single every day and it sucks, trust me on this! Why can't I have some fun too?* Plus, Cynthia was being boring. She didn't want to go to see male strippers or play craps; she just wanted to hang with her two best friends and have dinner. I wanted excitement, I wanted to be with Tom—and this was my opportunity.

Tom "surprised" us at the VooDoo Steakhouse in the Rio Hotel, where Justine and I had taken the bride-to-be. When he found us at our table he was already drunk. He'd probably been drinking since the plane. I introduced him to the girls and told them Tom just happened to be in town for business and wanted to stop by. Justine and Cynthia exchanged a "this is bullshit" look, which Tom didn't notice but I did. *Screw it*, I thought. When would I have a real chance to be alone with this guy to see if this could work between us? I needed to know if this was what I wanted, even if the only way to do that was for him to crash Cynthia's bachelorette party.

The three of us already had full cocktails, but Tom flagged down a passing waiter, not our waiter, for more. "We're going to need another round of drinks! Keep 'em coming!" And then he hijacked the night like a boozy terrorist, regaling us with stories about himself at a volume that attracted unwanted attention. When the bill came, Tom grabbed it, then stared straight at Cynthia and winked. "I got this. Good luck."

The next morning, I skulked back from Tom's room into the hotel room I was supposed to be sharing with Cynthia and Justine. They didn't seem happy to see me; in fact, I received a downright icy reception, which was pretty ungrateful if you think about it. It wasn't like I had brought Tom back to our room! I had stayed with him, leaving them to enjoy the room all to themselves. Hello! But also, Tom picked up the check! Why weren't they more appreciative? A thank-you might have been in order—instead I was getting dirty looks.

Somewhere, just beneath the surface of my bravado, I knew that hooking up with Tom hadn't been the right thing to do. Deep down in the pit of my stomach I felt shame—not just about leaving my friends for the night, but for seeing Tom, a married guy, in the first place. But I'd felt desperate and obsessed, and being drunk helped me to rationalize doing what I wanted. Drunk me didn't just act beneath my moral compass—drunk me took my moral compass, tossed it out the car window, drove over it, and then put the car in reverse and drove over it again just to make sure it was destroyed.

Now, sitting on the phone with Cynthia, I had to hear how my behavior had hurt her; I had to listen to how my actions had affected someone else and not argue or defend myself.

"It really ruined what I thought was going to be a special weekend. You made it about you. I kept waiting for you to say something about it but you never did." She was right. I never did because I was self-righteous and defensive. I thought if I acknowledged that I'd done something wrong, even to myself, it would be like pulling bricks from the delicately constructed foundation of my self-image.

"I'm really and truly sorry. There's no excuse for my actions," I said. "I was a shitty friend." And I meant it. I had selfishly put my own needs first and subsequently ruined her experience.

"It's okay. Thank you for apologizing."

The act of facing my shortcomings was profoundly uncomfortable and freeing at the same time. I wasn't perfect. But I hadn't died from admitting it. I knew that my defensiveness had been a survival tool when I was younger. Growing up with chronically angry parents and a stepfather who often gave me the silent treatment for months at a time, I'd had two choices, as I saw it: Get smaller and quieter, going along to get along, or say, "Fuck this," and fight, grow a thicker skin, and pretend nothing got to me. It was a survival skill that I'd been using for a long time. I wore my "fuck this" attitude like a winter parka, insulating myself from the negative elements of my childhood. But even after I'd moved out on my own and no longer needed the protection, I found I couldn't take it off; it had become a part of me.

But now, with the help of my sober friends and my sponsor, I was able to switch it out for a windbreaker . . . and then just a fuzzy sweater . . . and eventually a tube top. I was still sarcastic and cynical, but I was slowly able to look at my faults and take a little criticism without completely falling apart.

Once I got that apology out of the way, I felt like a weight had been lifted. This was a nice, altogether unfamiliar feeling, and I wanted more of it. And just like that, I was suddenly gung-ho to apologize to everyone from my past. I apologized to a high school friend from whom I'd borrowed seventy-five dollars I'd never paid back—she had zero recollection of the loan and only a vague recollection of me, but it didn't matter, because *I* did, and it had been bugging me for years.

Putting that check in the mail to her felt amazing! Better than amazing! Next, I apologized to a friend I'd cut off for an entire year a few years back. We'd since made up and hadn't mentioned our fallout, but I'd never told her that I was sorry for abandoning her when she was going through a tough time. Again, it felt great!

My sponsor talked me out of Facebook messaging an apology to a guy I'd dated for about six weeks, many years before. He'd told me he was falling in love with me after only a week of dating but almost immediately afterward he'd started getting distant, often telling me he was tired or under the weather when we were supposed to have plans. He'd already invited me to go camping with a bunch of his friends before he'd clearly decided he was over me, so, even though he tried to back out of it, I pretended everything was fine, insisted on going anyway, got super drunk, and apparently yelled at him and broke it off, desperate to become the breaker-upper before I could become the breaker-uppee. The next day I remembered none of it until he told me. He was married now with a kid but, whatever! I was ready to own my behavior!

"Let that one go," my sponsor said. "The best way of apologizing is for him to never have to hear from you again." Oh. I see. Okay. Cool, cool.

The more challenging apologies were when I didn't think I was wrong.

Sometimes I really didn't want to do it. Years ago I got a call from a mom at my kids' school—let's call her "Rumor," and no, it's not Rumer Willis, it's a made-up name. Now, Rumor was pretty gossipy, and even after quitting drinking and becoming a better person I was usually still up for some gossip. But this was darker than the normal stuff. She was implying that a mom we both knew had cheated on her husband and that her new baby wasn't her husband's child. "I don't know it for a *fact* but I'm about ninety-nine percent sure," Rumor said, sounding almost gleeful.

"But how do you know?"

"Okay, you can't tell anyone that I'm telling you this, because I don't want it coming back on me, but I saw her arguing with her husband last weekend at the fundraising gala. It looked like they were gesturing at Emily, and come on, Emily *definitely* doesn't look like her dad. I just put two and two together."

"So you're assuming Emily isn't his kid—because you saw them *arguing*?"

"It was the *way* they were fighting. I swear. It was obvious. I felt it."

"I think that's a pretty nasty rumor to spread over a *feeling*," I spat out. All of a sudden I was beyond pissed.

"I'm not spreading a rumor. I've basically said it to you and one other person who happens to agree with me!" Now I was furious.

"This is so fucked up!" I was yelling now. "What kind of shit do you say behind *my* back?" And then, before I could say anything I'd *really* regret, I hung up on her ass. Standing up to her felt so satisfying. I was definitely the better person, and she needed to be put on blast for being so horrible. The *only* hitch in my giddy-up was that our kids were good friends and I would have to deal with this bitch for years to come. But *fuck* her! Who gives a shit? I'd just ignore her! On the *other* hand, that was a long time to have to keep up being this mad. Oh well. I was up for the challenge.

I waited a day and then I decided to call my recovery friend, Shayna, and explain what had happened. She had bad news for me:

"I agree she sucks, but it sounds like you didn't behave much better. I hear a lot of self-righteous anger." Ugh. She wasn't wrong.

I just didn't like to hear it. This was still my pattern: fight or flight. Shut people out before they could shut me out. But it was confusing, because she had acted badly too!

"Do I have to apologize?" I had a sneaking suspicion I did.

"For your part. Send her a text and tell her you're sorry for how *you* behaved, that *you* overreacted, and then, from now on, refrain from engaging in gossip with her."

I sent the text and shortly after got this response: "Thanks for your apology. You were way out of line but it's all good." For a split second I was pissed again. What about what *she* did? Could she not see that it was wrong to spread vicious rumors about her friend and her friend's *child*? But then, miraculously, I had an epiphany: *Who cares?* It was over. I didn't have to carry around any ill will; my conscience was clear. I felt lighter, freer, and calmer—as if I'd taken half a Xanny! This apologizing was some good shit.

But the apology that really set me free was to my father, even though he was dead.

My relationship with Stanley had remained rocky since those early days in Los Angeles. I had a long list of grievances: He'd refused to pay child support, he spent his life addicted to pills, he'd used me to take him to the hospital under false pretenses to get more drugs, he stole from people, he'd *chosen* to not be in my life for the majority of my upbringing, he had only been interested in me once I was an adult and could lend him money or help him out in some way. Despite this, I'd tried time and time again to have some sort of relationship with him, possibly out of guilt, longing, love; I didn't know.

Years before he died, I'd made a last-ditch attempt to dig him out of his latest mess by getting him out of the apartment from which he was being evicted and into a pretty sweet assisted-living facility.

I'd gone to see quite a few old folks homes that were nightmare scenarios but had finally found a unicorn: This place served crab cakes for lunch, had 24/7 snack access, and, best of all, the manager agreed to let him pay only his SSI, which was about $840 a month—to be honest, I would've lived there myself.

Within the first week, he smuggled in prohibited appliances and argued with other residents; then, at the end of the first month, he refused to hand over his rent and was subsequently kicked out. All my months of hard work wasted. So yes, I was angry with him. The way I saw it, I'd had good reason to stay this way.

I hadn't spoken to him in over six years and I was less than three months away from delivering my twins when I got a call that he had been transferred from the county-run nursing home, where he'd ended up living, to the ER. At some point during the twenty minutes I spent deciding whether or not I'd go see him, he died. I honestly wasn't sure how to feel.

Despite the fact that he'd been married four times and had children from all four marriages, it was somehow left to me to manage the details of his death. After doing a little research, it seemed the simplest thing was to have him cremated. But now his ashes had been stored in a large nondescript box in my closet for the past few years because I wasn't sure what to do with him. I'd never gotten closure with my father while he was still alive—but I needed it now, and I knew an apology was my ticket to freedom.

In my estimation, I didn't have much to apologize for, clearly. I was the wronged party pretty much my whole life, wasn't I? Anyone could see that. Could there have been some way I'd contributed to my own misery? I doubted it but I decided that I would write him a letter and see if anything came up. Turns out there was maybe something, maybe even a few things that fell on my side of the ledger: Since my father had been semi-famous when I was young, I took pride in being his daughter. When I didn't feel like I belonged with my mother and stepfather, I imagined I belonged with Stan. I'd built a fantasy of moving to Los Angeles and reuniting with a loving dad, but hadn't included him—the real him—in any of my scenarios. This was an incredibly unrealistic expectation. And yet, when the truth didn't turn out how I'd imagined, I'd been angry. Was that entirely his fault? Could I assume any portion, even a small one, of the blame?

Hadn't I enjoyed invoking his name with teachers and other adults of his era when I was younger? And hadn't I continued to do that with older comedians I admired whenever his name came up in a conversation about comedy? "Oh, that's my dad," I'd say, not finding it necessary to elaborate that we didn't have much of a relationship.

My father was angry and bitter at the business, at old friends, at the world at large, and he never felt that his life turned out the way it should've, the way he deserved. He saw himself as underappreciated, and was quick to place blame on old managers who refused to pay him enough, comedians he claimed stole his bits, everyone but himself.

I found it nearly impossible to find empathy for him while he was still alive but, in death, could I appreciate that he'd done his best? Hadn't he done exactly what he was capable of doing? He'd made so many mistakes, but he hadn't made those mistakes *at* me. He'd made them in spite of me. He couldn't be a parent, not a real parent. But I could. I was capable of making better choices.

I had felt so pressured by him for attention and financial support. It had, at times, felt overwhelming, like a weighted blanket, suffocating me. But by not contacting me in the years before he died, hadn't he let me go? Could I have chosen to be less angry with him, given his limited ability to love me? Could I have set him free? Maybe I couldn't do it then, but I could do it now. I owed it to him.

And so, I took my letter and his ashes down to Malibu beach— Malibu, where he'd lived in his rental house at the height of his fame, when his world was bright with goals achieved but also possibility, the time before his popularity cooled and he'd soured.

Little-known fact—or possibly well-known fact that I was un- aware of: You aren't allowed to just go ahead and spread someone's ashes willy-nilly around a beach. It sounds romantic and we've seen it in a lot of movies—a whole family takes Dad's ashes to the coast of Ireland because he loved it there as a boy and everyone cries and sings a dirge while paying tribute to a life well lived. Maybe it's legal in Ireland, but in California, if you want to scatter ashes on public or private property, you're supposed to have written permission from the property owner, and if you want to spread ashes in the ocean, you need to be at least three nautical miles from shore.

So . . . I was going to have to be sneaky.

I drove to Malibu at dusk with the cardboard box holding my dad's cremains in my trunk, secured between my roadside assistance kit and a bag of clothes I kept meaning to donate to Goodwill. As I wound my way down the sixteen miles of Malibu Canyon Road, which connects the San Fernando Valley to the beach, I played CDs of his favorite jazz artists, from Charlie Parker to Billie Holiday, and I really tried to appreciate them, listening with his ear, not mine. I knew he'd like that. When track four, "I Get Along Without You Very Well," from Billie's album *Lady in Satin* came on, the growing melan- choly made me glad I'd nearly reached my destination.

I parked on Pacific Coast Highway in front of a random house and then grabbed the box from the trunk, putting a blanket over it in case someone spotted me. But besides a few surfer dudes changing out of sandy wetsuits near their van, there was no one around. I made my way down a path between two houses, took off my flip-flops, and stepped onto the sand of what I assumed was someone's private property. The beach smelled the way it always did when I was a kid: like salt water and driftwood and seaweed. I love the smell of the ocean, and I'm a sucker for any candle from Bath & Body Works with a name like Beach Cottage or Sea Breeze or Aquamarine.

I decided to sit on the ground under the wood pilings that were the foundation of some zillionaire's house while I sussed out my surroundings. It would have been less than ideal to get arrested, and I wasn't sure if people were real sticklers about ash spreading. But I didn't see a soul, so I walked a few feet to where the dry sand became wet sand, letting the tail end of a wave run over my feet, and then I sat on a rock. I felt the seat of my pants get instantly wet but didn't care.

The actual ashes were in a sealed plastic bag inside the box, so I had to rip it open like you would a bag of frozen vegetables. If you've ever dealt with human ashes, I don't have to tell you they don't actually look anything like ash—they're much coarser and contain pulverized bone fragments. But the good news is that they looked a lot like sand with tiny pieces of seashell mixed in, so as long as I didn't dump them all in one place, they would probably be indistinguishable from the rest of the beach. I was good to go. I was ready.

And so, with the sound of the waves as my background music, I sat and read Stanley my letter, apologizing for all the ways I could have been a better daughter and forgiving him for the ways he could've been a better father—because I didn't want him to have regrets wherever he was.

And then, with tears flowing, I said a prayer and scattered his ashes all around the beach, but joyously, just as if I were that family on the coast of Ireland paying tribute to a great man. And I set us both free.

Epilogue: In the End, There Is Gratitude

I'm at my brother and sister-in-law's house for Super Bowl Sunday. I brought my whole crew: Jon, my now fifteen-year-old twins, and my daughter who recently turned eighteen (I can't believe it). I live for these parties. There's beer, of course, and my husband will have one or two, but drinking isn't the focus—or maybe I just don't notice it as much. These days, instead of clocking how many people are drinking without me, I tend to be more aware of how many people are *not* drinking—how people laugh and talk and eat and parent without a beer or a glass of wine in their hand.

There's plenty of cherry-flavored Bubly sparkling water—my sister-in-law, Racquel, always has it on hand—she knows it's my favorite but she doesn't buy it specifically for me; it wouldn't occur to her anymore that I don't drink. It's been over fifteen years since she initiated that humiliating conversation with me about my drinking. In a few months, I'll have fourteen years of sobriety.

Racquel had that baby she wanted, and then a few years later she had another one. They're thirteen and nine already. And yes, she did all the professional pregnancy photo shoots and themed up those nurseries. She's 100 percent that bitch. Although she struggled in those early motherhood days with sleep deprivation and mood swings, she never started drinking too much. It just wasn't her deal.

But motherhood didn't make me drink too much. Becoming a mother triggered anxiety, and so I reached for what I'd always reached for when I experienced stress and anxiety whether due to fighting stage fright, trying to forge intimacy, or having a baby. It's my deal.

Maybe addiction is in my genes, stamped onto my DNA by an addict father—if that's the case, I'm keeping an eye on my kids for signs they may carry this thing too. I'm extremely open with my kids about my alcoholism. When they were younger, I explained it to them as simply an allergy to alcohol—I have a body that doesn't process alcohol well, so I just can't have it. But once they were old enough to understand, I went into greater detail. I want them to be able to spot it in themselves and not have any shame in their game. I'm not seeing it yet, but if it turns out it's a struggle for them, they know they can talk to me, I'll understand. And I can direct them to help. Or maybe my wino tendencies were a direct result of starting my drinking career too young. Or maybe there was an environmental factor like a chaotic childhood. Or maybe nothing caused it. Maybe I'm just someone who drank too much and couldn't stop.

I realize that there are a lot of people getting sober who have way worse stories: horrific car crashes, waking up naked in unfamiliar places with total strangers, finding mysterious bloodstains (or maybe I watch too many Netflix true-crime docs). The point is, my story *isn't* incredibly dramatic.

But that's the good news.

Nothing terrible had happened to me *yet*. But I had lost control of my drinking and was speeding downhill in a semi without solidly working brakes. I had a choice: I could either use that runaway-truck ramp to stop myself safely, or risk it all by continuing to drink. I'm so glad I turned off the road and made my escape.

Now here's where I tell you how grateful I am that I got sober. (Yeah, sorry.) When I first quit drinking, I would get enraged when I heard people talking about their gratitude. "I'm just so grateful for my sobriety! I have such a beautiful life and it's all due to quitting drinking!" I'd hear ex-drunkies say that stuff and I'd immediately wish they'd get chlamydia. *Why are these people so goddamned happy? What do they have to be happy about?* I felt anything but grateful when I first quit. I felt a lot of things: anger, shame, sadness, and confusion. *How did I get here? Why can't I control my drinking? Will I ever be able to drink again? This isn't fair! Look at all the people I know who drink more than I do! Why don't they have to quit drinking?* No, I was a long way from grateful. And yet, I had *decided* to quit. No one forced me.

But like that frog put in tepid water that's slowly brought to a boil, I didn't feel it all changing—my thinking, my attitude, my whole outlook—until it was too late and I became one of those grateful assholes. Feel free to wish me an STD.

For years I looked back at the amount of wine I drank and my compulsion to check out with contempt—I was my own harshest critic. But now I can offer myself some grace. I was trying to survive, and drinking alcohol, bingeing on sweets, staring at my phone: This was how I dealt with my demons, and I needed those coping mechanisms until I learned different ones.

Would I have quit drinking if I hadn't driven drunk that night? I don't know. I like to think that eventually something would have happened to wake me up to the fact that alcohol wasn't serving me anymore—because if nothing had ever happened, I might not have this life.

I've heard it said that what you focus on expands—it may have been *Oprah* or even, God forbid, *The Secret*. Let's not worry about that, but it makes sense to me. It sounds so corny, but it's true: My recovery helped me switch my focus to wanting what I already have instead of trying to get what I want.

And at this Super Bowl party, there are so many of my favorite things to focus on: time with my family; spicy chicken wings with blue cheese dressing; getting to hang out with my brother and sister-in-law, who have always had my back; and the company of friends.

I grab a paper plate and load it with Super Bowl staples plus a couple of frosted football–shaped cookies—progress, not perfection—and head over to put my initials in a bunch of boxes on the Super Bowl pool grid. Thank God I never got addicted to gambling! When I'm done, Racquel pulls me aside and asks if she can talk to me in the kitchen. This time it's about *The Bachelor*.

Acknowledgments

Let me start with a shout-out to my fabulous editor, Rebecca Strobel. Thank you for your excellent feedback and guidance, but mostly for believing that my story was one that needed to be told and then holding my hand through the scary parts. I want to thank the entire team at Gallery Books for their hard work, including Aimée Bell, Lucy Nalen, Tyrinne Lewis, Sally Marvin, Caroline Pallotta, John Vairo, Lisa Litwack, Kathryn Kenney-Peterson, and Jamie Selzer, plus my copy editor, Polly Watson. But I especially want to thank my publisher, Jennifer Bergstrom. You took a chance on me so many years ago and you continue to take a chance on me, and for that I'm eternally grateful. I'd also like to thank Patrick Price, my very first editor, for his support, insight, and advice. I'm so glad you found me all those years ago. To my OG mom friends: Lara Tochner, Cecily Lerner, and Julie Kasem. I'm so lucky to have raised my kids alongside such amazing women. Thanks to my friends Robyn Wisinski, Cecily Knobler, and Bonnie McFarlane for the true-blue friendship through the years. To my friend and podcast partner, Lynette Paradise, thank you for providing a place to share our thoughts on parenting, addiction, and, of course, murder. Here's to thirteen years of *For Crying Out Loud* and thirty more to come! And thanks to Caelan Biehn, our amazing producer! Thank you to Marielise for turning the light on and to Barbara

Hancock: Your support and love have meant everything to me. To all the women who were with me at the beginning, but need to be anonymous, I'm so grateful for your friendship and help over the past fourteen years. I love you all! Thanks to Laura Cathcart Robbins for your support, friendship, and inspiration. Thank you to Lisa Sundstedt for the years of friendship and for being my Eskimo. You've been a big part of this. To my friends who allowed me to use their names and tell stories about them in this book: Jamie Absalonson, Cynthia Perpich, Diana Horn, and Mike Landry; and the rest who didn't, you know who you are. To my shortstacks, Elby, Sadie, and Xander: This book is for you. Thanks for being such amazing kids—loving, kind, and so funny. Thank you for inspiring me to make the change required to become the mom you deserve. Thank you to Michael Wilder for having my back from the very beginning and all the way through. I couldn't ask for a better brother. And thank you to Racquel Wilder, my amazing sister-in-law and friend. I will always appreciate your straight-up honesty mixed with a ton of empathy. Thank you for planting the seed. And thank you to my other sister-in-law, Wende Wheeler, for all the support and love behind the scenes. Lastly, I couldn't do any of it, nor would I want to do any of it, without my husband, Jon Taylor. Thank you for loving me, listening to me, advising me, forcing me to paint an orange pop-wall (I like it now), being the best dad, and, most importantly, always wanting me to be my best self even if you were initially worried I wouldn't be as much fun. I love you, asshole.

About the Author

Stefanie Wilder-Taylor is an author, TV personality, and cohost of the popular podcast *For Crying Out Loud*. She also co-created and hosted the late-night comedy parenting show *Parental Discretion with Stefanie Wilder-Taylor* for NickMom on Nickelodeon. She's the author of *Sippy Cups Are Not for Chardonnay*; *Naptime Is the New Happy Hour*; *It's Not Me, It's You*; *I'm Kind of a Big Deal*; and *Gummi Bears Should Not Be Organic*. She's appeared on *Oprah*, *Good Morning America*, *20/20*, *The Dr. Oz Show*, *Dr. Phil*, *Larry King Live*, and the *Today* show on NBC. She lives in Los Angeles with her husband, her three delightful teenagers, and her dog, Penelope.